LOVE KEEPS ON GIVING!!!

by Dave Williams

DORRANCE
PUBLISHING CO
EST. 1920
PITTSBURGH, PENNSYLVANIA 15238

Dorrance Publishing Co
585 Alpha Drive
Suite 103
Pittsburgh, PA 15238
Visit our website at *www.dorrancebookstore.com*

ISBN: 979-8-8881-2036-1
eISBN: 979-8-8881-2536-6

LOVE KEEPS ON GIVING!!!

John 3:16 "For GOD So Loved."

Love Keeps On Giving!!!

Psalm 18:1-3 reads, "I will love thee, O Lord, my strength. The Lord is my rock, and my fortress, and my deliverer: my God, my strength, in whom I will trust: my buckler, and the horn of my salvation, and my high tower. I will call upon the Lord, who is worthy to be praised: so shall I be saved from mine enemies."

PREAMBLE

Let's pray: "Thank you Lord for the many blessings I have received from my early existence to this present moment. Oh Merciful Savior, thank you for the abundant blessings on the way. Include in this prayer all Your children!!! Some are saved and some are not. Bless each of our hearts and help us to seek Your will. Lord help us find peace, love and joy daily in our lives. I believe You want to meet all our needs that are in Your will. We ask these and other blessings in Jesus', Name, Amen."...Deacon Williams

John 3:16 reads, "For God so loved the world, that he gave his only begotten Son, that whosoever believeth in him should not perish, but have everlasting life." I fervently believe, "The love you give and receive is a reality that will lead you closer and closer to God as well as to those whom God has given you to love. It is our duty as children of God to always share love with all God's children!!!!!

This book shares how the wisdom and love from Dr. Martin Luther King Jr. helped mold three young boys, Creigs Beverly, Sam Cook and Dave Williams into successful men. These three young boys graduated from the Alabama State Laboratory High School (Lab High) in Montgomery, Alabama. Lab High was a semi-private school on the campus of Alabama State University where many of the teachers' children attended. Lab High had high academic requirements and most of their students attended colleges. Dr. Creigs Beverly was baptized by Dr. King and he followed him to Morehouse for his undergraduate degree. He later became the Dean of Social Work at Atlanta

University and finally retiring as a professor from Wayne State University School of Social Work in Detroit, MI.

Sam Cook was an astute businessman and worked for Montgomery Community Action Agency for many years. He was a close confidant of Dr. King and very engaged in fighting for equal justice in Alabama and in our world. He received his Bachelor and Masters from Alabama State University: a HBCU in Montgomery. He was a veteran of the US Army. More about Sam Cook's life and a photo of Sam and Dr. King from the Selma to Montgomery March appears later in this book.

Dave Williams was a student of Dr. King and was one of his first followers. He was a member of the Crusaders which Dr. King started in his church, currently Dexter Avenue King Memorial Baptist Church. Dave Williams loved sports and was a pretty good baseball and basketball player during his youth. We must always try to share love with everyone we have contact with on life's journey. We are all GOD's children and deserve respect. We are mandated to love GOD and love our sisters and brothers. Matthew 22:36-40 exclaim, "Master, which is the great commandment in the law? Jesus said unto him, Thou shalt love the Lord thy GOD with all thy heart, and with all thy soul, and with all thy mind. This is the first and great commandment. And the second is like unto it, Thou shalt love thy neighbour as thyself. On these two commandments hang all the law and the prophets." A few words of encouragement may save a lost soul from their evil ways. Without a shadow of doubt, I fervently believe that when you have trials or reach "Rock Bottom," if you hold on to GOD's hand, He will allow you to have His Favor and rebound to have "Success!!!"

It's not a coincidence that throughout my life, I have been on the cutting edge of History in America. My early involvement in the Civil Rights Movement empowered me to take proactive positions and oppose unfair actions on the children of GOD. I still believe today, as Dr. King stressed throughout his lifetime that divine love is the only path to peace. It is imperative that we always fear GOD and not man. Our commitment to GOD and guide for His love is found in 1 John 4: 7 – 20, "Dear friends, let us love one another, for love comes from GOD. Everyone who loves has been born of GOD and knows GOD. Whoever does not love does not know GOD, because GOD is love. This is how GOD showed his love among us: He sent his one and only

Son into the world that we might live through Him. This is love: not that we loved GOD, but that he loved us and sent his Son as an atoning sacrifice for our sins. Dear friends, since GOD so loved us, we also ought to love one another. No one has ever seen GOD: but if we love one another, GOD lives in us and his love is made complete in us. We know that we live in him and he in us, because he has given us of his Spirit. And we have seen and testify that the Father has sent his Son to be the Savior of the world. If anyone acknowledges that Jesus is the Son of GOD, GOD lives in him and he in GOD. And so we know and rely on the love GOD has for us. GOD is love. Whoever lives in love lives in GOD, and GOD in him. In this way, love is made complete among us so that we will have confidence on the day of judgment, because in this world we are like him. There is no fear in love. But perfect love drives out fear, because fear has to do with punishment. The one who fears is not made perfect in love. We love because he first loved us. If anyone says, "I love GOD," yet hates his brother, he is a liar. For anyone who does not love his brother, whom he has seen, cannot love GOD, whom he has not seen."

Let's pray: Thank you Lord for sharing your love, peace, joy and mercy with us to empower us to bless others. Thank you for giving us Your Words to guide us throughout this earthly journey. Lord, help us to learn more of You through Your words and be all that You want us to be, in Jesus Name, Amen. As I look back over my life, I thank GOD again for His grace and mercy. When I had doubt, He said, "Have faith, I am in control and I am working it out for your good." If GOD said it, that settles it!

A verse and the chorus of one of the great hymns of Mahalia Jackson, "If I Can Help Somebody" follows:

"If I can help somebody, as I pass along,
If I can cheer somebody, with a word or song,
If I can show somebody, how they're travelling wrong,
Then my living shall not be in vain.

Chorus:
My living shall not be in vain,
Then my living shall not be in vain
If I can help somebody, as I pass along,
Then my living shall not be in vain."

Yes, we are our brothers' and sisters' keeper. In order for the citizens, "We the People," to turn America in the right directions, we all must play our role. When we get involved in the activities of our block, community, city, state and nation, we all will benefit and help make the needed improvements. Lou Holtz, the famous football coach said, "When I die, my accomplishments will eventually be forgotten. But what I've invested in my players will continue to live on." Pastor Joel Osteen said, "The best legacy is not what we leave for people. It's what we leave in people. We all have things that we've learned: skills, talents, life experiences, wisdom. You have a wealth of knowledge that GOD has entrusted you with. You are not supposed to keep that to yourself. You should be passing that on to somebody else. We have a responsibility to transfer what we know to the next generation. Are you taking time to invest in your children? And if you don't have any children, how about your nieces and nephews? Your neighbors? The kid down the street? You and I have an opportunity to leave a mark that cannot be erased. Yes, eventually we're all going to die, but when you invest in somebody else, you will continue to live on. Your life can have influence for generations to come if you will take time to invest in people."

The following is an excerpt from Dr. Beverly and his wife's book, *Challenges of the Black Church In 21ˢᵗ Century America: Reverend Ernest L. Williams Collaborated on this Data:*

CAN THE BLACK CHURCH SURVIVE THIS?

Service

The service of the church is to fulfill the mandate of Christ "to go and teach all nations, baptizing them in the name of the Father, and of the Son, and of the Holy Ghost: Teaching them to observe all things whatsoever I have "commanded you" (Matthew 28:19-20).

One reason that the Black church is losing its footing in the current culture is because we are disconnected from Jesus Christ and his greatest commission. We allow everything to go on in our church settings, it is treated as any other agenda item to be discussed in length, voted on, and once again tabled. And if not tabled, it is given to the pastor to do by himself with no or little assistance from the congregation. The gospel is the primary purpose of the entire church and not the mission of one person or one particular group of the church.

First, let us be clear on what the gospel is. The gospel is the good news of Jesus's death atonement for man's sin. Thus, we are called to share the gospel of Jesus to sinners. To share in the good news of Jesus is more than lip service. Sharing the gospel is caring for others. The Gospel of Luke illustrates Jesus's care for the marginally rejected socially, economically, and religiously. Secondly, how can we communicate the gospel to every aspect of church life? When the gospel of Jesus Christ is our goal, every subgroup of the church must have that same focus.

It is because of the gospel that the church should be involved in social change. The church should have been the first to sound the alarm on police brutality of African Americans. Why? Because of racism, hatred, and institutional racism denies and betrays the gospel of Jesus Christ. However, just like the White church was silent on racism in the early nineteen hundreds, so is the Black church silent on issues of police brutality and other discrimination acts in this country.

So then what is the service of the church? The church is called to go outside of its walls to serve the community where it exists. This service is twofold. The church is called to serve those who are within its reach (current membership). However, if this is all we do, there would never be any growth. Secondly, the church is called to go outside of its reach with the gospel of Christ. How does that gospel look like? Christ's gospel is a message of forgiveness, love, caring, and restoration. In order to give the gospel, we must first live the gospel. John's gospel shows Jesus "abiding" with the believers. If the church is unwilling to abide with the people of its community, then that church will not survive. It is when we invest in our communities through our service that those communities will be attracted to us, and that is the only way Christ can draw people to himself.

What kinds of services can a church render to the community where it exists? Each church must access its own community concerning the needs. Most churches will already have people within their walls who are qualified to meet those needs. Most churches have nurses, social-psychological-related experts, teachers, and other professionals. These are valuable resources to render adequate services for any community. If we don't use the talents of our church members, others will. Can the Black church survive this? "This" refers to the current downward trend in society that is causing the church to be irrelevant socially, economically, and spiritually. I believe the church can survive "this" if we keep Jesus and his mission as ours. I believe there is hope for the Black church if we follow Job's example. The Bible says of Job, And the Lord turned the captivity of Job, when he prayed for his friends: also, the Lord gave Job twice as much as he had before. Then came there unto him all his brethren, and all his sisters, and all they that had been of his acquaintance before, and did eat bread with him in his house: and they bemoaned him, and comforted him over all the evil that the Lord had brought upon him: every man also gave him a piece of money, and everyone an earring of gold. So the Lord blessed the latter end of Job more than his beginning: for he had fourteen thousand sheep, and six thousand camels, and a thousand yoke of oxen, and a thousand she asses. He had also seven sons and three daughters. And he called the name of the first, Jemima: and the name of the second, Kezia: and the name of the third, Kerenhappuch. And in all the land were no women found so fair as the daughters of Job: and their father gave them inheritance among their brethren. After this lived Job an hundred and forty years, and saw his sons, and his sons' sons, even four generations. (Job 42:10–16)

What can we learn from Job with respect to our present condition within the Black church? First, God turned Job's situation around after he prayed for his friends. Job's friends were very critical of him. But Job prayed for them. The Black church must pray for this nation. In order for the Black church to overcome, it too must learn the prayer of forgiveness. Secondly, Job's family and friends all invested in him financially. (Job 42:11) Job was ruined, but his family and friends believed that God was not through with him. They took a risk to invest in such a one. The future of the Black church will involve taking risks. If God can turn Job's situation around, I believe the Lord can turn the Black church's situation around also. Thirdly, when God turned Job's captivity around, Job honored his three daughters equally with his sons. Job names his three daughters by name. The names of the sons are not mentioned. What a high honor Job placed on his daughters. Job knew that his future and the future of his family rested not only with his sons but also his daughters. The Black church must not forget to honor the sanctity of marriage and Black motherhood. If the Black race in America is to survive and thrive, the Black church must be the leading voice of paying honor and respect to Black women. If we don't, then the world will make claim to womanhood in a humanistic and anti-biblical fashion.

Lastly, notice in Job 42:16, the writer records, 'After this, Job lived a hundred and forty years." The Black church is in the midst of a "this" situation. I believe as Job, we will survive with God's help if we are adaptable, if we make the right investments, and if we make the Great Commission of Christ our main goal in the church. And then it will be said even of the church."

Psalm 27:14 declares, "Wait on the Lord: Be of good courage, And He shall strengthen your heart: Wait, I say, on the Lord!" Below is an email I received from New Jersey's US Senator Cory Booker and my response to him.

From: Cory Booker hello@corybooker.com
To: davewms43@yahoo.com
Sent: Tuesday, September 20, 2022
Subject: We don't talk enough about Love

Dave,

Throughout my career in politics, I've had one guiding principle: Love. Love is the reason why, as a first-time candidate running for Newark City Council, I went on a hunger strike to draw attention to the desperation facing the most vulnerable communities in our city. Love motivated me to run for mayor, and after coming up short the first time, love motivated me to get back up and try again. Love is what carried me through four years of Donald Trump, when on some days it seemed it was our country itself telling us that it didn't truly love us. In the times we're living through, there's no such thing as too much love — it's what keeps folks safe, gives us hope when we have none, and inspires us to create the America we know is possible.

I am so grateful that you have chosen to come on this journey with me, because that too is an act of love. There are many forces inside and outside of politics that will still seek to divide us, but I am confident that if we stick together there is no obstacle that can stand between us or stop us from fulfilling our promise to one another — to build a government of, by, and for the people where no one gets left behind. Thank you for choosing love. Our movement is stronger for having you with us.

Love,
Cory

Dear Senator Booker:

You are so right! Enjoy my recent email to my social media contacts.

Be Encouraged My Brothers

Greetings My Brothers:

A few sentiments to forecast better days are ahead. A recent email I received from a minister read, "We have all faced moments in our lives when the pressure mounts beyond what we feel we can handle, and we find ourselves thinking that we do not have the strength to carry on. Sometimes we have just gotten through a major obstacle or illness only to find another one waiting for us the moment we finally catch our breath. Sometimes we endure one loss after another, wondering when we will get a break from life's travails. It does not seem fair or right that life should demand more of us when we feel we have given all we can, but this is the way life works.

When we look back on our lives, we can see that we have survived many trials and surmounted many obstacles, often to our own amazement. In each of those instances, we had to break through our ideas about how much we could handle and go deeper into our hidden reserves. Think of it like a frozen lake: it appears impenetrable, but when we break through it, we find a deep reservoir. When we break through the thought that we don't have more to give or to even fall back on, we can find a well of energy and inspiration trapped beneath. Sometimes we break through by cutting a hole in our resistance with our willpower, and sometimes we melt the ice with compassion for our predicament and ourselves. Either way, each time we break through, we reach a new understanding of the strength we store within ourselves. When we find ourselves up against that barrier of thinking we cannot handle our situation, we may find that the kindest choice is to love ourselves and our resistance too. We can simply accept that we are overwhelmed, exhausted, and stretched and offer ourselves loving kindness and compassion. If we can extend the unconditional warmth of a mother's love to ourselves, before we know it, the ice will begin to melt."

I am sharing my recent letter to President Obama and his wife with excerpt of my soon to be released book in this email. **Be Encouraged My Brothers.** I still believe our best days are ahead!!!!! Proverbs 3:5-6 reads, "Trust in the LORD with all thine heart: and lean not unto thine own understanding. In all thy ways acknowledge him, and he shall direct thy paths."

Dear President Obama and 1st Lady Michelle Obama:

As you are aware, The Obama Presidential Center will be a place to reflect and grow, connect and create: to tap into your own sense of purpose and discover the change you want to make in the world. It will be a place to honor history while inspiring young people **to write chapters of their own.**

Attached is your personal excerpt from my soon to be released book, Love Keeps On Giving. I hope you enjoy and will pledge to share a few copies with your staff and contacts upon release in a few weeks!!! I believe everyone need a little peace, joy and love on this earthly journey! You are my second hero since I met Dr. King in his living room, Montgomery, AL, in the summer of 1955 at age of eight with a group of church boys called the Crusaders. I am also a yellow dog Democrat and my book provides true

American History from Afro-Centric lens. I fervently believe that it is primarily through the same lens that the ideas, values and experiences of people of African descent can be understood unequivocally. I am prayerful you will enjoy this excerpt and issue an executive order, (erase, I forgot you aren't Prez anymore) LOL: Assist me as you can. Thank you for consideration and may God's Favor continue to cover you and your family.

Love and Prayers,
Dave Williams, Author, MSW and DAV

Regardless of our race/ethnicity, gender, socioeconomic status or our situational issue, GOD is always ready to meet our needs. When we spend daily time in GOD's Words and obey Him, we get closer to GOD. His Holy Spirit transforms our lives. We view our lives differently. We think and act with more peace and love with our contacts. The closer we get to GOD, the easier the road to "Success" becomes! Jesus said in John 15:5, 'Apart from me you can do nothing.' One of the underlying messages of this book is to have GOD's faith filled Words bring you encouragement to help you achieve your preordained destiny and become a "Success." I fervently believe that our greatest source of wealth evolves from our relationship with GOD. The wonderful truth is, GOD blesses those who walk in faith and believe in Him for victory. GOD always shows favor to those who strive to help the least of our society. I love to read the history of people who give their all to make this a better world.

To me, being a blessing to others is one of the most important spiritual principles on this journey of life. The ultimate challenge and value of a man's life is what he leaves for posterity. It bears repeating that any communication that I received from President Obama brought me not only mental stimulation but spiritual enlightenment and personal encouragement. On June 8, 2015, the following e-mail was received from President Obama with Senator Edward Kennedy's letter attached:

The White House
Washington

On a day in early September of 2009, I received the following letter from Senator Edward Kennedy. He'd written in May of that year, shortly after he learned that his illness was terminal. He asked that it be delivered to me upon his death. It is a letter about the cause of his career—what he called "that great unfinished business of our society"—health care reform. "What we face," he writes, "is above all a moral issue: that at stake are not just the details of policy, but fundamental principles of social justice and the character of our country."

Senator Kennedy never stopped asking what he could do for his country. Today, tens of millions of Americans are better for it. And while Teddy didn't live to see his life's work signed into law, more than five years after its passage, the spirit of his words ring true. This is, fundamentally, about the character of our country. Doing right by one another. It's who we are.

Tomorrow, I will deliver remarks about health care in America. Get a history of where we've been, and let me know you'll be watching.

Thank you,
President Barack Obama

Edward Kennedy
Massachusetts
United States Senate
Washington, DC 20510-2101
May 12, 2009

Dear Mr. President,

I wanted to write a few final words to you to express my gratitude for your repeated personal kindness to me – and one last time, to salute your leadership in giving our country back its future and its truth. On a personal level, you and Michelle reached out to Vicki, to our family and me in so many different ways. You helped to make these difficult months a happy time in my life. You also made it a time of hope for me and for our country.

When I thought of all the years, all the battles, and all the memories of my long public life, I felt confident in these closing days that while I will not be there when it happens, you will be the President who at long last signs into law the health care reform that is the great unfinished business of our society. For me, this cause stretched across decades: it has been disappointed, but never finally defeated. It was the cause of my life. And in the past year, the prospect of victory sustained me—and the work of achieving it summoned my energy and determination.

There will be struggles—there always have been—and they are already underway again. But as we move forward in these months, I learned that you will not yield to calls to retreat—that you will stay with the cause until it is won. I saw your conviction that the time is now and witnessed your unwavering commitment and understanding that health care is a decisive issue for our future prosperity. But you also reminded all of us that it concerns more than material things: that what we face is above all a moral issue: that at stake are not just the details of policy, but fundamental principles of social justice and the character of our country.

And so because of your vision and resolve, I came to believe that soon, very soon, affordable health coverage will be available to all, in an America where the state of a family's health will never again depend on the amount of a family's wealth. And while I will not see the victory, I was able to look forward and know that we will—fulfill the promise of health care in America as a right and not a privilege.

In closing, let me say again how proud I was to be part of your campaign – and proud as well to play a part in the early months of a new era of high purpose and achievement. I entered public life with a young President who inspired a generation and the world. It gives me great hope that as I leave another young President inspires another generation and once more on America's behalf inspires the entire world. At the Denver Convention where you were nominated, I said the dream lives on. And I finished this letter with unshakable faith that the dream will be fulfilled for this generation, and preserved and enlarged for generations to come.

With deep respect and abiding affection.

Senator Booker's email gave me confirmation that *Love Keeps on Giving* is a must read for all literate Americans. It is full of compassion and will provide its readers with the strength and motivation to do their part to make this a better world.

The Skylar Herbert Scholarship was created in the WSU School of Social Work by Dave Williams. He stated that, "During the coronavirus pandemic in April of 2020, as a Wayne State University (WSU) alumnus, I was emotionally moved by the story of two first responders, a great couple, Ebbie and Lavondria Herbert. Their 5 year- old daughter, Skylar Herbert died from Covid-19, and I created **The Skylar Herbert Endowed Scholarship** in her honor at WSU School of Social Work. At her death, Skylar was believed to be the youngest person in Michigan to die from COVID-19."

(12-30-2021 —- Just learned of my friend's death and penned these sentiments which I'm sharing to encourage others who may have a bowed down head.)

A Few of God's Best

Always remember that when we share love, God is in the midst. Even in grief and times of uncertainty, try to show love to uplift a bowed down head. Let's pray: Almighty GOD, thank you for bringing us to another level on this journey of life. I plead Your mercy to help us to continue to trust and obey You as we travel to the end of this earthly domain. As I persevere and try to encourage my brothers and sisters, let Your will be done in and through them. Lord, thank you for my ups and downs on this journey of life. You have led me all the way and I'm much obliged and offer You many thanks. Right now, I ask You to have Your way in your children's lives. Please forgive us of our sins and those who have trespassed against us. Lord, we surrender our all to You today and we know You have made great plans for the rest of our lives. Thank you Most Kind Master for blessing me from my early existence to this moment. You have been so good to me and I will forever give You the glory and praise. I submit everything to You and I stand firmly on Your Words in 1 Peter 5:6-7, "Humble yourselves therefore under the mighty hand of GOD, that he may exalt you in due time: Casting all your care upon him: for he careth for you."

O Merciful Father, thank you for the life of Loretta McCall and Your leading her into a place of rest and peace today. We surrender our brokenness to You and open our hearts to receive Your healing and favor. Lord, have mercy on this family: touch the sick and those who are grieving the loss of a loved one today. Soothe their heartaches and pain and let them know You are with them. Jesus, I ask at this moment that You will touch every heart and mind sharing this sentiment. Help us to get in Your will and let You handle every situation. Help us to read and obey Your Words daily and receive Your power to navigate the rest of this earthly journey. We ask these and other blessings in Jesus Miraculous Name, Amen.

As I speak these words spiritually, Loretta and the other individuals named are saying Amen!!! I hear them saying " "Tell The Truth and Shame The Devil." Three of my best friends when I left Montgomery, Alabama in 1992 were Carrie Simmons, Loretta Howard McCall and Samuel George Cook. They were true friends and would give you the shirt off of their back. They never wanted you to ask to borrow money but never said no. They may have said not today but I will see about tomorrow. Each of these persons worked for years with the Montgomery Community Action Agency. Each knew the Lord Jesus Christ as their Personal Savior. Each finished Alabama State University.

As a retired MSW from Wayne State University Graduate School of Social Work – Detroit, Michigan, and Vietnam Veteran, I loudly and with deep sorrow say, God gave them much. They gave all they could to help all the people they could. They lived good lives and were blessed. So long my friends and save my seat at the Lord's Eternal Supper with the other Angels!!!

I close with my salute to Loretta with my version of Edgar Guest's poem, "People Like Him." People liked her, not because she was rich or known to fame: She had never won applause As a star in any game. Her way was not a brilliant style, She didn't have a forceful way, But she had a gentle smile And a kindly word to say. Never arrogant or proud, On she went with manner mild: Never quarrelsome or loud, Just as simple as a child. Honest, patient, brave and true: Thus she lived from day to day, doing what she found to do, in a cheerful sort of way. Wasn't one to boast of gold or belittle it with sneers, Didn't change from hot to cold, Kept her friends throughout the years.

Sort of woman you like to meet, Any time or any place, There was always something sweet and refreshing in her face. Sort of woman you'd like to be: Balanced well and truly square:

Patient in adversity, Generous when her skies were fair. Never lied to friend or foe, Never rash in word or deed, Quick to come and slow to go, in a neighbor's time of need. Never rose to wealth or fame, Simply lived, and simply died, But the passing of her name. Left a sorrow, far and wide. Not for glory she'd attained, Nor for what she had of pelf, Were the friends that she had gained, But for what she was herself.

One of the most emotional and painful letters I have ever written appears below. In an email, I tearfully stated:

"All God's children need to be encouraged and affirmed. Christians should always provide their friends and contacts with spiritual nourishment and refreshing in their time of need."

The letter below was sent to Detroit mayoral candidate, Attorney Anthony Adams after he lost his bid for Mayor of Detroit on November 2, 2021:

Dear Attorney Adams:

From your attendance at Detroit's Club Opium on West Eight Mile Road to your appearance on the Mildred Gaddis Show through your ads on MSNBC Joy Reid Show, you taught this Vietnam Veteran, you wanted to fight to help African -Americans. You gave your best efforts and I salute you and your team for your courageous and valiant efforts! From my about 6:30am arrival at Cooke School and North Rosedale Park Community Center throughout my canvassing for your campaign in Brightmoor: through 6 and 7 Mile Precincts: through Greenfield and Puritan Precincts, voting was light and victory seemed pale. As we had discussed earlier we needed about 30,000 votes on Election Day and about half of absentee ballots led by Unions push for Mayor Duggan. Hold your head high and walk proud as you and your lovely wife pursue 'your future dreams.' I am sharing this excerpt you may recall from my first book.

CHAPTER TWO
Great Odds

One of my favorite scriptures I read when I need comfort is found in Ephesians 6:10-13: "Finally, my brethren, be strong in the Lord, and in the power of His might. Put on the whole armour of GOD, that ye may be able to stand against the wiles of the devil. For we wrestle not against flesh and blood, but against principalities, against powers, against spiritual wickedness in high places. Wherefore take unto you the whole armour of GOD, that ye may be able to withstand in the evil day, and having done all, to stand."

We must try to maintain an optimistic outlook and harbor only positive thoughts in our daily lives. When we have an optimistic mind, we stay positive and focus only on the thoughts that are conducive to our well-being and progress. Positive thoughts will increase our chances of "Success" in any endeavor. When you're sure that you are worthy and that achievement is within your grasp, you start to relax and look for solutions rather than dwelling on problems. Someone once said, "What the mind expects, it finds." Anticipate wealth, good health, happiness, joy and accomplishment, then if it's GOD's will, you may experience each of these. Always try to think positively and with persistence, you can condition your mind to dismiss negative thoughts and actions.

Matthew 17:20 reads, "If you have faith as a mustard seed, you will say to this mountain, 'move from here to there,' and it will move: and nothing will be impossible for you." GOD has planted seeds within each of us. He has predestined that those things in our heart come to pass. You may have had more than your share of unfair things happen in your life. You probably have plenty of reasons to just settle where you are. But understand, the depth of your past is an indication of the height of your future. If you've been through a lot of negative things in the past, it just means that your future is bigger and brighter and greater than you can even imagine. Go ahead and step out, embrace and claim all that GOD has for you. Are there dreams and promises that you've let go of? Are there things that GOD has placed in your heart, but because of time, because of disappointments, you've given up on them? Today is the day to give your dreams a new beginning. Yes, it's your season to be blessed!!

Let's pray: My Father, My Master, My Provider, My Lord and Savior, I believe You want me to prosper and be in good health. Today I declare by Your Words, I am healed of all infirmities that exist in my body. Jesus, I know that You have brought me thus far and I feel certain that You will be with me and lead me to the end of this journey. Father, I thank you for the destiny that You have placed in my heart. I will maintain a positive outlook and I have faith that what You have for me, is for me. I choose to stand in faith knowing that You are working behind the scenes on my behalf. I am confident that I will embrace all that You have for me, in Jesus' Name, Amen.

Dave wrote in an e-mail on February 13, 2008:

Senator Clinton,

The 4th quarter has just begun: this is where true champions get their composure to be victorious. I'm with you all the way and I still believe you will win!!!

Dave

Senator Clinton wrote in an e-mail on February 13, 2008:

Dear Dave:

All through this hard-fought campaign for the Democratic nomination, you and I have met challenge after challenge head-on. Every time they start to count us out, we prove them wrong. And we're going to keep proving them wrong as many times as we need to until we win the White

House. You and I know that only the people, not the pundits, get to decide where this race for the Democratic nomination will end up. And, before very long, the people who depend on us the most — working families who have been hard-hit by the failed policies of the Bush administration — will have their say in states like Wisconsin, Ohio, Rhode Island, Texas, Pennsylvania and others.

Don't forget who we're fighting for: families who need universal health care, people struggling to survive the Bush economy, folks desperately trying to hold onto their homes, students grasping for the American dream. They're the reason we need to work hard, and we need to win. And winning means having the passion, energy and resources to aggressively compete in crucial upcoming primaries. When we embarked on this journey, you and I promised each other we'd stick together through every point and every moment of opportunity. That's what we've got to do — right here, right now. Are you with me?

Let's get it done,
Hillary Rodham Clinton

P.S. Remember, no matter how many times they try to count us out, you and I will keep counting on each other to help drive our campaign to victory in the weeks ahead.

GOD is in the blessing business and He can do whatever He wants, whenever He chooses. President Barack Obama is a good example of GOD helping a man become successful in spite of great odds. After defeating Senator Clinton and the other Democrats, he was elected the first African - American President of the United States. President Obama displayed a righteous spirit, self-confidence and savvy when he named Senator Clinton as Secretary of State.

 Humbly Submitted,

Dave Williams, MSW and Vietnam Veteran

July 21, 2020
Bloomberg Philanthropies
25 East 78th Street
New York, New York 10075

Honorable Mike Bloomberg:

I submit this request on behalf of David Williams, a former student of mine, and a Vietnam Veteran. David is attempting to bring and apply all of the principles and techniques of central city wholistic development to an area in Detroit, Michigan known as the Cooley Project.

David is a man of high intelligence, has a deep and abiding love for humanity and has never resisted putting himself in harm's way to benefit, protect and develop the God given potential of others. He is a 100% disabled veteran.

In order to carry out the development initiatives of the Cooley Project rooted in the "Greenwood Initiative," he will need economic assistance. I have no idea what your criteria is for rendering economic assistance to programs and projects, but I can assure you that whatever financial assistance you can render to David will not only be appreciated, but also put to demonstrable use! Even an incubator grant would be significant. We are living in dangerous and difficult times. We need to do all we can to "keep hope alive." The recent passing of Congressmen John Lewis is a vivid reminder that freedom, equality, and justice for all continues to be a dream, and not a reality, for all in America. I do hope that you can find your way to help David. His organizations EIN # is 84-2249309 and his organization is under a 501-C3 designation. He can be reached at davewms43@yahoo.com.

Sincerely,
Dr. Creigs Beverly
Retired Professor Emeritus
Wayne State University
Detroit, Michigan

On November 6, 2018, I had two reasons to be joyful. First, I learned that the Democratic nominee for Michigan's Governor, Gretchen Whitmer had won her election. Then, I read online that Chief Judge Robert N. Davis of the United States Court Of Appeals For Veterans Claims, stated in his order that, "After further review, the Court re-docketed this as a petition for extraordinary relief. The Court apologizes to Mr. Williams for the delay in the adjudication of his case." Judge Davis went on to say, "Ordered that Mr. Williams, within 30 days from the date of this order, identify which of the claims listed in the July, 2014 Board decision are still pending. It is further ordered the secretary, within 30 days from the date Mr. Williams files his response, file an answer to the petition that addresses its specific allegations and provides any documentation necessary to aid in the Court's resolution of this matter."

During my vigorous canvassing, literature distribution and volunteer work for the Democrats, I had sent in several letters to the Detroit newspapers. A portion of one letter reads, "As a combat veteran of the Vietnam War, I know the importance of having good people in command. With less than a month to our General Election, Tuesday, November 6th, it's time for all hands to get on deck to ensure a fighter for Michigan is elected to lead our state. No campaign is perfect, but I'm proud of the fact that Governor's candidate, Gretchen Whitmer and Garlin Gilchrist, her running mate, are taking the time to make their rounds throughout Michigan to hear the concerns of citizens statewide. I'm doing my part to help them!!!

On August 2, 2022, the Republican primary for Governor was won by Tudor Dixon. She will compete with Governor Whitmer in the November General Election. Governor Whitmer said, "The road to Election Day starts right now. Make no mistake: This is going to be a tough fight in one of the most competitive elections in the country." We need everyone to assist and encourage your contacts to make sure they register and vote. A 20% turn-out in Detroit is not acceptable. Yes, that is what the voting results indicated for the August 2nd Primary!!!

I fervently agree with the Michigan Chronicle endorsement, "Whitmer is tested, tough, and resilient when making executive decisions about the well-being of people. She has proven time and time again, especially doing this pandemic, that she is not afraid to make decisions, even if unpopular with much of the population. While the governor is a leader for all, she recognizes and is making significant strides to close racial gaps of inequity that have affected underserved populations in Michigan, especially African Americans, for multiple decades.

It is my desire and hope from writing this factual first-hand American history, my readers and their contacts lives will be immensely benefitted and this data will be passed down for many generations!!!! Included in this project are sound advice and spiritual reflections of President Barack Obama, Judge Damon Keith, Senator Ted Kennedy, President Ronald Reagan, Nat Turner, Rev. Martin Luther King Jr., Mary McLeod Bethune, Dr. Creigs Beverly, Don Siegelman and other social and political leaders. "Have you ever wondered why some persons are happy and act as though they are successful, while others seem doomed for failure?" Williams said. "This book is written to help you think, start making right choices and become a success for the rest of your life. It is written as a guide to anyone who wants to improve their lives." As a social worker, Williams has devoted his career to making life better for those who are less fortunate. While serving in the U.S. Army in Vietnam, and while growing up in Montgomery, Ala., during the Civil Rights Struggle, Williams says, "I learned and still believe God is in control. That's my message for those persons whose spirits are low and appear to have reached rock bottom."

A portion of a letter I received from Senator Reverend Raphael G. Warnock on July 30, 2022 read:

Dear Dave,

America has a choice to make. We can embody the aspirations of January 5, or we can be the ugliness of January 6. Are we going to give in to the forces of division and demagoguery in our country or are we going to push closer to the ideal of E Pluribus Unum - out of many, one? On January 5, 2021, Georgia elected me the first Black U.S. Senator from Georgia. I grew up in public housing as the son of two preachers——a mother who grew up picking cotton and a father who spent his days restoring broken cars and his Sundays restoring broken people.

And that same day, Democrat retook the Senate because Georgia also elected a Jewish Senator named Jon Ossoff. and I like to think that Dr.

Martin Luther King Jr., whose pulpit I occupy, and Rabbi Abraham Joshua Heschel, who linked arms with Dr. King in the cause of civil rights, were smiling that day.

But the next day, January 6, the forces of division and hatred ransacked the U. S. Capitol. A tragedy and a crime whose full and awful dimensions we are still learning... one that metastasized into voter suppression bills all across the country. We don't get to pretend **it didn't happen. It happened.**

Each represented a path for America—- a path of vision and a path of division—-a country where we join hands in common endeavor or where we raise our hands against one another in conflict. And we have to choose.

Maybe this doesn't seem like the most auspicious moment for a choice. Those of us who rejoiced on January 5 are feeling the dispiriting outrage of rights being revoked. We're tempted by despair when we see January 6 denialism persist, voting rights bills filibustered, and the Supreme Court overturning Roe v. Wade and making it harder to address climate change. I'm writing because, with democracy itself at stake, I believe it's exactly the time to choose. The choices we make——as voters, as supporters of campaigns, as citizens—— are a sort of prayer for the kind of world we desire for ourselves and our children. A democracy is the political enactment of the spiritual ideal that all of us have a spark of divine.

Sincerely,
Reverend Raphael G. Warnock
U.S. Senator

1 Peter 4:8 reads, "And above all things have fervent love for one another, for love will cover a multitude of sins." After this poem by Lucille Clifton, taken from Dr. Beverly's book, Dave Williams complete life story is unfolded! Hopefully you will be enlighten and I am prayerful you will enjoy reading this first-hand true History!!!

We Know This Place

We have been on this piece of ground longer than the government. We know this place. We have walked it and worked it, fought its wars and filled its factories. We know this place. We have learned it the hard way, the blood way, the lesson that lasts, America cannot surprise us. We know this place. We bear responsibility for what we know. We are the family of tribes. The new people. We live across the whole face of this country. We are urban and rural and suburban. We speak all its languages. We know its secrets. We are its secrets. We have survived. We do survive. We are the children of the ones they could not kill. Our presence confirms us. The question now is not: Will there be an us? The question now is: What kind of us will there be? Today is the name of possibility. Today contains the traces of the past and the seeds of tomorrow. Tomorrow is vision or illusion. We must choose vision! One of the functions of the present is to dream the vision of the future from the memory of the past. Remember the love of our grandmothers. Remember it for our grandchildren. We know that we can be better than we are. Even the best of us. We are responsible for what we know. Here is the name of the place where we must begin to accept, to embrace that responsibility. Now is the name of when we must begin. The present is the last name of the past and the first name of the future. The present is what we are in. Let us be!" Be encouraged my brothers and sisters, let's share more love, I am prayerful you will be enlightened from these sentiments. Again Lord, I thank you for Your love, grace and mercy!!!!!

To my DAV members and supporters, I feel you today! As a lifetime member of the **Disabled American Veterans** (DAV), which is a nonprofit that provides a lifetime of support for veterans. I feel blessed to support DAV's mission since I know firsthand the dire struggles that our members endure after returning home. I am God's advocate to help make life better for all His children!!!

TABLE OF CONTENTS

ACKNOWLEDGEMENTS

"To GOD Goes The Glory." When GOD is placed first in your life, everything else will flow according to GOD's plan. Let's pray, "Lord, thank you for Your all-knowing. You have been so good to us and we take these moments to reflect on our past and look to our future with great expectation. Thank you for being the Author and Finisher of our faith. Lord, we will continue to trust You the rest of this earthly journey. Forgive us of shortcomings and sin. Restore a righteous spirit within us, in Jesus Name we pray, Amen.

Thanks next to my first love and life-time soulmate, Patricia Ann Williams. What I like most about Pat is her desire to help people! She always is true to GOD first, Pat second and her husband third. GOD has been a blessing to us and I fervently believe our best days are in front of us. I believe that those blessings we have prayed would come to pass and those desires we diligently believed for ourselves, our children and loved ones are imminent. GOD is Awesome!!

Thanks goes out to everyone who listened to my smallest thought in the completion of this book project. The following is written in memory of my brother, Dr. Booker Taliaferro Williams Jr. He was my hero, mentor, confidant and eternal source for my wisdom in many areas. His ideas and support are missed: his life lessons are imprinted in me. He had a great run and believed in GOD. One writer said it this way, "To determine a person's strength, just take a look at what Satan, his enemies or detractors are throwing at them. When you endure or overcome mighty obstacles, you will find abundant blessings that GOD has preordained for you."

Recommended Words of Daily Meditation and Self-motivation

Sometimes, you have to move yourself out of the way: Let go, trust GOD and He will take care of the situation... GOD is a right-now GOD... I have great worth... I am loved and I will share love... I have Favor... I have great expectation for my present and my future. I will be a "Success!!!" "For With GOD, Nothing Shall Be Impossible." (Luke 1:37)

Time Out!!

To me, former President Barack Obama can be considered a disciple of Dr. King. As you may have read, I am a Vietnam Veteran and one of Dr. Martin Luther King's first followers. He started an organization in his church, now Dexter Avenue King Memorial Baptist Church in Montgomery, Alabama in 1955. This group of church boys was called the Crusaders. We rode to these meetings with a neighbor, Ms. Verdie Davie and Ms. Lamie Davis, her assistant. Among the members were students from Alabama State Lab High School, my alma mater: Pastor Thomas Jordan, Dr. Levi Watkins, Dr. Norman Walton, Howard Alexander and Dave Williams and two of his three brothers. We read Bible stories and discussed family issues. It was the mission of our group to become godly men. Soon there were Crusaders in other churches in Montgomery. We always closed our meetings with snacks and repeating Luke 1:37 which reads, "For with God nothing shall be impossible." This still is one of my favorite Scriptures. It was true then and I believe history has shown, **Dr. King was an anointed child of God who died trying to help the least of God's children.**

What comes from your heart reaches the heart of others. There is nothing like spiritual truths! Eldridge Cleaver was an American writer and political activist who became an early leader of the Black Panther Party. One of his most memorable quotes says, "If you are not a part of the solution, you are a part of the problem." This update includes four new extensive chapters (24 - 27) which reiterate the overall premise for writing this book, reflect on GOD's presence in daily helping His children. These added chapters may be considered, "A Book Within A Book." This updated text, to me, is the apex of this writing project and will hopefully help you solve most problems that you may encounter on your journey of life!!!

Proverbs 13:20 states in part, "Walk with the wise and become wise." (NIV) Throughout this book, it is exclaimed that God always provide His children what they need when they have faith in Him!!! Each of us was created to give and receive love. God is always in control and places people in our lives to help us on our journey of life. In my opinion, Valerie Heard and Michelle Simmons are two of the greatest teachers and friends God put on this earth. I've witnessed firsthand their abilities to impart knowledge and love into their students in the Montgomery Public Schools. They are uniquely gifted to help God's children navigate their lives into successful careers. They are my lifelong friends although they're retired in Montgomery and I'm in Detroit. I salute both of them for their spiritual encouragement and shared wisdom over the years.

Success is not just measured by your job, nor by your bank account, the size of your home nor what kind of car you drive. John 10:10 reads, "The thief cometh not, but for to steal, and to kill, and to destroy: I am come that they might have life, and that they might have it more abundantly." GOD wants to shower you with abundant blessings! Success include our physical, spiritual and emotional state of mind. If we have good relationships, peace of mind and enjoy our lives with contentment and having GOD as the center of our actions, then "Success" is imminent. Success does not have to be money or fame but fulfilling your God given destiny. Being a native of Montgomery, Alabama, I have always tried to keep up with the struggle for justice in America. I was in tears when President Barack Obama said in his speech on March 7, 2015 in memory of the Selma to Montgomery March 50th Anniversary, "The air was thick with doubt, anticipation, and fear. They comforted themselves with the final verse of the final hymn they sung: No matter what may be the test, GOD will take care of you: Lean, weary one, upon His breast, GOD will take care of you.

There are places, and moments in America where this nation's destiny has been decided. Many are sites of war – Concord and Lexington, Appomattox and Gettysburg. Others are sites that symbolize the daring of America's character – Independence Hall and Seneca Falls, Kitty Hawk and Cape Canaveral. Selma is such a place. In one afternoon fifty years ago, so much of our turbulent history – the stain of slavery and anguish of civil war: the yoke of segregation and tyranny of Jim Crow: the death of four little girls in Birmingham, and the dream of a Baptist preacher – met on this bridge.

As is true across the landscape of American history, we cannot examine this moment in isolation. The march on Selma was part of a broader campaign that spanned generations: the leaders that day part of a long line of heroes. We gather here to celebrate them. We gather here to honor the courage of ordinary Americans willing to endure billy clubs and the chastening rod: tear gas and the trampling hoof: men and women who despite the gush of blood and splintered bone would stay true to their North Star and keep marching toward justice. They did as Scripture instructed: 'Rejoice in hope, be patient in tribulation, be constant in prayer.' And in the days to come, they went back again and again. When the trumpet call sounded for more to join, the people came – black and white, young and old, Christian and Jew, waving the American flag and singing the same anthems full of faith and hope."

"An idle mind is the devil's workshop." Although, this often quoted cliché is not found in the Bible, 1 Peter 5:8 states, "Be sober, be vigilant: because your adversary the devil, as a roaring lion, walketh about, seeking whom he may devour." Yes it is true that when you take your focus off GOD and His Word, and allow your mind to wander or dwell on ungodly things, you open yourself up to doing or saying wrong things. You place your righteous lifestyle in danger of falling under the control of the enemy. When it comes to righteous living, the enemy is always on your trail to tempt you to do wrong.

When facing any adversity, we should pray unceasingly and ask GOD to help us fight our battle. Psalm 24:7-8 read, "Lift up your heads, O ye gates: and be ye lift up, ye everlasting doors: and the King of glory shall come in. Who is this King of glory? The Lord strong and mighty, the Lord mighty in battle." When GOD is fighting for us, every adversity will be turned to victory. GOD will make our enemy a footstool. He will richly bless us and give us double for our trouble! One of Rev. James Cleveland's songs entitled, "I Don't Feel No Ways Tired" chorus goes, "I don't feel no ways tired, I've come too far from where I started from. Nobody told me that the road would be easy, I don't believe He brought me this far to leave me." It is often said that, "Successful people maintain a positive focus in life no matter what is going on around them.

They stay focused on their past successes rather than their past failures and on the next action steps they need to take to get them closer to the fulfillment of their goals." Ecclesiastes 9:11 exclaims, "I returned, and saw under the sun, that the race is not to the swift, nor the battle to the strong, neither yet bread to the wise, nor yet riches to men of understanding, nor yet favour to men of skill: but time and chance happeneth to them all."

Humbly I write today that before you begin to read this insightful and true African - American and Caucasian History lesson, I want to share my introductory remarks with you. This book was divinely inspired to me and "To GOD Always Goes The Glory." It is a true account of growing up Black but practicing diversity in spite of segregation and facilitating good race relations through unbridled communications with leaders of America both Black and White. These shared discussions all point to the "Dream of Dr. King's Beloved Community" which is later discussed. We all have a direct order from GOD to do our part to make this a better world. We are all GOD's children. We can and we must get along peacefully on this earth. Success on our earthly journey comes to those who have a dream, pursue it passionately and trust God to direct their steps.

The following was a speech I wrote during the 2009 Detroit Mayoral Race for candidate Dave Bing's visit with my church family:

2-8-09 – "Thanks Pastor Langford for allowing this opportunity for Detroiters.

Psalm 19:14 states: 'May the words of my mouth and the meditation of my heart be pleasing in your sight, O LORD, my Rock and my Redeemer.' (NIV)

Rev. Al Sharpton, US Senator Debbie Stabenow, former candidate for Governor, Geoffrey Fieger, current Governor Jennifer Granholm, former Mayor Dennis Archer and others have visited Christland seeking votes. Christland has been a longtime polling place in Detroit. We are not only a spiritual enlightening church but a highly community oriented church. Our soup kitchen has helped many deprived citizens of Detroit on a weekly basis.

My three favorite sports are basketball, football and politics. Since I can't play the first two any longer, I get my excitement from participating in political campaigns and playing chess. We have a great opportunity to get Detroit moving in a positive direction on February 24th in the Mayor's race. Christland is blessed to have one of the candidates visit us today, Mr. Dave Bing.

I first met Mr. Bing in 1968 when I came to Detroit to work for the summer to earn money for college in Alabama. He and some of his Piston teammates allowed a few college guys to play a pick-up game with them at the Fisher YMCA where we were staying. He also opened up my first saving account at NBD Bank, across from the Y and encouraged me to do well in college.

Mr. Bing is the grandson of a Baptist minister. He is a Christian and a man of integrity. He has served as a Trustee at Hartford Memorial Baptist Church for 27 years. A few weeks ago he had me in tears from one of his sermons to some local ministers and concerned voters. Mr. Bing is a very compassionate man who has donated much money for needy persons and causes in the Metropolitan Detroit area and throughout the US. He has assisted every Mayor elected in Detroit from the election of Coleman Young. He helped elect former President Bill Clinton and was deeply involved in reaching voters for our current President, Barack Obama. He has been a successful basketball player and businessman. I feel certain he will be a great CEO for Detroit. Without any further ado, let's give a warm Christland welcome for our next Mayor, Mr. Dave Bing."

Although this initial visit was cancelled and Pastor Allen Langford introduced Mayor Bing on his rescheduled visit, I learned a great lesson. Many times on your journey of life, you will not get credit for your efforts and acts of kindness. Continue to do positive acts anyway. If you don't receive due reward on this earth, an eternal reward by GOD awaits the righteous and is of more value than anything you can receive on this earth!!

Always remember, "When you respect the game of life: learn all you can: do critical thinking before you make your decisions: trust your spiritual compass and allow God to daily guide you: Your Success Is Imminent."

FOREWORD

Both David (Dave) Williams and I grew up in Montgomery, Alabama. We each personally knew the Reverend Dr. Martin Luther King, Jr. and we each experienced the civil rights movement firsthand via the Montgomery Bus Boycott. Though grounded geographically in the red clay of Alabama, our developmental paths were quite different. You will read his story in the pages to follow and I am convinced after having done so, you will more fully appreciate your own life and your own search not only for self, but also for community.

When David asked me to write the Foreword to his book, I was at first reluctant to do so. My reluctance to do so was based on the passage of so many years when our lives never crossed. I therefore felt that I couldn't do justice to his book.

Then, as we continued to discuss his book and the purpose for which it was written, my mind flashed back to the mid-1990s. At that time I was a Professor of Social Work at Wayne State University in Detroit, Michigan teaching graduate courses in the History of American Social Welfare and Mental Health and Social Policy.

At the beginning of the second semester, on a very cold January night as I opened my class, there sat David Williams. Decades had passed since I had seen him. At that moment the realization hit me that time and distance from a person are not nearly as important as the foundation established when first you met.

David Williams has had a remarkable life. He has both influenced and been influenced by many. He not only shares his life experiences, but he also contextualizes them within biblical underpinnings.

I not only recommend this book for reading, but I also request that before doing so, each person get quiet enough and still enough to hear what you haven't heard before. Discover what was heretofore unknown to you and perhaps most important of all, do for others what you heretofore haven't done. If David Williams has a legacy, and he most surely does, then it lies in the last aforementioned insight. From Professor to former student: Well Done!

Creigs Beverly, Ph.D.
Professor Emeritus, Wayne State University

PROLOGUE

John 3:16 states, "For GOD so loved the world, that he gave his only begotten Son, that whosoever believeth in him should not perish, but have everlasting life." John13:34-35 reads as follows: "A new commandment I give unto you, That ye love one another: as I have loved you, that ye also love one another. By this shall all men know that ye are my disciples, if ye have love one to another." If we love one another as GOD ascribed, we will have a better community of nations.

GOD wants His children to prosper and have "Success"!! Throughout our discourse, I have enclosed passages mostly from the King James Version of the Bible that have provided me with immeasurable vitality in my hours of despair, uncertainty and insecurity. GOD's Word is no respecter of person: it applies to everyone in the same manner. The Bible is our blueprint to "Success" and it always provides us with the wisdom we need. Feed on GOD's Words daily to receive the strength we'll need to prosper and overcome any adversity that may come our way. Let's pray: Almighty GOD, Maker of Heaven and Earth, thank you for this day. Lord, first I want to ask You to forgive me of all my sins: I'm sorry and I want to be saved. I believe You died on the cross for me and You arose from the grave with all power in Your hands. Please GOD, continue to bless each reader and their circle of influence. Continue to lead and protect us and our families. Give us more love for each other and more love for You. Thank you for all the blessings You have allowed us to receive from our early existence until now!!! We pray that You will continue to help us to grow spiritually and mentally. Bless us financially. Give us continued physical well-being. Help us to do those things that are right and good in Your sight. Give us peace of mind and true happiness. We love You Lord, we honor You Lord and we will continue to obey and trust You to meet our every need and those desires You want us to have. Lord, bless us as we continue to march toward justice, Your "Beloved Community and Success." We make this supplication, in Jesus' Name, Amen.

From a lad when I was just learning to read, I heard that David was a man after GOD's own heart. 1 Samuel 13:14 reads, "But now your kingdom will not endure: the Lord has sought out a man after his own heart and appointed him leader of his people, because you have not kept the Lord's command." Acts 13:22 reads, "After removing Saul, he made David their king. He testified concerning him: I have found David son of Jesse a man after my own heart: he will do everything I want him to do." (NIV) I didn't exactly know what this meant but since I was named David, I wanted to seek after the heart of GOD. I believed GOD's heart was always good and He would bless each of us if we did His will. To this day, even when I got off track, I would repent and try to seek GOD's heart. I fervently believe that with GOD's help, we can succeed at any endeavor we strive to achieve. If we read and reverently study GOD's Words, pray unceasingly, worship and honor GOD, He will see that we are after His heart and GOD will help us to be a "Success."

This book is dedicated in memory of my biggest role model and confidant, my brother, Dr. Booker Taliaferro Williams Jr. He was the person who always encouraged me and pushed me to excel from an early age. He went home to be with the Lord on April 10, 2009. I will best remember him as the epitome of Paul's words to Timothy found in 2 Timothy 4:7-8, "I have fought the good fight, I have finished the race, I have kept the faith. Now there is in store for me the crown of righteousness, which the Lord, the righteous Judge, will award to me on that day and not only to me, but also to all who have longed for his appearing."

This book tells the readers about some of the life experiences of David (Dave) M. Williams growing up Black in Alabama. Dave was raised during the height of segregation and the Black experience to receive equal treatment and justice in America. From my viewpoint, political competition is just like playing a professional sport. The participants always play to win. Sometimes democratic politics is unpredictable. Such was the case in the early stages of the Barack Obama versus Hillary Clinton presidential contest in 2008. There was an ongoing concern and no one could figure out whether Whites would actually vote for a Black candidate. Looking from historical lens, I did not think Senator Obama had a chance and volunteered to help Senator Clinton's campaign.

Throughout this literary work, it is my paramount objective to give the readers and their contacts the mental stimulation to do their part in order to make this a better world. I believe soon and very soon, it is about time for the return of our Lord and Savior to judge mankind. Man has reached the point where he appears to be content with self-annihilation. This book is a spiritual and secular journey that is accurate and written to offer a historical perspective for current and future generations. I am confident you will enjoy reading this work as much as I found enjoyment and peace while writing it. Hebrews 13:5-6 states, "Let your conversation be without covetousness: and be content with such things as ye have: for he hath said, I will never leave thee, nor forsake thee. So that we may boldly say, 'The Lord is my helper, and I will not fear what man shall do unto me'."

The contents of the following e-mail to a local political activist and a letter from President Obama and his wife, Michelle, kind of sum up my political career and indirectly suggest Dr. King's "Beloved Community" which we will discuss later.

My good brother,

At the age of eight in Montgomery, I met Dr. Martin Luther King Jr. in his living room with a group of church boys called the Crusaders. This was prior to the Montgomery Bus Boycott. He told us three things which left an indelible imprint on my heart and guided my life to this day. He said, 'Always keep GOD first, try to get a good education and always give something back to your community.' I have helped fight for justice and equality in Alabama/US since that date. I have met personally Marty, Bernice, Dexter, Ralph, Rosa, Atty. Fred Gray,

E. D. Nixon, Rose and Hank Sanders, J L Chestnut, Stokely, John Lewis, Big James Orange, Andy, Hosea, Jesse and all the wannabees (self-proclaimed civil-rights historical participants who came to Montgomery). I ran for the Alabama House of Representatives in 1983 and lost to the incumbent. I have fought racism and injustice in US and in Vietnam. I have worked in the Alabama Governor's Office and Attorney General's Office. During her first run for Governor, Jennie Granholm called me her secret weapon. I worked hard for Freman. I worked two years for DPS. I am on my last campaign and I feel Hillary will be a great President in spite of her past shortcomings.

For your personal and confidential information, I just e-mailed the following to Senator Clinton:

Dear Senator Clinton:

I am a Vietnam Veteran and unemployed. I am a loyal Clinton supporter and had the best time of my life at the Arkansas/California Ball during President Clinton's last Inauguration. I want to repeat this great moment and I am submitting my resume for consideration of employment. Since I am unemployed I will relocate to Washington and travel anywhere I'm needed. I have worked extensively in many campaigns as community organizer, assistant campaign manager, literature design, opposition research, t-shirt distribution and door-to-door canvassing.

Thank you in advance for your prompt and positive consideration.

Dave Williams, MSW
So brother, stay involved and all we can do is hope for the best.

Barack and Michelle Obama 11-18-08

Dear Mr. Williams,

The victory we achieved on November 4 means so much to so many — but to all of us, it is a stirring affirmation of our country's most fundamental promise: America is a place where anything — we choose to dream together, anything for which we choose to work together — is possible. Ours was never the likeliest campaign for the presidency. We didn't start with much money or many endorsements. Our campaign was not hatched in the halls of Washington — it was built by working men and women, students and retirees who dug into what little savings they had to give five dollars and ten dollars and twenty dollars to this cause. It grew from the millions of Americans who volunteered, and organized, and proved that more than two centuries later, a government of the people, by the people and for the people has not perished from the Earth.

Dave, this is your victory. But even as we celebrate, we know the challenges are the greatest of our lifetime — two wars, a planet in peril, the worst financial crisis in a century. The road ahead will be long. Our climb will be steep. And we will be asking you to join in the work of remaking this nation the only way it's been done in America for 221 years — block by block, brick by brick, calloused hand by calloused hand. What began 21 months ago in the depth of winter must not end on a night in autumn. This victory alone is not the change we seek — it is only the chance for us to make that change.

Dave, this is our moment. This is our time — to put our people back to work and open doors of opportunity for our kids: to restore prosperity and promote the cause of peace: to reclaim the American Dream and re-affirm that fundamental truth — that out of many, we are one: that while we breathe, we hope, and where we are met with cynicism, and doubt, and those who tell us that we can't, we will respond with that timeless creed that sums up the spirit of a people: Yes We Can. For now, please accept our deepest thanks. We will never forget you.

Sincerely,
Barack ObamaMichelle Obama

Have you ever wondered why some persons are happy and act as though they are successful or they truly may be middle or upper class? While, if you look around your house, neighborhood, city, state or the United States, you will see too many of my brothers and sisters seemed doomed for failure. This book is written as a helping tool. It is written to provide an answer to the question about wondering. It is written to help you think, start making right choices and become a successful person for the rest of your life. It is written as a guide to anyone who wants to improve their lives. A special message is intended for those persons whose spirits are low and appear to have reached "Rock Bottom." It is especially written for those persons who feel desolate, deprived, and finding it hard to survive in these trying days of the last five to six years. I think the bottom fell out for me in 2005 to 2006!!! "For with GOD nothing shall be impossible." (Luke 1:37)

Again I say, "If you should suffer (Rock Bottom) for what is right, you are blessed (Success)." GOD said, "You don't need to reach 'Rock Bottom.' Follow my Words and I'll make you a 'Success!!'"

Biblical Abbreviations used: NIV – New International Version: NKJV – New King James Version: AMP – Amplified Bible

CHAPTER ONE
Divine Assignment

One of my favorite jobs was my position as a clinical therapist with a private agency. I truly enjoyed helping people solve their problems. My entire life from the age of eight years of age, I have been fighting to help the less fortunate. Detroit is, in my opinion, a melting pot by day and except for on nights when the "Wings, Lions or Tigers" are playing, a mostly Black, urban city. Detroit is located in Michigan, one of the most economic deprived areas in the United States. Due to having a history of dependence on the automobile industry for economic survival, foreign investment in cars has caused Detroit to greatly suffer. The first gainful employment I had was at the Engine Plant at Ford's Rouge Plant in Dearborn, Michigan in 1967. The Dearborn Plant was in a suburb about twenty miles from Detroit. This assembly line experience turned out to be the evolution of me becoming a man.

This was the summer of the Detroit riots. I really learned to survive in an urban setting that summer working in an automobile factory and enduring the environment permeated by violence from the riots. In late May-1967, I began working a summer job in Detroit to earn money for college. I fearlessly continued to catch the bus to the Dearborn Engine Plant during the riots when I didn't catch a ride with other workers. I trusted GOD for protection during this period of turmoil. As I recollect and the local papers reported, The Detroit Riot began on July 23, 1967 when undercover police officer raided an after-hours nightclub. The club was located at 12th Street and Clairmount Avenue. I lived in an apartment with my brother, Booker, on the corner of Seward/Woodrow Wilson, one block from 12th Street and about half mile from

Clairmount. In the club, about 82 people were arrested who were found inside having a party for two returning Vietnam Veterans. After these persons were arrested, looting and fires spread all over Detroit. Within 48 hours, the National Guard was mobilized, to be followed by the 82nd Airborne on the riot's fourth day. As police and military troops sought to regain control of the city, violence escalated. At the conclusion of 5 days of rioting, 43 people were dead, 1189 injured and over 7000 people had been arrested. According to a survey by the Detroit Free Press, the main issue on the minds of Detroit's Black residents was police harassment and police brutality leading up to the riot.

During the 1967 riots, I was engulfed by Psalm 91:1-16, "He who dwells in the shelter of the Most High will rest in the shadow of the Almighty. I will say of the LORD, He is my refuge and my fortress, my GOD, in whom I trust. Surely he will save you from the fowler's snare and from the deadly pestilence. He will cover you with his feathers, and under his wings you will find refuge: his faithfulness will be your shield and rampart. You will not fear the terror of night, nor the arrow that flies by day, nor the pestilence that stalks in the darkness, nor the plague that destroys at midday. A thousand may fall at your side, ten thousand at your right hand, but it will not come near you. You will only observe with your eyes and see the punishment of the wicked. If you make the Most High your dwelling— even the LORD, who is my refuge. Then no harm will befall you, no disaster will come near your tent. For he will command his angels concerning you to guard you in all your ways: they will lift you up in their hands, so that you will not strike your foot against a stone. You will tread upon the lion and the cobra: you will trample the great lion and the serpent. Because he loves me, says the LORD, I will rescue him: I will protect him, for he acknowledges my name. He will call upon me, and I will answer him: I will be with him in trouble, I will deliver him and honor him. With long life will I satisfy him and show him my salvation."

My last seventeen years have been spent in Detroit working as a social worker for the most part. I have had some success but many "Rock Bottom" experiences that have made me almost give up on ever being successful. As of today, I feel superb as I attempt to complete this work to uplift your mind, body and spirit.

While visiting my hometown of Montgomery, Alabama in 2005, I bought a T-shirt that said, "I am the ancestor of an enslaved people, I have the mentality of a runaway slave." The slave preacher, Nat Turner, believed that GOD had called him to lead his people out of slavery. Turner believed that if you believed in something badly enough, you could make it come true. Turner said, "I was ordained for some great purpose in the hands of the Almighty. The Spirit instantly appeared to me and said the Serpent was loosed, and Christ had lain down the yoke he had borne for the sins of men and I should take it on and fight against the Serpent."

The words on this T-shirt reminded me of my first meeting with Dr. King, who led the fight against segregation. Although this was mentioned previously, these words are worth being repeated: I remember vividly at the age of eight, Dr. Martin Luther King Jr. in his living room in Montgomery, Alabama saying to a group of church boys called the Crusaders, "Always remember to keep GOD first, get a good education and give something back to your community." I feel these words are very pertinent today and Dr. King was giving us his formula for "Success." These words have been my compass throughout my journey of life and probably led me to a career in social work.

Dr. Benjamin Elijah Mays was an outspoken critic of segregation and major mentor to Dr. King. He was president of Morehouse College in Atlanta, Georgia from 1940 to his retirement in 1967. Dr. Mays was a minister who focused on the dignity of all human beings and the disparity between American democratic ideals and American social practices which were the key messages of Dr. King and the Civil Rights Movement. Dr. Mays gave the eulogy at Dr. King's funeral in 1968. He died in 1984 and was buried on the campus of Morehouse College.

One of my favorite quotes of Dr. Mays is, "It must be borne in the mind that the tragedy in life doesn't lie in not reaching your goal. The tragedy lies in having no goal to reach. It isn't a calamity to die with dreams unfulfilled, but it is a calamity not to dream. It is not a disaster to be unable to capture your ideal, but it is a disaster to have no ideal to capture. It is not a disgrace not to reach the stars, but it is a disgrace to have no stars to reach for. Not failure, but low aim is a sin."

Howard University (HU) in Washington, D.C. has been known as the Mecca of Black education since its founding in 1866. According to HU historical documentation, it was first established as a seminary for Black clergymen but soon became a college for liberal arts and medicine. The aforementioned Dr. Benjamin Mays was Dean of the School of Religion at HU in 1934 until he went to Morehouse in 1940. Today HU is comprised of 12 schools and colleges and about 11,000 students. HU continues to attract the nation's top students and produces more on-campus African-American PhD's than any other university in the world. I was fortunate enough to attend one year studying social work at HU in 1972-1973. This was one of the highlights of my education. A mediocre graduate of Alabama State University in Montgomery, Alabama, I was overwhelmed by college life in D.C.. I spent a great deal of my time while in D.C. visiting Senate Hearings and getting a firsthand look at how our government works. After my first year, I had to return to Montgomery to provide for my 8-month old daughter and family.

After the death of my brother, I saluted him with the following sentiments that GOD gave me for comfort and to share with others:

EXIT

Sooner or later, everyone must exit this life! Lord, we are calling on You right now to help us get prepared for our exit. You have promised that You would never turn away anyone who calls on You. For Your Words say, 'Whoever shall call on the name of the Lord will be saved!' We believe and we are sorry for our unbelief! Save us Lord and forgive us of our sins from this world and prepare us for Your eternal kingdom.

In the book of Psalms, David often asked GOD to intensify his awareness of life's fragility. He said in Psalm 39:4, 6: 'Lord, make me to know my end, and to appreciate the measure of my days. Let me know and realize how frail I am – how transient is my stay here. Surely every man walks to and from: each one heaps up riches, not knowing who will gather them.' (AMP) David's increased awareness of his own fragility increased his desire to know GOD, the only Life that is lasting! This confirmed for David the utter uselessness of allowing himself to be in turmoil due to seeking earthly riches. You can be encouraged that life's uncertainty makes us more aware that we will be home with the Lord soon. We must try to understand the positive changes GOD may want us to make in order to have a more fulfilled life.

Some things aren't done for you to understand. GOD does not make mistakes. He is always good and His decisions are preordained. Don't fear death!

GOD wants you to know that He is standing right by your side. His strength is by you to carry you through your earthly journey. He wants you to know that not only did Jesus die to abolish the power of death, but the power that any fear of death may hold over you as well. His Words explain that Jesus became like us so that, by going through death, He might, 'Make of no effect him who had the power of death, that is, the devil: And also that He might deliver and completely set free all those who through the fear of death were held in bondage throughout the whole course of their lives.' (Hebrews 2:14-15) With GOD, death is not a termination, it is a transition, from earthly life to life with Him which is eternal and will never cease. Death is for the Christian a setting free from the bondages of our physical bodies and the sin of this world. Death gives us the freedom to be with GOD. Rejoice – you may be leaving one home, but in GOD's grace you are going to a better one.

OUR PRAYER

Heavenly Father, thank you for Your revelation. Let Your power of victory over death and over the fear of death, now deliver me from all bondage. No longer will apprehension over the passage from this life into Your Life in heaven, make me sick or afraid. For to be absent in the body is to be at home with You. I praise You for the renewal of my mind and the new freedom I now feel to go on in Your name. Lord, I will trust You and honor You forever, in Jesus' Name, Amen."

Each of us has a divine assignment to fulfill on our short stay here on this earth. GOD knew us from our conception. He brought me through my early and middle years. GOD will lead me the final miles of this destination on earth. GOD wants each of us to complete our divine assignment. Whether we complete our assignment is left up to us, our conscience, our obedience and GOD's favor. The favor of GOD is worth more than houses or land. It is of more value than silver or gold. GOD's favor will help us achieve whatever we conceive in our mind if it is in His will.

CHAPTER TWO
Great Odds

One of my favorite scriptures I read when I need comfort is found in Ephesians 6:10-13: "Finally, my brethren, be strong in the Lord, and in the power of His might. Put on the whole armour of GOD, that ye may be able to stand against the wiles of the devil. For we wrestle not against flesh and blood, but against principalities, against powers, against spiritual wickedness in high places. Wherefore take unto you the whole armour of GOD, that ye may be able to withstand in the evil day, and having done all, to stand."

We must try to maintain an optimistic outlook and harbor only positive thoughts in our daily lives. When we have an optimistic mind, we stay positive and focus only on the thoughts that are conducive to our well-being and progress. Positive thoughts will increase our chances of "Success" in any endeavor. When you're sure that you are worthy and that achievement is within your grasp, you start to relax and look for solutions rather than dwelling on problems. Someone once said, "What the mind expects, it finds." Anticipate wealth, good health, happiness, joy and accomplishment, then if it's GOD's will, you may experience each of these. Always try to think positively and with persistence, you can condition your mind dismiss negative thoughts and actions.

Matthew 17:20 reads, "If you have faith as a mustard seed, you will say to this mountain, 'move from here to there,' and it will move: and nothing will be impossible for you." GOD has planted seeds within each of us. He has predestined that those things in our heart come to pass. You may have had more than your share of unfair things happen in your life. You probably have plenty of reasons to just settle where you are. But understand, the depth

7

of your past is an indication of the height of your future. If you've been through a lot of negative things in the past, it just means that your future is bigger and brighter and greater than you can even imagine. Go ahead and step out, embrace and claim all that GOD has for you. Are there dreams and promises that you've let go of? Are there things that GOD has placed in your heart, but because of time, because of disappointments, you've given up on them? Today is the day to give your dreams a new beginning. Yes, it's your season to be blessed!!

Let's pray: My Father, My Master, My Provider, My Lord and Savior, I believe You want me to prosper and be in good health. Today I declare by Your Words, I am healed of all infirmities that exist in my body. Jesus, I know that You have brought me thus far and I feel certain that You will be with me and lead me to the end of this journey. Father, I thank you for the destiny that You have placed in my heart. I will maintain a positive outlook and I have faith that what You have for me, is for me. I choose to stand in faith knowing that You are working behind the scenes on my behalf. I am confident that I will embrace all that You have for me, in Jesus' Name, Amen.

According to newspapers accounts, "In December 2008, President-elect Barack Obama's national security team, faces the challenge of managing two wars and various ongoing foreign policy crises even as it helps the president-elect shape what he called 'a new beginning, a new dawn of American leadership' in the world.

In announcing his choices of Sen. Hillary Rodham Clinton (D-N.Y.) to be secretary of state, Defense Secretary Robert M. Gates to continue in office and retired Marine Gen. James L. Jones to serve as national security adviser, Obama laid out a vision of an America whose global stature is restored and whose military, diplomatic and economic power are balanced with one another and with 'the power of our moral example.'

But he acknowledged that 'grave' and 'urgent' national security issues, including the wars in Iraq and Afghanistan, potential conflict between Pakistan and India, and economic crisis at home and abroad, require immediate attention. The challenge will be balancing those immediate priorities handed over by the Bush administration — what the Obama camp calls the' inheritance issues' — with national and international expectations for the longer-term changes he pledged during the campaign.

The members of his new team, Obama said yesterday, 'Share my pragmatism about the use of power, and my sense of purpose.' Three other Cabinet selections announced were Eric H. Holder Jr. as attorney general, Arizona Gov. Janet Napolitano as secretary of homeland security and Susan Rice as U.S. ambassador to the United Nations.

Obama repeatedly emphasized his intention to expand U.S. diplomacy while buttressing the size and capabilities of the military, and he stressed the interconnectedness of national security and economic issues. Rice, who served as a senior foreign policy aide to Obama during the campaign, listed an ambitious global agenda – 'to prevent conflict, to promote peace, combat terrorism, prevent the spread and use of nuclear weapons, tackle climate change, end genocide, fight poverty and disease.'

But 'you have to manage the legacy' of the Bush administration 'while trying to move forward on priorities,' one Obama adviser said. 'The balance is showing that you're serious about what's important — what you said during the campaign — without overloading the agenda. It's more important to have success that shows you're making progress than a long, uncompleted pass.'

In addition to the pressing issues in Iraq, Afghanistan, Pakistan and India, Obama must quickly decide whether to continue negotiations begun by President Bush on North Korea and the Israeli-Palestinian conflict, how to deal with Iran, and what to do about the U.S. detention facility at Guantanamo Bay, Cuba. Preparations must be made for three major summits — NATO, the Group of 20 and the Summit of the Americas — scheduled within three months of the inauguration.

At his news conference, however, questions focused less on policy than on how the eclectic personalities standing behind Obama and in front of American flags — particularly Clinton, Gates and Jones — would mesh. Asked how he would avoid having a 'clash of rivals' rather than the smoothly functioning team he portrayed, Obama said he expected "vigorous debate" and described himself as 'a strong believer in strong personalities and strong opinions.'

'One of the dangers in the White House, based on my reading of history,' Obama continued, 'is that you get wrapped up in groupthink and everybody agrees with everything and there's no discussion and there are no dissenting views.'

Obama turned playful when a reporter reminded him of the sharp criticisms he leveled at Clinton during the campaign, including equating her travels as first lady to having tea with foreign leaders. Obama waved off the question, saying the press was merely "having fun" by stirring up quotes from the campaign.

'Differences get magnified' during campaigns, Obama said. 'I did not ask for assurances from these individuals that they would agree with me at all times. I think they understood and would not be joining this team unless they understood and were prepared to carry out the decisions that have been made by me after full discussion.'

'On the broad core vision of where America needs to go,' he said, 'we are in almost complete agreement. There are going to be differences in tactics and different assessments and judgments made. That's what I expect: that's what I welcome. That's why I asked them to join the team. But understand, I will be setting policy as president,' he added. 'I will be responsible for the vision that this team carries out, and I expect them to implement that vision once decisions are made.' The announcements confirmed weeks of speculation and secret negotiations. Gates had never closed the door on staying in office but repeatedly insisted that he wanted to retire to his home in Washington state. Discussions with Clinton were not solidified until agreement was reached over public release of the names of donors to the foundation established by her husband, the former president.

Jones was said to have resisted repeated entreaties from Obama until early last week. His concerns, according to a source who discussed the matter with the former NATO commander, centered on avoiding the problems that plagued Bush's first term, including a weak National Security Council and end runs around national security adviser Condoleezza Rice by then-Defense Secretary Donald H. Rumsfeld and Vice President Cheney.

Another Obama adviser said the president-elect's team has studied Bush's attempt to put together a first-term team of national security heavyweights, only to see discipline collapse among warring factions. With Jones, the adviser said, Obama felt he had found 'a very substantial person who can make the system work.' Obama kept coming back, the source said. Everything [Jones] told him about the reasons he didn't want the job, [Obama] said, 'I can fix that.' Jones is said to have emerged with guarantees that he would have Cabinet rank and be the main foreign policy conduit to and from the president.

Clinton stood without expression yesterday as Obama, the former rival she once called 'naïve' on some aspects of foreign policy, praised her 'extraordinary intelligence and remarkable work ethic.' Obama continued: 'She is an American of tremendous stature who will have my complete confidence, who knows many of the world's leaders, who will command respect in every capital, and who will clearly have the ability to advance our interests around the world. Hillary's appointment is a sign to friend and foe of the seriousness of my commitment to renew American diplomacy and restore our alliances.' Clinton cracked a smile when Obama described her as a 'tough campaign opponent.' In her own remarks, she said that 'if confirmed, I will give this assignment, your administration and my country my all.' A source close to the transition and familiar with discussions between Clinton and Obama described her as confident that she will have the president's ear when she needs it, and as unconcerned about the potential for rivalry with Jones and Gates. 'She knows how the White House works,' the source said of the former first lady."

President Obama's victory reminded me of one of my favorite Biblical fights, David slays Goliath. This story is found in 1 Samuel17:40-51(NIV), "Then he took his staff in his hand, chose five smooth stones from the stream, put them in the pouch of his shepherd's bag and, with his sling in his hand, approached the Philistine. Meanwhile, the Philistine, with his shield bearer in front of him, kept coming closer to David. He looked David over and saw that he was only a boy, ruddy and handsome, and he despised him. He said to David, 'Am I a dog that you come at me with sticks?' And the Philistine cursed David by his GODs. 'Come here,' he said, and I'll give your flesh to the birds of the air and the beasts of the field!' David said to the Philistine, 'You come against me with sword and spear and javelin, but I come against you in the name of the LORD Almighty, the GOD of the armies of Israel, whom you have defied. This day the LORD will hand you over to me, and I'll strike you down and cut off your head. Today I will give the carcasses of the Philistine army to the birds of the air and the beasts of the earth, and the whole world will know that there is a GOD in Israel. All those gathered here will know that it is not by sword or spear that the LORD saves: for the battle is the LORD's, and he will give all of you into our hands.' As the Philistine moved closer to attack him, David ran quickly toward the battle line to meet him. Reaching into his bag and taking out a stone, he slung it and struck the Philistine on the forehead. The stone sank into his forehead, and he fell face down on the ground. So David triumphed over the Philistine with a sling and a stone: without a sword in his hand he struck down the Philistine and killed him. David ran and stood over him. He took hold of the Philistine's sword and drew it from the scabbard. After he killed him, he cut off his head with the sword. When the Philistines saw that their hero was dead, they turned and ran."

Within the Holy Bible, if we read studiously, engulf its scriptures and obey GOD's Words, the path to "Success" will be found. In my witnessing and testimony in this writing, it is my desire to be a messenger for GOD and lead many persons to salvation and a more enriching/successful life. It is my aim to exclaim that GOD is the only way to "Success." In this text, "Success" has reference to both the secular and spiritual connotation. The level and power of our faith often determine our degree of "Success." This is reinforced in Mark 11:23-24: " For verily I say unto you, That whosoever shall say unto this mountain, Be thou removed, and be thou cast into the sea: and shall not doubt in his heart, but shall believe that those things which he saith shall come to pass: he shall have whatsoever he saith. Therefore I say unto you, what things soever ye desire, when ye pray, believe that ye receive them, and ye shall have them." True faith in GOD will assure you of being as successful as you want to be. By all means, let us not forget that, He cannot be fooled: you must be genuine.

I am still hopeful that eventually there will be peace on earth. John 14:27(NIV) states, "Peace I leave with you: my peace I give you. I do not give to you as the world gives. Do not let your hearts be troubled and do not be afraid." At an early age, maybe the second grade, I learned that, "What comes from the heart goes to the heart." Words from the heart motivate us and give us a deep personal connection to what is being communicated. On this journey thus far in my life, I have been quite an activist in the political arena. Over my career, I have been involved with many of the leaders of our country from my initial inspirational meeting with Dr. Martin Luther King Jr. Heartfelt words from another can make an indelible imprint. They may ring as true tomorrow as they were the day they were communicated.

As you may know or will learn, life is an amazing journey. It is full of opportunities, disappointments, excitement and the unknown. GOD's Words say, "Wherefore gird up the loins of your mind, be sober, and hope to the end for the grace that is to be brought unto you at the revelation of Jesus Christ." (1 Peter 1:13) In other words, don't give up, keep on believing, expecting and declaring that good things will happen for you each day. Without question, I believe GOD has predestined our purpose while on this earthly journey.

Biblical wisdom can provide us with renewed hope. The following is shared with certainty that if you daily declare, you will receive spiritual uplift and restoration.

1. We are saved by the words of our testimonies.
2. I can do all things through Christ who strengthens me.
3. If thou canst just believe, all things are possible to him that believes. Lord help us with our unbelief.
4. If you have the faith the size of a mustard seed, you can say unto your mountain, be thou removed and the mountain will be cast into the sea.
5. Nothing is impossible with GOD.
6. For we are made partakers of Christ if we hold to the beginning of our confidence steadfast unto the end.
7. We shall live and not die.
8. The thief cometh to kill, steal and destroy but I have come so that you might have life and that life more abundantly.
9. Give and it shall be given unto you: good measure, pressed down, shaken together and running over shall men give unto your bosom. And it shall be given unto you in the same measure withal it is meted.
10. Seek, ask, knock and the door shall be opened unto you.
11. Weeping may endure for a night, but joy cometh in the morning.
12. The Lord rewards those who diligently seek Him.
13. GOD will bless you for your diligence above all that you can ask or imagine.

Isn't it strange how one moment life can be exciting and fulfilling? It seems that your dreams appear to be coming true. Then, in an instance, a sudden misfortune occurs and your dream becomes a nightmare. Many people who have faced a sudden accident or tragedy know about life taking a downturn. Just when things appear to be coming together and are moving in the right directions, disaster can happen and cause misery. We now feel like an earthquake struck, the roof caved in and our life has become miserable.

We can end this misery and strife by telling ourselves, "I have had enough of this turmoil. I will not be a slave to this fear, uneasiness and confusion. I am going to seek GOD's guidance and trust Him for deliverance." GOD is always ready to help us!! He awaits our invitation for Him to step in. He is our shelter in the time of storm. He will free us from our despair when we seek His mercy. Even though you may not know what tomorrow holds, you have the blessed assurance that you know Who holds tomorrow. GOD will never leave you nor forsake you. Yes, those trials may seem difficult, but if you just trust in Him, He will show you that there is nothing impossible with Him. He is not slack in His promises. He will never fail His children. He has never forsaken the righteous. Hold on to the promise that "many are the afflictions of the righteous, but the Lord will deliver you out of them all!"

Remember you can always, "Cast all your care upon Him: for He careth for you." 1Peter 5:7 Let's pray: Most Gracious and Almighty GOD, please forgive us of our multitude of sins. We submit all our concerns to You today. Lord, we thank you for Your love, guidance and comfort in our time of trials and tribulations. When we were weak, You lifted us up. When there were tears and heartaches, You came in with Your soothing Spirit. Lord, as we continue on life's journey, we are casting all our cares upon You. We trust and we believe You will lead us safely to our destiny. We ask these and other blessings, in Jesus' Name, Amen.

CHAPTER THREE
Setting The Stage

Let's set the stage for this journey from "Rock Bottom to Success," my hometown, Montgomery, Alabama: the capital of the State. It is located on the banks of the Alabama River in the central part of the State. It is located about 100 miles south of Birmingham and about 175 miles southwest of Atlanta. According to Alabama's History, Montgomery was incorporated in 1819 and the State Capitol was moved to Montgomery from Tuscaloosa in 1847. Montgomery's current population is about 201,000 persons. I liked Montgomery because it never snowed while I was growing up there. It had an ideal climate for pleasant living: it was not too extreme during the winter nor summer seasons. The annual average temperature was about 65 degrees.

Montgomery was a very religious city having over 200 churches during my youth. I joined Beulah Baptist Church when I was about 8 years of age. We often walked the two miles to church each Sunday. Beulah laid the foundation for my religious experience. I was an active participant in the Sunday School, the choir and the Crusaders, a group of church boys learning and trying to spread the Words of GOD. Rev. Willie Frank Alford, Sr. was my pastor until his death. Beulah has always actively participated in the spiritual, cultural, and educational life of the Montgomery community. Beulah's congregation entertained the Alabama Baptist Missionary State Convention of which Dr. W. F. Alford was president until his homegoing. He also served on the Board of Directors for the National Baptist Convention, USA Inc. On August 25, 1989, the homegoing of Dr. Willie Frank Alford was held at the Beulah Baptist Church led by President T. J. Jemison of the National Baptist Convention, USA., inc.

Beulah has a rich history. It served as the first "classroom" of the State Normal College, now Alabama State University. There were many civil, political and spiritual meetings held in Beulah's sanctuary, including but not limited to the Civil Rights Mass Meetings of the sixties, The Emancipation Celebration, Montgomery Antioch District Sunday School and Baptist Training Union Congress, Youth Rally of the Southeast District, and the Montgomery Antioch Women's Convention. GOD blessed the congregation with another servant on December 24, 1989. Rev. Porter Osby, Jr., accepted the call to Beulah. Under his energetic leadership, many projects begun by Rev. W. F. Alford have been expanded while others were launched.

Reflecting back, it was the love of GOD that enabled my parents to provide for their six children. We all graduated from college, although my father only completed the third grade and my mother was a high school graduate. My parents, both deceased, loved the Lord and going to church was mandatory in the Williams' home. The children enjoyed church because we met other keen Christian children at church and we enjoyed singing in the choir.

Like in most families, my mother was the homemaker and pillar of strength in the Williams' family. She instilled spiritual and moral values in her six children that helped us navigate our endeavors. She was led by Psalm 37:25- "I have been young, and now am old: yet have I not seen the righteous forsaken, nor his seed begging bread." Mother was mainly a housewife but she sometimes earned money by keeping preschoolers and working at a beauty shop. She was a stern disciplinarian and demanded excellence in our school work. She enjoyed church work and was one of the leaders of our Crusaders' group. She sang in the choir and the older children did also. Due to my mother teaching preschoolers, my oldest sister and my elder brother, who is deceased, had careers in education. My parents may not have had much worldly goods but they were quite wealthy in their faith in GOD. My parents were a GOD-fearing couple and were blessed accordingly. My mother passed on October 9, 1980 reading her Bible. A great deal of the inspiration to write this book derived during those days of grief for me. My mother lives spiritually within me and my siblings because of her life lessons she taught us. My mother never distrusted GOD and she taught us the importance of reading the Bible for strength and consolation. She taught us the importance of attending church and learning of GOD's Words. My dear mother taught her children that through hard work and a love for GOD, all obstacles can be removed. My mother taught us well the value of obtaining a good education.

We were raised in a neighborhood one block from the Tulane Courts housing project. As many low-income housing projects did, Tulane Courts had the propensity to develop many wayward children. Although we had many friends and playmates that lived in Tulane Courts, the Williams' children had to abstain from inappropriate behavior. Certain principles were internalized in the Williams' children. In essence they were: (1) Work hard at all endeavors. (2) Have high morals and try to live a Christian life. (3) Always believe and trust GOD. As mentioned earlier, we all became members of Beulah Baptist Church at early ages. We all attended Alabama State Laboratory High School which was part of the Alabama State College domain. I regretted going to this school at times because it often meant grocery money had to be used to pay tuition. This school was a semi-parochial school consisting of grades 1-12 for about 500 students. It initially was a teacher training facility for Alabama State College. This school was one of the best schools in Montgomery for gifted minority minds. Some of the most scholarly students in Montgomery got their educational roots at "Lab High." Civil Rights icon, Rosa Parks, attended "Lab High" in the 10th and 11th grades. I developed self-confidence and positive tools for learning at "Lab High" where I was a student from the 2nd through the 12th grades. I was never haunted by a feeling of inadequacy growing up Black due to the strong academic foundation of "Lab High."

One of the poems that was required learning in the 6th grade was a poem by George Linnaeus Banks. It reads as follows:

"WHAT I LIVE FOR"

I live for those who love me,
Whose hearts are kind and true:
For the heaven that smiles above me,
And awaits my spirit too:
For all human ties that bind me,
For the task that GOD assigned me,
For the bright hopes yet to find me,
and the good that I can do.
I live to learn their story
Who suffered for my sake:

17

To emulate their glory,
And follow in their wake:
Bards, patriots, martyrs, sages,
The heroic of all ages,
Whose deeds crowd History's pages,
And Time's great volume make.
I live to hold communion
With all that is divine,
To feel that there is a union
Twixt Nature's heart and mine:
To profit by affliction,
Reap truth from fields of fiction,
Grow wiser from conviction,
And fulfill GOD's grand design.
I live to hail that season
By gifted ones foretold,
When men shall live by reason,
and not alone by gold:
When man to man united,
And every wrong thing righted,
The whole world shall be lighted,
As Eden was of old.
I live for those who love me,
For those who know me true,
For the heaven that smiles above me,
And awaits my spirit too:
For the cause that lacks assistance,
For the wrong that needs resistance,
For the future in the distance,
And the good that I can do.

My father worked at the Montgomery Fair Department Store as a cook and janitor. Ms. Rosa Parks also worked at this downtown retail store as a seamstress. My father was a good worker and well liked because of his cooking skills. We were poor but we were taught to be grateful for whatever blessings we received. I can never forget one day in December in 1955, dad came home early. He had been fired due to Ms. Parks refusing to give up her seat to a white man. Having six children and the baby about a month old, I know dad felt that he was at "Rock Bottom."

Mother believed the Lord would step in and she comforted dad by her strong spirituality. Within a few days, through the facilitation of Mr. David Mussafer, my dad found work. Mr. Mussafer was a wealthy Jewish businessman who my father had respected so much that he named me in honor of him. Yes, my full name is David Mussafer Williams. When my father took me to visit him, Mr. Mussafer always gave me encouragement and money to buy clothes. Later my father found employment at Bellingrath Junior High School where he worked until he retired. My parents knew firsthand the meaning of Psalm 34:17-18, "The righteous cry, and the Lord heareth, and delivereth them out of all their troubles. The Lord is nigh unto them that are of a broken heart: and saveth such as be of a contrite spirit."

Montgomery has come a long way in the area of race relations. Much of the overt segregation that existed in 1955, the birth year of the modern Civil Rights Struggle, is barely visible today. In my opinion, this can be attributed directly to the relentless efforts and seeds planted by Dr. Martin Luther King Jr. I am not going to write any lengthy account of Dr. King, because we all are quite familiar with the works of this great man. According to his biography, Dr. Martin Luther King became pastor of the Dexter Avenue Baptist Church in Montgomery, Alabama in 1954. Always a strong worker for civil rights for members of his race, Dr. King was, by this time, a member of the executive committee of the National Association for the Advancement of Colored People, the leading organization of its kind in the nation. He was ready, then, early in December 1955, to accept the leadership of the first great Negro non-violent demonstration of contemporary times in the United States, the bus boycott described by Gunnar Jahn in his presentation speech in honor of the laureate. The boycott lasted 382 days. On December 21, 1956, after the Supreme Court of the United States had declared unconstitutional the laws requiring segregation on buses, Negroes and whites rode the buses as equals. During these days of boycott, King was arrested, his home was bombed, he was subjected to personal abuse, but at the same time he emerged as a Negro leader of the first rank.

I feel impelled to write that this man had a significant influence on me while he lived in Montgomery. As I previously mentioned, it was at a meeting of a group of church boys called the Crusaders, that I first met Dr. King face to face. A lad of about eight years of age, I will never forget the meeting at his home where he came in and talked with the boys in our organization. The thing that impressed me the most was Dr. King's command of words. He really instilled in all of us, a value of self-worth and he advised us to always look to

Jesus to direct us. He told us that no matter how bleak or dismal our path may get, GOD could move in and make a way for us to have "Success." He told us to always believe in Jesus and look to Him for our help in time of trouble.

I will never forget the news account of his message when his home was bombed and Montgomery's Blacks were quite angry. Dr. King told a group of angry Blacks that had gathered for revenge, "My wife and baby are okay. I want you to go home and put away your weapons. Violence is not the way to solve our differences. Jesus said, 'He who lives by the sword will perish by the sword.' We must meet hate with love." Needless to say, violence was avoided from those Blacks that day. I truly believe and many historians agree that over the last hundred years, Dr. King had one of the most significant roles in changing human relations, not only in this country, but the entire world. He made an indelible imprint on this soul while he was only a child trying to determine his destiny. The first time I was arrested was at the age of 15, following Dr. King in a march in Montgomery. I spent about three days in jail because we, "Refused to disperse and leave area as ordered." Due to having so many underage children arrested, the Montgomery Courts dismissed without trials many of the cases. I felt blessed to be released.

CHAPTER FOUR
Vietnam

Dr. King spoke out on the war in Vietnam in 1967. He received many threats and upset many politicians and other leaders in America because of his refusal to remain silent regarding the Vietnam War. He said that, "a time comes when silence is betrayal." Dr. King listed seven major reasons for making his Vietnam speech part of his divine assignments and mandated that he spoke out in opposition to the war. (1) He felt the Vietnam War had an adverse effect on the Civil Rights Struggle. The war drew men, skills and resources from helping the poor. (2) Dr. King believed that Blacks were being sent to fight a war and were dying in higher proportions in Southeast Asia for liberties they were being denied in America. (3) Dr. King felt that he couldn't tell his followers in America to be non-violent while Americans were killing and losing lives in Vietnam. (4) "No one who has any concern for the integrity and life of America today can ignore the present war." America can't be saved when it is destroying the deepest hopes of men around the world. (5) Dr. King received the Nobel Peace Prize in 1964. He felt that the Nobel Peace Prize was his commission to work harder for the brotherhood of man all over the world. (6) Dr. King said that his ministry for Jesus Christ, who died for his enemies, mandated that he oppose the war. (7) Dr. King believed he had to speak for the weak, voiceless and victims of America. Dr King said, "I believe that the Father is deeply concerned especially for his suffering and helpless and outcast children, I come tonight to speak for them."

One of the most emotional and disgusting days of my life occurred on April 4, 1968. My hero, Dr. King, was assassinated and I was suspended from

Alabama State College. That night after Dr. King was killed several local students had purchased gasoline and were trying to start a riot on campus. I was subsequently named as one of these students and told to miss the rest of that semester to cool my head. I went to Detroit and found work and later was drafted by the U.S. Army.

I entered the Army in January 1969 after being AWOL for about a month. I tried hard not to go and did all I could not to go for fear of being shipped to Vietnam. I was sworn in and sent to Fort Benning, Georgia. The mission of Fort Benning was to provide the world's best Infantry Soldiers and trained units: to provide a power projection platform that could deploy soldiers and units anywhere in the world on short notice. I did not like being in the Army but I attempted to make the best of a bad situation. I made high enough scores on the entry aptitude tests to enter the Non-Commissioned Officer School at Fort Benning. This environment was a miniature Montgomery with Blacks still being victims of segregation. Since I was always a good athlete, this helped me tremendously navigating the rough spots of Fort Benning. Excelling in sports was my equalizer against racism. After completion of the NCO Academy at Fort Benning, I was sent to Fort Polk, Louisiana for further training. Here I worked with new recruits in preparing them for Vietnam. It was reasonably tough going at each of these military facilities but I have always been a survivor! One thing throughout my life has been constant: I never lacked self-confidence. Often this has caused me problems, for I never have shied away from a good fight.

The inevitable finally arrived and I received orders to go to Vietnam in January 1970. GOD's Words say in Isaiah 41:10, "So do not fear, for I am with you: do not be dismayed, for I am your GOD. I will strengthen you and help you: I will uphold you with my righteous right hand." Normally, I passionately hate to think back on my days in Vietnam. To illustrate how GOD's blessings sometimes are mysterious, it is imperative that I recapitulate some experiences of life in the Vietnam War.

When I read or hear of the increased drug problems in the U.S., I remember that while in Vietnam, drugs were the order of the day. It was in Vietnam that I first learned what it meant to get high on grass and amphetamines (speed). Grass was the drug of choice for most of my 15 to 20 friends who played ball and hung out together. We would get high mostly coming in from combat missions but sometimes while traveling to combat areas. I quit using when I decided I was endangering myself and others by being high on missions. With GOD's help, I stopped harming my body and mind. I decided to get my high from recommitting my life to GOD. My advice to my comrades who felt they had to have drugs to endure the war environment was to get high on GOD. Mother had sent me a Bible and it brought me great consolation in the jungles of Vietnam. GOD's Words proved to be a refuge in the time of trouble.

GOD's blessings sometimes are disguised. To draw me away from my friends and get me clean from drugs, I was infected with malaria fever. Malaria is sometimes a deadly disease. It is caused by the bite of an anopheles mosquito that has bitten a person who has the disease. After I contracted the disease, I was hospitalized in a secured area on Cam Ranh Bay. After the initial symptoms were arrested, I was allowed to go swimming daily when I did not have other patient duties. I was hospitalized for about thirty days and it really felt good to be free from combat.

After I was discharged from the hospital, I returned to my unit and was assigned a base camp job. I was blessed to be given a week of rest and relaxation (R&R) in Hawaii. When I returned from R&R, within a couple of months, I applied for entry into college again. I was accepted for the fall semester and received a three-month early release from the military to go back to college.

I left Vietnam the first week in October 1970 and was in a classroom the second week of October. It was a most uplifting experience to get away from the combat and monsoon season of Vietnam. "Thank you again, Oh Merciful Father, for being with me." I could have very well been killed, as many of my friends and comrades who lost their lives in Vietnam. It indeed is a blessing to be writing today and reflecting on my experience in the most costly war in terms of monetary expenses and physical lives, that the U.S. has been engaged. We lost over 58,000 U.S. military persons in Vietnam. I graciously recall that I had been assigned to an infantry unit that frequently engaged in contact with the Viet Congs and came back hardly with a scratch. It is amazing how GOD provides protection for those persons who truly believe in Him. Again, I must thank my "Dear Mother" for teaching me at an early age about GOD and the value of prayer.

To summarize my Vietnam survival experience by a reference from the Holy Bible, I think it is appropriate to use the following passages from Psalms

34: 6 - "This poor man cried, and the Lord heard him, and saved him out of all his troubles. 7 – The angel of the Lord encampeth round about them that fear him, and delivereth them. 11 – Come ye children, hearken unto me: I will teach you the fear of the Lord. 13 – Keep thy tongue from evil, and thy lips from speaking guile. 14 – Depart from evil, and do good: seek peace, and pursue it. 15 – The eyes of the Lord are upon the righteous, and his ears are open unto their cry. The face of the Lord is against them that do evil, to cut off the remembrance of them from the earth. 17 – The righteous cry, and the Lord heareth, and delivereth them out of all their troubles. 18 – The Lord is nigh unto them that are of a broken heart: and saveth such as be of a contrite spirit. 19 – Many are the afflictions of the righteous: but the Lord delivereth him out of them all. 20 – He keepeth all his bones: not one of them is broken. 21 – Evil shall slay the wicked: and they that hate the righteous shall be desolate. 22 – The Lord redeemed the soul of his servants: and none of them that trust him shall be desolate."

CHAPTER FIVE
Bachelor Degree

My episode in Vietnam reaffirmed my belief that those who truly believe in GOD and ask His guidance shall not perish but have everlasting life. Let's pray: "Lord, enable my belief in You to be strengthen today and take my life and use me for Your service. Amen."

Yes, it was while I was in Vietnam, I learned how to really pray and try to establish more rapport with GOD. If you were assigned to an infantry unit that, almost daily faced combat situations, you would have learned to also depend on GOD. My faith was quite strong and I believe I had a special angel protecting me in Vietnam. Throughout my tour in Vietnam, I was blessed, as GOD heard my supplications and the prayers of relatives and friends. James 5:16 says, "Confess your faults one to another, and pray one for another, that ye may be healed. The effectual fervent prayer of a righteous man availeth much." Although many of my friends and comrades were injured and paid the ultimate sacrifice, death, GOD spared me from all harm during this treacherous time in the Vietnam War. I vowed that I would forever give GOD praises and honor as long as I lived. I fervently believed that GOD wanted me to uplift and glorify His name to others before I departed this journey on this earth.

My faith became stronger because of the Vietnam experience and I learned the revelation of the Words found in Hebrews 11:1-12,39,40 – "Now faith is being sure of what we hope for and certain of what we do not see. This is what the ancients were commended for. By faith we understand that the universe was formed at GOD's command, so that what is seen was not made out of what was visible. By faith Abel offered GOD a better sacrifice than Cain did. By faith he was commended as a righteous man, when GOD spoke well of his offerings. And by faith he still speaks, even though he is dead. By faith Enoch was taken from this life, so that he did not experience death: he could not be found, because GOD had taken him away. For before he was taken, he was commended as one who pleased GOD. And without faith it is impossible to please GOD, because anyone who comes to him must believe that he exists and that he rewards those who earnestly seek him. By faith Noah, when warned about things not yet seen, in holy fear built an ark to save his family. By his faith he condemned the world and became heir of the righteousness that comes by faith. By faith Abraham, when called to go to a place he would later receive as his inheritance, obeyed and went, even though he did not know where he was going. By faith he made his home in the promised land like a stranger in a foreign country: he lived in tents, as did Isaac and Jacob, who were heirs with him of the same promise. For he was looking forward to the city with foundations, whose architect and builder is GOD. By faith Abraham, even though he was past age—and Sarah herself was barren—was enabled to become a father because he considered him faithful who had made the promise. And so from this one man, and he as good as dead, came descendants as numerous as the stars in the sky and as countless as the sand on the seashore. These were all commended for their faith, yet none of them received what had been promised. GOD had planned something better for us so that only together with us would they be made perfect." (NIV) "When I think of the goodness of Jesus and all He has done for me. My soul cries Hallelujah, thank GOD for saving me."

After I was discharged from the Army, I returned to Montgomery to resume my study at Alabama State College on the G.I. Bill. When I returned to Alabama State in 1970, it was now a University. It was great being home having most of my body in good conditions. Montgomery had made some great strides. Alabama's History reveal that currently there are five colleges and universities in Montgomery with an estimated enrollment in excess of 15, 000 students. According to documentation from my undergraduate school, Alabama State had its beginning in 1866 in Marion, Alabama as the Lincoln Normal School. In 1887, the institution moved to Montgomery and was renamed the Alabama Colored Peoples University. In 1929, the name changed to the State Teachers College at Montgomery and later to Alabama State College.

On June 26, 1969, it became Alabama State University. It has produced more teachers than any other Alabama institution. Alabama State has equipped some of the most prominent Americans with their educational nurturing. I am a sincere believer in the axiom that "it is not where you come from that determines your 'Success' but how well you apply yourself in a particular learning environment." As it is written in Proverbs12:11, "He that tilleth his land shall be satisfied with bread: but he that followeth vain persons is void of understanding." With GOD overseeing your learning, He will enable you to obtain the necessary wisdom to make you a "Success."

I received a Bachelor Degree in Sociology/History in May 1972 from Alabama State University. I also got married in May and went to Howard University in September 1972. While at Howard I worked full time as a counselor for ex-drug offenders and carried 14 hours in graduate school. Life appeared to have me in a vise-grip and was moving much too fast for me. I thought I could keep up this frenetic pace but soon found out I couldn't. I left D.C. in 1973 to return to my family and find work in Alabama.

In 1979, I began using marijuana again. This led to the divorce of my first wife in July 1980. Things continued to spiral downward when I lost my mother in October 1980 and lost my job in November 1980. I was at "Rock Bottom." When you are at the bottom of the pit, GOD can come in and instantly change your circumstance if you submit to Him.

This reminded me of the story of Joseph in the Bible. It tells how Joseph went from the "Pit To The Palace." Out of jealousy, Joseph's brothers threw him into a pit and sold him into slavery because their father loved him the most. He was loved more because he was born when their father was in old age and their father gave him an ornamented robe. The following is taken from Genesis 39:2-5, "The LORD was with Joseph and he prospered, and he lived in the house of his Egyptian master. When his master saw that the LORD was with him and that the LORD gave him success in everything he did, Joseph found favor in his eyes and became his attendant. Potiphar put him in charge of his household, and he entrusted to his care everything he owned. From the time he put him in charge of his household and of all that he owned, the LORD blessed the household of the Egyptian because of Joseph. The blessing of the LORD was on everything Potiphar had, both in the house and in the field." (NIV)

Genesis 39:20–23, "Joseph's master took him and put him in prison, the place where the king's prisoners were confined. But while Joseph was there in the prison, the LORD was with him: he showed him kindness and granted him favor in the eyes of the prison warden. So the warden put Joseph in charge of all those held in the prison, and he was made responsible for all that was done there. The warden paid no attention to anything under Joseph's care, because the LORD was with Joseph and gave him success in whatever he did." (NIV)

Genesis 41:39-43, "Then Pharaoh said to Joseph, 'Since GOD has made all this known to you, there is no one so discerning and wise as you. You shall be in charge of my palace, and all my people are to submit to your orders. Only with respect to the throne will I be greater than you.' So Pharaoh said to Joseph, 'I hereby put you in charge of the whole land of Egypt.' Then Pharaoh took his signet ring from his finger and put it on Joseph's finger. He dressed him in robes of fine linen and put a gold chain around his neck. He had him ride in a chariot as his second-in-command, and men shouted before him, 'Make way!' Thus he put him in charge of the whole land of Egypt." (NIV)

Yes, what was meant for evil, GOD turned into a blessing for Joseph. GOD can do the same for any of his children who believe in Him and seek His help. "Success" is a process, a step-by-step movement toward a goal that one wants to reach. Everyone wants instant gratification. We want to be wealthy, renown and have great "Success." No one wants to take the required often slow steps that may lead to "Success." When you are sincerely ready to make changes in your behavior or daily actions, if you submit to GOD's will, GOD will give you the ability to do what is necessary to make those changes you desire or He thinks you need. At some point on this journey of life, we all will fall short of our goals or fail at some endeavor. A person who immediately gets back up after a failure, ask GOD for help, is usually the one who will succeed or has a greater chance of achieving "Success" or reaching a specific goal. Lord, thank you for ministering to my spirit. Thank you for picking me up and turning me on the right path again. I am ready to go on in Your Name, Amen.

CHAPTER SIX
Two Governors of Alabama

George Corley Wallace Jr. is recorded in History as one of the premier segregationist ever known. I worked in his final campaign for Governor of Alabama and saw up close that he was a born-again Christian. He daily tried to show love and true remorse regarding his past political views. After recovering from his gunshot wound of a 1972 assassination attempt, Wallace had sought forgiveness and apologized to the Black people of Alabama for his segregationist past. Wallace was forgiven by Black Alabama voters and was re-elected by their substantial votes. During his final term as Governor from 1983 to 1987, he appointed many Blacks to key government offices.

I received a letter dated February 29, 1984, from Governor Wallace. I believe the words he shared personally with me were from his heart and I felt proud to be the recipient of his spiritual revelation. When I had read his letter, I thought about the words in Philippians 4:19, "And my GOD will supply all your needs according to His riches in glory in Christ Jesus." Governor Wallace wrote in his letter:

Dear Dave:

Thank you so much for your letters and the copy of your manuscript. I sincerely apologize for taking this long to respond, but perhaps you can use some of the following for your book. As a young boy, I was raised in a family that had Bible devotion at breakfast. My father and my mother read me Bible stories before I was able to even read myself, and my grandfather and my father carried me to the camp meetings at Indian Springs in Georgia in the summers as a little boy. I think that I first found and came to know Jesus Christ when I was in the panhandle of Florida.

Dave, I know from experience that GOD is alive and that Jesus saves. And I know that I, like many people, have been in the valley of the shadow of death, and I know that when I was there that I asked GOD to let me live if it be His will, but if it not be His will, that I cast my lot with Him.

I would say to you, Dave, and to all people, if you have Jesus Christ in your heart and in your soul, then by the worldly standard that we some-times measure things you are a multimillionaire.

As Governor, I have dedicated and rededicated my life to our Lord and Savior Jesus Christ. I can certainly say that being a Christian has helped me to be a leader for the people of Alabama.

In closing, always remember if you have Jesus Christ in your heart and He has you in the hollow of His hand, you are whole, And I am whole. With the kindest regards and best wishes, I am.

Sincerely,
George C. Wallace
GCW: hh

One of the best Senators, in my opinion, ever sent to Washington from Alabama was Senator Howell Heflin. According to his biography, Howell Heflin was born on June 19, 1921 and was the nephew of a prominent white supremacist politician, James Thomas Heflin. During World War II, from 1942 to 1946, he served as an officer in the United States Marine Corps. He was awarded the Silver Star for valor in combat and recipient of two Purple Heart medals, seeing action on Bougainville and Guam. In 1978, Heflin was elected as a Democrat to the United States Senate to succeed John Spark-man. He remained in the Senate, where he rose to become Chairman of the Select Committee on Ethics, until January 3, 1997. Senator Heflin died on March 29, 2005 of a heart attack. The following letter was received from Senator Heflin:

United States Senate – Committee on Agriculture, Nutrition, and Forestry
Washington, DC 20510-6000
October 13, 1989
Dave Williams
559 South Court # D-2
Montgomery, Alabama 36104

Dear Dave:

Thank you for your recent letter and the accompanying material explaining the things that are being done by the people of Rice Temple AOH Church of GOD, to fight illegal drugs. I would like to extend my congratulations to the members of Rice Temple for putting forth such a positive effort to combat this menace that has invaded our society.

I regret to inform you that I do not know of any federal funding that is available for the type of program you have at Rice Temple. Generally, federal funds may not be granted to religious institutions due to church/state restrictions. I would suggest that you contact the Alabama Department of Economic and Community Affairs which may be able to assist you. You may also have some success by soliciting donations from businesses in the Montgomery area.

Again, I want to thank you for the good work you are doing at Rice Temple Church of GOD. Although I have been unable to be of much assistance concerning this request, please do not hesitate to contact me in the future if the need for my assistance should arise.

Sincerely,
Howell Heflin

After I received Senator Heflin's letter, I wrote a proposal for a friend that attended this church and subsequently received a $25,000 grant to help fund this program. An overview of this program is below:

Rice-Temple Assistance Program (RAP)

Statement of Program

Except for law enforcement officials, there is no active or direct involvement with persons in the defined areas to help alleviate drug and alcohol abuse. Due to the high incidence of crime in these areas, most community resources are fearful of attacking the problem from a caring and helping standpoint.

Numerous calls, letters, and other personal contacts have been made to our church regarding assistance with the drug and alcohol problem. Many persons who have been affected by this problem have demonstrated a strong interest and desire to have something done. There is no strategy that will cure drug abuse and in working jointly with other community resources, RAP plans to help alleviate this problem.

Goals

1. To help reduce drug dependency and abuse:
2. To help save taxpayers' dollars by helping to reduce crime and destruction of property and lives:
3. To help establish better family and neighbor relations:
4. To provide twice a week discussions or therapy sessions.

Objectives

1. To provide a forum for community resources, residents, and other officials to seriously try to find solutions to the drug and alcohol abuse problem:
2. To coordinate services and activities for residents of Caroline Courts, Clayton Courts, Cleveland Courts, and other west side disadvantaged areas where drug and alcohol abuse is of epidemic nature:
3. To help youths to learn about drug and alcohol abuse: stimulate discussion groups and create support groups for family and friends.

How Effects of Assistance Will Be Measured

1. Percentage of participation by target group and community:
2. Reduction in crime and drug activity as reported by law enforcement data:
3. On-going feedback through weekly discussions.

GOD is our father and His heart is for us to prosper and be in good health. 3 John 1:2 says it this way: "Beloved, I wish above all things that thou mayest prosper and be in health, even as thy soul prospereth." If one wants to grow in the Words of GOD, it is mandatory to study the Bible daily!! We must pray unceasingly and ask GOD to give us the wisdom to understand His Words and do His will. The Bible is the vehicle that GOD provided to carry us throughout our earthly journey and help us to reach our eternal home.

An old story states, "A patient noticed a Bible on the doctor's desk. He asked, 'Doctor, do you, a psychiatrist, read the Bible?' The doctor said, 'I not only read it, I study it. It's the greatest textbook on human behavior ever put together. If people would absorb its message, a lot of us psychiatrists could close our offices and go fishing.' The psychiatrist picked up the Bible and turned to Ephesians 6:13 and read four words by Paul, 'Having done all, stand.' This means when you have done your best: you have tried various solutions for a problem or situation you are facing: you feel as though you are running in circles and not getting satisfaction: all you need to do is stand still and allow GOD to help you. He will give you that peace of mind you are seeking.

From the beginning to the end, the Bible illustrates that the human soul, spirit and conscious are battlegrounds where good struggles with evil. GOD wants us to be prosperous, happy, and enjoy our lives every day. The sky is the limit when we realize that GOD's unconditional love forgives and forgets and He expects us to do the same. GOD wants us to follow the advice of John Wesley: 'Do all the good you can, by all the means you can, in all the ways you can, in all the places you can, at all the times you can, to all the people you can, as long as ever you can.'

Ecclesiastes 9:8-9 states, 'Each day is GOD's gift. It's all you get in exchange for the hard work of staying alive. Make the most of each one!' Roman 8:31 says, 'If GOD is for us, who can be against us?' GOD provides all our needs and those desires He wants us to have just as He does for the sparrows. When we are mistreated and it appears we have a door of opportunity closed in our face, GOD sees this experience. We must continue to trust Him to open another door with bigger and better things in store for us."

One of the finest gentlemen I have met in my life is the former Governor of Alabama, Donald Eugene Siegelman. I consider Don Siegelman, my friend. He has helped me personally on many occasions. Don is the only person in the History of Alabama to be elected to serve in all four of the top statewide elected offices: Secretary of State, Attorney General, Lieutenant Governor and Governor. I worked for Don when he was Attorney General. When I moved to Detroit and was seeking employment, Don wrote the following reference letter which helped me to get a job:

To Whom It May Concern:

Mr. David Williams worked for me when I was Attorney General of Alabama. David was an excellent employee with high work ethic standards. He was loyal and completed each and every task to my complete satisfaction.

During Mr. Williams' tenure with the office of the Attorney General he related to me a problem which had occurred while he was working with the Department of Human Resources. The situation seemed so outrageous and unfair that I told David I would investigate the matter and see if it could be expunged. I left office before this matter was completed and David had no way of knowing that it had not been expunged.

David Williams is a good person and was a good employee for the State of Alabama. If you have further questions, please call me.

Sincerely,
Don Siegelman

In 2006, Don Siegelman was convicted on corruption charges from his last term as Governor. There has been an ongoing controversy due to counteraccusations that his prosecution was intentionally wrongful, engineered by former President George W. Bush, presidential advisor, *Karl Rove* and officials of the *U.S. Department of Justice* to gain political advantage. On September 23, 2009, Don Siegelman sent me the following in an e-mail: "My case is now before the U.S. Supreme Court. For the first time in history, *First Amendment Law Professors*_and former state Attorneys General, 91 of them, both Democrats and Republicans have filed briefs saying in essence that I should not have been prosecuted!" I am prayerful and I fervently believe that Don will eventually receive justice in this matter. In my opinion, Don Siegelman is the victim of a political lynching by former President George Bush, Karl Rove and their

operatives! I sent the following letter to support the innocence of Don Siegelman during his litigation:

February 6, 2007
Honorable Mark E. Fuller, Chief
United States District Judge
P.O. Box 711
Montgomery, AL36101-0711

Dear Judge Fuller:

I am a native of Montgomery, Alabama and a graduate of Alabama State University. Guardian angels rescued me on two perilous occasions that left an
indelible imprint on my life. While a combat infantry soldier in Vietnam in
1970, an angel rescued me in the midst of a horrific firefight when many of
my comrades lost their lives. Again, in 1989 in Montgomery while despon-
dent, unemployed and penniless an angel named Mr. Don Siegelman hired
me as a field worker in his bid for Alabama's Attorney General. Mr. Siegelman gave me renewed hope. After his victory in the Attorney General's race,
I was appointed to a position in the Attorney General's Press Office.

I got married and moved to Michigan in 1992. Mr. Siegelman demonstrated his compassion again by writing the enclosed letter which assisted
me to become employed (Exhibit 1). I returned to graduate school in 1995
and completed my MSW as a Dean's Scholar (transcript – Exhibit 2). As
the enclosed brochure indicates, I have begun my own consultation business (Exhibit 3). Without reservation, I feel through divine intervention,
Mr. Siegelman was the catalyst that turned my life around.

Mr. Don Siegelman is a good and courageous man. Because of his visionary leadership and compassion, Alabama is a better state for all GOD's
children. Unequivocally, I pray that this Honorable Court will extend
mercy on this man who has tried to help instill justice, equality and opportunities for all people.

Sincerely,
David M. Williams, MSW

CHAPTER SEVEN
Master's Degree

After moving to Detroit in 1992, I got remarried to a native of Montgomery, Patricia (Pat) Williams, who had been living in Detroit since 1972, I felt revived. Pat and I were high school sweethearts for a period of time. I met Pat when she was in the 9th grade at Booker Taliaferro Washington High School (The Yellow-jackets). Our first meeting was at a dance at the Houston Hills Community Center, the local weekend place to be on the eastside. She was a charming young lady and a great dancer and I also thought I was a pretty good dancer. She lived about a mile from the center in Tulane Courts. I lived about two miles from the center on Hall Street. We enjoyed our company then and ended up getting married almost thirty years after we first met. We have been married for over seventeen years and in my opinion, Pat is one of the best RN in the profession. Pat has been a pillar of strength during our marriage and I often sing to her Bette Midler's song "Wind Beneath My Wings", which goes, "Did you ever know that you're my hero? You're everything I wish I could be. I could fly higher than an eagle, for you are the wind beneath my wings."

Pat practices her profession 24-7 wherever she may be positioned. We both have children from previous marriages. GOD joined us together and He doesn't make mistakes. Psalm 22:4-5 reads, "Our fathers trusted in you: they trusted, and you delivered them. They cried to you, and were not ashamed." GOD is Omnipresent/ present everywhere: Omnipotent/ All Powerful: Omniscient/ Knows Everything: Why shouldn't everyone trust a GOD like this?

I worked for the State of Michigan for a few years and decided I wanted to go back to graduate school. With Pat's permission, I applied to Wayne State

University full time to try to complete my masters in social work (MSW). One of the requirements for entry into Wayne State University graduate program was to submit a personal interest statement. I submitted the statement below:

Personal Interest Statement- Submitted as Requirement for Master of Social Work (MSW) Program

I feel my myriad of experiences in Social Work related positions dictate that I obtain a MSW degree in order to help formulate policies in this current wave of welfare reform. By completing your MSW program, I will be better equipped to identify the human, financial, technical or organizational resources available to assist the disenfranchised and needy of our society.

My entire adult life has been devoted to making life better for those who are less fortunate. While serving in the U.S. Army in Vietnam, and while growing up in Montgomery, Alabama during the Civil Rights Struggle, I have witnessed first-hand the inequities experienced by African-Americans. I vowed to avail myself to opportunities to improve my knowledge and skills in order to assist those in need.

Finally, without equivocation, I believe completion of your MSW program will enable me to assist with empowering those disenfranchised persons who do not want a hand-out but only want someone sensitive to their plight and committed to helping them escape hopelessness. It is my desire to obtain MSW and continue to be a bridge for others to cross from deprivation.

Respectfully Submitted,
David M. Williams 2-15-95

According to Wayne State University (WSU) documentation, WSU is a comprehensive university with 13 colleges and schools. WSU is Michigan's only urban research university, located in the heart of Detroit's University Cultural Center. WSU has about 350 academic programs, including 126 bachelor's degree programs, 139 master's degree programs, 60 doctoral degree programs and 30 certificate, specialist and professional programs. One of WSU goal is to develop mutually beneficial partnerships with the Metro-Detroit communities as a catalyst for the region's social, cultural, economic and educational enrichment.

WSU is among the nation's leaders in preparing people for professional practice.

Wayne State University School of Social Work has both undergraduate and graduate programs leading to the Bachelor of Social Work (BSW) or Master of Social Work (MSW) degree. The school is nationally known for the quality of its educational programs. The MSW program consists of two academic years of full-time study for a total of 60 credits, 30 each year. The credits are a combination of curriculum and 10 credits in field education (three full days a week of supervised practice in a social agency). Typically, students are enrolled in 15 credits for each of four semesters. The first year of graduate study is called the "Core Year" and, as mandated by the Council of Social Work Education (CSWE), provides a foundation of basic social work knowledge and skills for all students. The second year of graduate study is designated the "Advanced Year." Students select their concentration area toward the end of the Core Year or as they enter the Advanced Year.

I enjoyed my two years at WSU and the rigors of graduate school. I was named a "Dean's Scholar" and my tuition was paid by a grant for my second year. My second year Field Placement was the Black United Fund, inc.(BUF). I learned the intimate details of constructing budgets and implementing objectives and goals. BUF is a non-profit charitable agency. I graduated from WSU in May 1997. Upon leaving BUF, they gave me a farewell party and a plaque which I still cherish. It reads as follows:

NEW BIRTH

'Success is not measured by what we have, but rather who we have.'

Mr. David Williams, the Black United Fund of Michigan, inc.(BUF) is proud to have had the opportunity to work with someone who exemplified the real meaning of "Joy and Happiness."

Choosing to go back to college and pursue your master's degree was probably the best decision you could have ever made, because you took a chance and stepped out in faith in order to make your dream a reality. We salute you for achieving educational "Excellency."

After two years of course work, papers, lectures and research, you finally accomplished your goal. This goal is in fact "a new birth." It is time of birth because you now have the opportunity to birth a new career, on a new level, with new ideas that did not come from course work or textbooks, but from GOD, who freely give us wisdom and understanding.

Your internship here at BUF has been both a pleasant and educational experience. We thank GOD for your kind and unselfish spirit. Your willingness to roll up your sleeves and lend a helping hand will always be remembered. You have touched our lives in such a way, that wherever you go and whatever you decide to do, others will see your "light of enthusiasm and will follow in your footsteps. You are a light that sits upon a hill and cannot be hid. We congratulate you and wish you GOD's best as you go forth into the community and do what you do best, "Shine!"

According to her biography, Dr. Mary Jane McLeod Bethune was born on July 10, 1875 and expired on May 18, 1955. Dr. Bethune was an American educator and civil rights leader best known for starting a school for *Black students in Daytona Beach, Florida that eventually became Bethune-Cookman University and for being an advisor to President Franklin D. Roosevelt. Dr.* Bethune dedicated her life to the education of both whites and blacks about the accomplishments and needs of Black people, writing in 1938, "If our people are to fight their way up out of bondage we must arm them with the sword and the shield and buckler of pride - belief in themselves and their possibilities, based upon a sure knowledge of the achievements of the past. Not only the Negro child but children of all races should read and know of the achievements, accomplishments and deeds of the Negro. World peace and brotherhood are based on a common understanding of the contributions and cultures of all races and creeds.

Dr. Bethune said, "Sometimes as I sit communing in my study I feel that death is not far off. I am aware that it will overtake me before the greatest of my dreams – full equality for the Negro in our time – is realized. Yet, I face that reality without fear or regrets. I am resigned to death as all humans must be at the proper time. Death neither alarms nor frightens one who has had a long career of fruitful toil. The knowledge that my work has been helpful to many fills me with joy and great satisfaction."

Referred to as her "Last Will and Testament," Dr. Bethune wrote, "Since my retirement from an active role in educational work and from the affairs of the National Council of Negro Women, I have been living quietly and working at my desk at my home here in Florida. The years have directed a change of pace for me. I am now 78 years old and my activities are no longer so strenuous as they once were. I feel that I must conserve my strength to finish the work at hand. Already I have begun working on my autobiography which will record my life-journey in detail, together with the innumerable side trips which have carried me abroad, into every corner of our country, into homes both lowly and luxurious, and even into the White House to confer with Presidents. I have also deeded my home and its contents to the Mary McLeod Bethune Foundation, organized in March 1953, for research, interracial activity and the sponsorship of wider educational opportunities.

Sometimes I ask myself if I have any other legacy to leave. Truly, my worldly possessions are few. Yet, my experiences have been rich. From them, I have distilled principles and policies in which I believe firmly, for they represent the meaning of my life's work. They are the products of much sweat and sorrow. Perhaps in them there is something of value. So, as my life draws to a close, I will pass them on to Negroes everywhere in the hope that an old woman's philosophy may give them inspiration. Here, then is my legacy.

I LEAVE YOU LOVE.
Love builds. It is positive and helpful. It is more beneficial than hate. Injuries quickly forgotten quickly pass away. Personally and racially, our enemies must be forgiven. Our aim must be to create a world of fellowship and justice where no man's skin, color or religion, is held against him. "Love thy neighbor" is a precept which could transform the world if it were universally practiced. It connotes brotherhood and, to me, brotherhood of man is the noblest concept in all human relations. Loving your neighbor means being interracial, inter-religious and international.

I LEAVE YOU HOPE.

The Negro's growth will be great in the years to come. Yesterday, our ancestors endured the degradation of slavery, yet they retained their dignity. Today, we direct our economic and political strength toward winning a more abundant and secure life. Tomorrow, a new Negro, unhindered by race taboos and shackles, will benefit from more than 330 years of ceaseless striving and struggle. Theirs will be a better world. This I believe with all my heart.

I LEAVE YOU THE CHALLENGE OF DEVELOPING CONFIDENCE IN ONE ANOTHER.

As long as Negroes are hemmed into racial blocs by prejudice and pressure, it will be necessary for them to band together for economic betterment. Negro banks, insurance companies and other businesses are examples of successful, racial economic enterprises. These institutions were made possible by vision and mutual aid. Confidence was vital in getting them started and keeping them going. Negroes have got to demonstrate still more confidence in each other in business. This kind of confidence will aid the economic rise of the race by bringing together the pennies and dollars of our people and ploughing them into useful channels. Economic separatism cannot be tolerated in this enlightened age, and it is not practicable. We must spread out as far and as fast as we can, but we must also help each other as we go.

I LEAVE YOU A THIRST FOR EDUCATION.

Knowledge is the prime need of the hour. More and more, Negroes are taking full advantage of hard-won opportunities for learning, and the educational level of the Negro population is at its highest point in history. We are making greater use of the privileges inherent in living in a democracy. If we continue in this trend, we will be able to rear increasing numbers of strong, purposeful men and women, equipped with vision, mental clarity, health and education.

I LEAVE YOU RESPECT FOR THE USES OF POWER.

We live in a world which respects power above all things. Power, intelligently directed, can lead to more freedom. Unwisely directed, it can be a dreadful, destructive force. During my lifetime I have seen the power of the Negro grow enormously. It has always been my first concern that this power should be placed on the side of human justice.

Now that the barriers are crumbling everywhere, the Negro in America must be ever vigilant lest his forces be marshalled behind wrong causes and undemocratic movements. He must not lend his support to any group that seeks to subvert democracy. That is why we must select leaders who are wise, courageous, and of great moral stature and ability. We have great leaders among us today: Ralph Bunche, Channing Tobias, Mordecai Johnson, Walter White, and Mary Church Terrell. [The latter now deceased]. We have had other great men and women in the past: *Frederick Douglass, Booker T. Washington, Harriet Tubman,* and *Sojourner Truth.* We must produce more qualified people like them, who will work not for themselves, but for others.

I LEAVE YOU FAITH.

Faith is the first factor in a life devoted to service. Without faith, nothing is possible. With it, nothing is impossible. Faith in GOD is the greatest power, but great, too, is faith in oneself. In 50 years the faith of the American Negro in himself has grown immensely and is still increasing. The measure of our progress as a race is in precise relation to the depth of the faith in our people held by our leaders. Frederick Douglass, genius though he was, was spurred by a deep conviction that his people would heed his counsel and follow him to freedom. Our greatest Negro figures have been imbued with faith. Our forefathers struggled for liberty in conditions far more onerous than those we now face, but they never lost the faith. Their perseverance paid rich dividends. We must never forget their sufferings and their sacrifices, for they were the foundations of the progress of our people.

I LEAVE YOU RACIAL DIGNITY.

I want Negroes to maintain their human dignity at all costs. We, as Negroes, must recognize that we are the custodians as well as the heirs of a great civilization. We have given something to the world as a race and for this we are proud and fully conscious of our place in the total picture of mankind's development. We must learn also to share and mix with all men. We must make an effort to be less race conscious and more conscious of individual and human values. I have never been sensitive about my complexion. My color has never destroyed my self-respect nor has it ever caused me to conduct myself in such a manner as to merit the disrespect of any person. I have not let my color handicap me. Despite many crushing burdens and handicaps, I have risen from the cotton fields of South Carolina to found a college, administer it during its years of growth, become a public servant in the government of our country and a leader of women. I would not exchange my color for all the wealth in the world, for had I been born white I might not have been able to do all that I have done or yet hope to do.

I LEAVE YOU A DESIRE TO LIVE HARMONIOUSLY WITH YOUR FELLOW MEN.

The problem of color is worldwide. It is found in Africa and Asia, Europe and South America. I appeal to American Negroes — North, South, East and West — to recognize their common problems and unite to solve them. I pray that we will learn to live harmoniously with the white race. So often, our difficulties have made us hypersensitive and truculent. I want to see my people conduct themselves naturally in all relationships — fully conscious of their manly responsibilities and deeply aware of their heritage. I want them to learn to understand whites and influence them for good, for it is advisable and sensible for us to do so. We are a minority of 15 million living side by side with a white majority. We must learn to deal with these people positively and on an individual basis.

I LEAVE YOU FINALLY A RESPONSIBILITY TO OUR YOUNG PEOPLE.

The world around us really belongs to youth for youth will take over its future management. Our children must never lose their zeal for building a better world. They must not be discouraged from aspiring toward greatness, for they are to be the leaders of tomorrow. Nor must they forget that the masses of our people are still underprivileged, ill-housed, impoverished and victimized by discrimination. We have a powerful potential in our youth, and we must have the courage to change old ideas and practices so that we may direct their power toward good ends. Faith, courage, brotherhood, dignity, ambition, responsibility — these are needed today as never before. We must cultivate them and use them as tools for our task of completing the establishment of equality for the Negro. We must sharpen these tools in the struggle that faces us and find new ways of using them. The Freedom Gates are half-ajar. We must pry them fully open. If I have a legacy to leave my people, it is my philosophy of living and serving. As I face tomorrow, I am content, for I think I have spent my life well. I pray now that my philosophy may be helpful to those who share my vision of a world of Peace, Progress, Brotherhood, and Love."

CHAPTER EIGHT
Judge Damon Keith

When I was in the 7th grade, one of my favorite readings was *The Reader's Digest*, "My Most Unforgettable Character." While I worked as a substitute teacher at Winship Middle school, I distributed to all my classes and other teachers a biography on Judge Damon Keith. It was titled, "One of My Most Unforgettable Characters – Honorable Damon Jerome Keith." Many of the students did not know who Judge Keith was and I gave them a life lesson on this great American.

In 1997, after having knee surgery from playing basketball, I started rehabilitation at Ford's Center for Athletic Medicine. Subsequently I became a member of Fitness Works, a contracted fitness center which offered memberships to the public and provided the medical staff with the environment needed to ease a recovering athlete through rehabilitation and back to participating in sports. One of the persons who worked out at the center regularly was U.S. Appeals Court Judge Damon Keith. I had heard a lot about Judge Keith but talking with him personally made me more cognizant of why he is a great American. Judge Keith graduated from Howard University Law School in 1949 and earned a LL.M from Wayne State University (WSU) in 1956. In 1993, Judge Keith established a unique law collection at WSU in Detroit that traces the contributions of Black lawyers and judges to American jurisprudence. The centerpiece of the collection is a traveling exhibit called "Marching Toward Justice."

Over the years since our meeting, Judge Keith has shared with me documents and information which I will forever cherish. The following was taken from a Summary Biography Judge Keith sent me: "Judge Keith was born in Detroit, Michigan, and has served as a judge on the United States Court of Appeals for the Sixth Circuit since 1977. Prior to his appointment to the Court of Appeals, Judge Keith served as Chief Judge of the United States District Court for the Eastern District of Michigan. As a member of the federal judiciary, Judge Keith has consistently stood as a courageous defender of the constitutional and civil rights of all people. In United States v. Sinclair, commonly referred to as the Keith Decision, the Supreme Court unanimously affirmed Judge Keith's landmark ruling prohibiting President Nixon and the federal government from engaging in warrantless wiretapping in violation of the Fourth Amendment. Judge Keith was heralded for that decision because he was a prime example of an independent federal judge. He had the courage to say no in the face of a presidency which likened itself to a 'sovereign. One writer said, 'The strength of the judiciary is rooted in just such independence as that displayed by Keith.'

In the case Detroit Free Press v. Ashcroft, Judge Keith stood up to President George W. Bush during the aftermath of 9/11. Writing for a unanimous United States Court of Appeals panel, Judge Keith memorably declared, "Democracies die behind closed doors," and ruled it unlawful for the Bush administration to conduct deportation hearings in secret whenever the government asserted that the people involved might be linked to terrorism. In his September 2, 2002 op-ed entitled, Secrecy is Our Enemy, New York Times columnist Bob Herbert lauded Judge Keith's opinion as 'forceful' and 'eloquent,' noting, 'You want an American hero? A real hero? I nominate Judge Damon J. Keith of the United States Court of Appeals for the Sixth Circuit.'

Judge Keith has also vigorously enforced the nation's civil rights laws, most notably in the areas of employment and education. In Stamps v. Detroit Edison Co., Judge Keith ruled the Detroit Edison Company had practiced systematic racial discrimination, resulting in fines against the company of $4 million and against the employee union of $250,000, and an order for the company to institute an aggressive affirmative action program. Within the context of education, in Davis v. School District of Pontiac, Judge Keith found that the city had unlawfully built schools to coincide with segregated housing patterns. Accordingly, he ordered the implementation of city-wide busing to promote integration and to guarantee equal protection under the law for all children.

Judge Keith's fidelity to the U.S. Constitution has been well recognized. In 1985, Chief Justice Warren E. Burger appointed Judge Keith Chairman of the Bicentennial of the Constitution Committee for the Sixth Circuit. In 1987, Judge Keith was appointed by Chief Justice William Rehnquist to serve as the National Chairman of the Judicial Conference Committee on the Bicentennial of the Constitution. In 1990, President George H.W. Bush followed suit and appointed Judge Keith to the Commission on the Bicentennial of the Constitution. In recognition of Judge Keith's service to the Bicentennial Committee, Bill of Rights plaques commemorating this important constitutional anniversary bear Judge Keith's name. These plaques adorn the walls of courthouses and law schools throughout the United States and Guam, as well as the FBI Headquarters and the Thurgood Marshall Federal Judiciary Center in Washington, D.C.

In 1998, Judge Keith was chosen to receive the Edward J. Devitt Distinguished Service to Justice Award. The recipient of the Devitt Award is selected each year by a panel comprised of a United States Supreme Court justice, a federal circuit judge, and a federal district court judge, and honors the recipient as an outstanding federal judge of national stature.

In January 2000, at the Eighth Annual Trumpet Awards in Atlanta, Georgia, Turner Broadcasting Systems presented Judge Keith with the Pinnacle Award. In February 2000, Judge Keith's career was profiled by Court TV as part of a program saluting 'America's Great Legal Minds' in honor of Black History Month. The National Urban League also presented Judge Keith with its highest honor, the Whitney Young Award, at its National Conference in July 2004.

In 2005, Harvard University's Department of Afro-American Studies included Judge Keith in its African American National Biography, a collection of biographies profiling eminent African Americans. Also in 2005, Judge Keith served as co-chair of the National Victory Celebration for the Farewell to Mrs. Rosa Parks, organizing memorial services across the country for Mrs. Parks. Twenty-six years earlier, Judge Keith had proudly presented Mrs. Parks with the NAACP's highest honor, the Spingarn Award, in Louisville, Kentucky.

As a community leader, Judge Keith organized local businessmen to provide housing for Mrs. Parks, after she was robbed and physically assaulted in her house. In 2004, Judge Keith was again responsible for rallying members of Detroit's African-American business community, this time to save the city's Charles H. Wright Museum of African-American History from bankruptcy. The Detroit Board of Education has dedicated one of its primary schools in his honor, naming it *The Damon J. Keith Elementary School*.

Humbly, I note that Judge Keith and I have a few things in common. We both attended HU and WSU. We both were rooted in living a GODly life from an early age. We both are Deacons at local churches. We both have tried to make our world better for all GOD's children. Finally, we both fervently believe in Luke12:48, "For unto whomsoever much is given, of him shall be much required: and to whom men have committed much, of him they will ask the more."

Judge Keith is the recipient of numerous awards, most notably, the NAACP's highest award, the Spingarn Medal, whose past recipients include Rev. Martin Luther King, Jr., Justice Thurgood Marshall, Mrs. Rosa Parks, and General Colin Powell. Judge Keith has received over forty honorary degrees from colleges and universities across the country. Harvard University, on June 5, 2008 gave him an honorary degree which stated, "Avatar of independence, champion of equal justice under law, a just and humane jurist who has shared and shaped the action and passion of his time."

One day Judge Keith chuckled when I told him that I felt like the luckiest man in the world: meeting both Dr. King and Judge Keith face to face. Judge Keith's life is a testimony to the power of one person to improve the fortunes of so many in our society. He put it this way, "I am thankful to GOD that I am on the second highest court in the country and have had the opportunity to practice a personal philosophy that is so deeply engraved in me – that whoever you are, you should work to make things better – to make a difference." Yes, without a doubt, Judge Keith is a great example of how GOD can lead you to "Success" if you trust Him.

CHAPTER NINE
Reach Out And Help Others

The Hatch Act of 1939 is a United States federal law whose main provision is to prohibit federal employees (civil servants) from engaging in partisan political activity. In my opinion and I'm sure many other citizens of Michigan feel that John Engler was the worst Governor in History. During his term as Governor from 1991 to 2003, he cut spending for social problems like mental health and welfare, he reduced spending for public education and he attacked public employees unions. He made sure his allies had plenty funds in their corporate welfare. His ultra-conservative policies made him one of the darlings of the Republican Party. I have always been an optimist and from a lad had great spiritual belief that GOD is involved in all our actions. John Engler was known to punish anyone who opposed his way of governance. I have no doubt he continuously violated the Hatch Act. I believe when we do what the Spirit tells us to do we should not be concerned about opposition. I was terminated from the State of Michigan by John Engler's cronies because the local newspaper editor published the letter below I submitted:

Detroit Free Press, "Letter to the Editor," March 14, 2000

Reach Out, Help Others

I am a welfare services specialist with the Michigan Family Independence Agency. As Gov. Engler likes to exclaim, we have made tremendous strides in reducing the welfare rolls. But as a professional social worker who works with families that become involved with Children Protective Services, I feel that too many of our citizens are disfranchised. It is the mandate for all public servants to help the least of our society enjoy some of the American dream.

Our spiritual vision should implore us to help develop and implement strong policies to assist the less fortunate. We must innovate and facilitate programs to help those citizens who need a little more assistance in order to escape the cycle of poverty. To survive and meet the basic needs of life is a challenge to far too many of our average citizens.

We can and must do better. It behooves us to improve our relationships with persons we have contact with in our daily activities. We can work together to seek happiness or perish from self-destruction.

David M. Williams, Detroit

About the same time I sent this letter to the Detroit Free Press, I mailed John Engler a proposal which I had sent to the Register of Copyrights (ROC). I received a copyright registration effective date of May 31, 2000 for my proposal entitled Enrichment and Counseling Center (ECC). The proposal stated, "The primary focus and objective of ECC's is to help advance mankind by providing high professional services and programs for the community, city and state. ECC's would provide at affordable prices comprehensive and intensive therapy for children and adults." Since we had MSW's in-house, I thought it would be cost-effective to utilize state MSW's for counseling instead of using private contractors. John Engler acknowledged receipt of my proposal by writing me the letter that follows, dated May 3, 2000:

Dear Mr. Williams:

Thank you for taking the time to share your concerns with me. Your information and opinions help keep me informed on matters that are most important to the people of Michigan.

I have taken the liberty of forwarding your concerns to Mr. Douglas Howard, director of the Michigan Family Independence Agency, for his review.

Mr. Howard's office will contact you if he has any questions or needs further information.

Thank you again for contacting my office.
Sincerely,
John Engler, Governor

After I received this letter, the pressure to make me resign was unbearable. The final straw occurred when my supervisor accused me of pushing her. I was suspended while an investigation was launched. Being a disciple of Dr. King, I have rigidly followed the non-violent philosophy throughout my life, except for when I was drafted for the Army. This accusation brought me great pain. This demonstrated clearly the limits your enemies would go to achieve their goals. I was terminated from state services on October 3, 2001, just after the September 11, 2001 terror attacks that had our nation in great uncertainty. "Rock Bottom" had struck again.

Although I have always been an optimist and had great spiritual belief, this hurt tremendously for a while. I still believed in the end, right always win. Psalm 27:1-14 brought me some relief: "The LORD is my light and my salvation, whom shall I fear? The LORD is the stronghold of my life, of whom shall I be afraid? When evil men advance against me to devour my flesh, when my enemies and my foes attack me, they will stumble and fall. Though an army besiege me, my heart will not fear: though war break out against me, even then will I be confident. One thing I ask of the LORD, this is what I seek: that I may dwell in the house of the LORD all the days of my life, to gaze upon the beauty of the LORD and to seek him in his temple. For in the day of trouble he will keep me safe in his dwelling: he will hide me in the shelter of his tabernacle and set me high upon a rock. Then my head will be exalted above the enemies who surround me: at his tabernacle will I sacrifice with shouts of joy: I will sing and make music to the LORD. Hear my voice when I call, O LORD: be merciful to me and answer me. My heart says of you, 'Seek his face!' Your face, LORD, I will seek. Do not hide your face from me, do not turn your servant away in anger: you have been my helper. Do not reject me or forsake me, O GOD my Savior. Though my father and mother forsake me, the LORD will receive me. Teach me your way, O LORD: lead me in a straight path because of my oppressors. Do not turn me over to the desire of my foes, for false witnesses rise up against me, breathing out violence. I am still confident of this: I will see the goodness of the LORD in the land of the living. Wait for the LORD: be strong and take heart and wait for the LORD."

I filed a lawsuit against the State of Michigan but one of the lowest points in my life occurred when I read the order below:

Case # 04=429878-CD

Williams v State of Michigan, Family Independence Agency et al

Order Granting Defendant's Motion For Summary Disposition

At a session of Court, held in the Wayne County Circuit Court, City of Detroit, County of Wayne, State of Michigan, on the 9th day of December, 2005.

Present: Honorable Cynthia Diane Stephens, Circuit Judge This action having come before the Court on Defendant's motion for summary disposition, plaintiff having filed a response, and the Court having considered the briefs and arguments of the parties:

IT IS ORDERED that, for the reasons stated on the record on December 9, 2005, Defendant's motion is granted, and Plaintiff's claims of age discrimination, retaliation for opposing age discrimination, sex discrimination and race discrimination are dismissed with prejudice.

This order resolves the last pending claim and closes the case.

Hon. Cynthia D. Stephens
Circuit Judge

On this Veterans' Day, November 11, 2009, as I am writing to complete my book, I feel full of the Holy Spirit. GOD continues to give me His Words to exclaim and to help His children. While researching through some old documents, I discovered an e-mail which stated the following:

Important Life Lessons

Sometimes, in order to not repeat the mistakes of the past, we have to look back/reflect and then move boldly into the future. A few of my favorite historical motivators are listed below. A little wisdom and account of their important **life lessons (Bold print)** are reviewed briefly to enlighten, encourage and motivate.

GOD

GOD can do anything but fail. If we believe in Him and trust Him, He will provide our every need and those desires He wishes for us to have. Let us pray: 'Almighty GOD, I am rich beyond measure because I am created in Your image. I am created to do Your good work, making Your world a more beautiful place to live for future generations. Thank you for all Your blessings, AMEN.' 2 Chronicles 7:14 – 'If my people, which are called by my name, shall humble themselves, and pray, and seek my face, and turn from their wicked ways: then will I hear from heaven and will forgive their sin, and will heal their land.'

Harriet Tubman

Excerpt from a letter to Harriet Tubman written by Frederick Douglass, August 29, 1868: 'I have had the applause of the crowd and the satisfaction that comes of being approved by the multitude, while the most that you have done has been witnessed by a few trembling, scarred, and foot-sore bondmen and women, whom you have led out of the house of bondage, and whose heartfelt 'GOD bless you' has been your reward. The midnight sky and the silent stars have been witnesses of your devotion to freedom and of your heroism. Excepting John Brown - of sacred memory - I know of no one who has willingly encountered more perils and hardships to serve our enslaved people than you have. Much that you have done would seem improbable to those who do not know you as I know you.' **You don't need public approval or a pat on the back to do what you feel is right and in the best interest of your community/nation.**

Dr. Martin Luther King Jr.

A speech that Dr. Martin Luther King Jr. gave on April 4, 1967 is the first time Dr. King openly linked Vietnam to the Civil-Rights Struggle. Dr. King explained how his views on Vietnam came into focus as he observed resources once aimed to help wipe out poverty in the U.S. be shifted to the Vietnam war. This is quite similarly to the current policies where fighting and rebuilding Iraq has caused devastation to our economy and our way of life throughout urban communities.

'Then came the buildup in Vietnam, and I watched the program broken and eviscerated as if it were some idle political plaything of a society gone mad on war, and I knew that America would never invest the necessary funds or energies in rehabilitation of its poor so long as adventures like Vietnam continued to draw men and skills and money like some demonic destructive suction tube.'

I remember as an infantry soldier in Vietnam, we use to say, 'When the going gets tough, you dig in and fight harder.' You are ready!! Now go forth and make a difference. As Dr. King said, **'I refuse to accept the view that mankind is so tragically bound to the starless midnight of racism and war that the bright daybreak of peace and brotherhood can never become a reality.... I believe that unarmed truth and unconditional love will have the final word.'**

Mrs. Maryann Mahaffey

According to the Detroit Free Press (July 28, 2006), former Detroit City Council member, Maryann Mahaffey made considerable personal sacrifice. 'Discounting herself, Mrs. Mahaffey dedicated her life to the uncompromising pursuit of justice, fairness and equal treatment for all regardless of race, gender or social status.' Until the end of her life on July 27, 2006, she was an example of the Girl Scouts mission to build individuals of courage, confidence and character, who make the world a better place to be.' **'Never forget the task ahead of us is never as great as the power of GOD behind us.'** Thank you GOD for these life lessons that are full of truths."

John14:27 reads, "Peace I leave with you, my peace I give unto you: not as the world giveth, give I unto you. Let not your heart be troubled, neither let it be afraid." I didn't get my day in court but I vowed I would continue to look forward. I prayed and renewed my trust and faith in GOD. I still believed GOD is too wise to make a mistake and too just to allow wrong to triumph over right. When the obstacles are great, GOD gets more Glory when He is allowed to help us overcome them. After you do all you can, turn it over to GOD and He will direct your path. Proverb 3:5-6 read, "Trust in the LORD with all thine heart: and lean not unto thine own understanding. In all thy ways acknowledge him, and he shall direct thy paths." GOD assured me not to be bitter but from this trial become better. I am a living witness that if we run to GOD, He will be our shelter in the time of storm.

Throughout my travel on this earthly journey, I have learned the need for GOD is inevitable. One song that confirms this to me and I enjoy singing is, "I Need Thee Every Hour." A portion of it goes, "I need Thee every hour, most gracious Lord: No tender voice like Thine can peace afford. I need Thee, O I need Thee: Every hour I need Thee: O bless me now, my Savior, I come to Thee. I need Thee every hour, stay Thou nearby: Temptations lose their power when Thou art nigh. I need Thee, O I need Thee: Every hour I need Thee: O bless me now, my Savior, I come to Thee."

The prayer of St Francis of Assisi hangs on our bathroom wall. When I need an emotional uplift and some words of restoration, I usually read these words, "Lord, make me an instrument of Thy peace: where there is hatred, let me sow love: where there is injury, pardon: where there is doubt, faith: where there is despair, hope: where there is darkness, light: and where there is sadness, joy. O Divine Master, grant that I may not so much seek to be consoled as to console: to be understood, as to understand: to be loved, as to love: for it is in giving that we receive, it is in pardoning that we are pardoned, and it is in dying that we are born to eternal life. Amen."

CHAPTER TEN
Winship Detention Model

I sent copies of my proposal to the next Governor, Jennifer Granholm, Michigan Senators and some of their Representatives. I received a letter from Senator Debbie Stabenow that reads as follows:

Dear Mr. Williams:

Thank you for contacting me about your interest in establishing Enrichment and Counseling Centers in Michigan through the Family Independence Agency. I appreciate you taking the time to share your ideas with me.

Since the issue you raised is under the jurisdiction of Michigan and the State Legislature, your representatives in Lansing would be better able to respond to you. If you have not already done so, I would urge you to contact your State Senator and State Representative in Lansing.

Thank you again for contacting me. Please do not hesitate to contact my office in the future on a federal issue of concern to you.

Sincerely,
Debbie Stabenow, United States Senator

In 2005, a friend of mine informed me by e-mail that the state department where I formerly worked the Family Independence Agency was now called the Department of Human Services (DHS) and advertised the following:

Clinical Social Workers Vacancies (sixteen) - Please post that we are seeking qualified applicants to fill sixteen permanent Clinical Social Worker positions within the Wayne County Department of Human Services. The Clinical Social Worker completes and oversees a variety of professional assignments to provide casework and treatment services. ECC's (Family Resource Centers/ FRC) were established by the State of Michigan as I had proposed to former Governor John Engler, Gov. Jennifer Granholm, Sen. Debbie Stabenow and others. According to state documentation, Governor Granholm initiated Family Resource Centers with 20 sites in 2003. She is quoted as saying: "This is not a pilot: it is a movement. Currently, expansion sites are identified by: density of DHS clients within a school, degree of local district support, and strength of collaborative leadership within a community. The goal is that FRC development will be cost neutral to the department."

Sometimes people, in this case me, don't get credit for their ideas and miss out on deserved compensation. GOD knows our heart and He knows every action we make to help his children. He won't forget and He will provide our reward. In Colossians 3:23-25 is found, "Whatever you do, work at it with all your heart, as working for the Lord, not for men, since you know that you will receive an inheritance from the Lord as a reward. It is the Lord Christ you are serving. Anyone who does wrong will be repaid for his wrong, and there is no favoritism." (NIV)After my departure from the State of Michigan, I was employed as a substitute teacher with the Detroit Public Schools (DPS) at Winship Elementary and Middle School from January, 2002 to June, 2003. This was a rude awakening for me due to the many fights I had to intervene to break-up and issue disciplinary actions to students that were involved. Substitute teachers were getting little or no respect in DPS. The principal often assigned me to the auditorium where many students that misbehaved in classes were sent for detention. For this reason, I developed "The Winship Detention Model" below and submitted it to the principal who tried to implement. This detention model was patterned after a proposal I did in graduate school.

The Winship Detention Model

Too often in today's world more time is spent in explaining or justifying the underachievement and underdevelopment of our youths rather than seeking lasting solutions. The preceding statement is especially true for those youths residing in Detroit's inner city and are attending the Detroit Public Schools.

The arguments range from school board ineptness to administrative incompetence: from dysfunctional families to community indifference: from economic exploitation to personal character flaws: the list goes on infinitely. There is perhaps some truth to all of these conclusions, but the question becomes whether we choose to wallow in a quagmire of indifference, perpetual justification and social disconnect, or whether we choose to transcend the negative overall and at least attempt to create the new and qualitatively different. Winship hopefully will choose the latter.

What is the basis for this optimism? When we think back to the trials and tribulations of our ancestors and what they were able to accomplish under the most inhumane and horrific conditions any people have ever known, and yet produced what they did, what possible excuse could exist for today's youths? Let's be clear here, yes racism and unequal opportunity continue to exist, but these are pale in comparison to what our ancestors endured and overcame.

Sharecroppers sent their children to college with nickels and dimes. Great institutions of higher learning were built with nickels and dimes: great churches were built with nickel and dimes, great businesses were built with nickels and dimes and yes, great communities were built with nickels and dimes. This was done long before the Civil Rights Movement, affirmative action and any number of compensatory justice programs. The legacy of discipline and excellence was established long before such constructs as the culture of poverty: benign neglect: intellectual inferiority: character defects and urban predator reached the American lexicon. It is clear that sometimes you need to go back in order to go forward.

The Winship Detention Model has four major program objectives:

- The first is to identify a cohort of middle school youths in DPS deemed to be academically and socially at risk based upon factors such as low educational achievement: multiple out of home placements: experimentation with alcohol and drugs: gang involvement, excessive school detentions and contact with the juvenile justice system.

- The second objective is to involve these youths in a program of personal ascension, where discipline replaces thoughtless spontaneity: excellence replaces mediocrity: hope replaces defeatism: vision replaces myopia: planning replaces reactions to uncertainty: and love replaces false consciousness.

- The third objective is to try to seek a good fit between the needs of program participants and the resources, both human and material to meet those needs in a proactive and developmentally transcendent way.

- The fourth objective of the program would be to work with and follow these students through their high school educational matriculation, raise their graduation from high school persistence index score and document the process for future replication.

I believe it is our task as American citizens to speak truth to systems that are not working in the best interest of helping to improve humanity, in this instance our children. Even when pressed by inner desires to voice concerns over things that appear wrong, many people tend to turn their head or remain silent. As I stated elsewhere, Dr King referred to this as, "Silence of betrayal."

Paul brought encouragement to Timothy and I found solace in this time of uncertainty by reading, 2 Timothy 1:7-12 (NKJV) "For GOD has not given us a spirit of fear, but of power and of love and of a sound mind. Therefore do not be ashamed of the testimony of our Lord, nor of me His prisoner, but share with me in the sufferings for the gospel according to the power of GOD, who has saved us and called *us* with a holy calling, not according to our works, but according to His own purpose and grace which was given to us in Christ Jesus before time began, but has now been revealed by the appearing of our Savior Jesus Christ, who has abolished death and brought life and immortality to light through the gospel, to which I was appointed a preacher, an apostle, and a teacher of the Gentiles. For this reason I also suffer these things: nevertheless I am not ashamed, for I know whom I have believed and am persuaded that He is able to keep what I have committed to Him until that Day."

GOD draws close to us when we draw close to Him. You can accomplish this by doing your part by communicating with GOD and giving your heart to

Him. Reading GOD's Words found in the Bible, praying and worshipping Him brings us closer to Him. The closer you become to GOD, the more you will experience His love, protection and blessings. Reflecting back to the 1955 Montgomery Bus Boycott and other incidents of denial of justice due to being Black: seeing the deaths of comrades and the intense combat struggles of Vietnam: when I think of the rigors of undergraduate and graduate school: employment mistreatment and the ongoing daily challenges of life: I feel so blessed that GOD was right by my side, fighting each battle. For this and other blessings, I will continue to praise and honor Him daily. When I thought about giving up, GOD assured me that He would make a way and told me not to quit!!

Our purpose on this earth is to praise, honor and worship GOD and utilize our GOD given talents to help mankind. Our daily prayer should include asking GOD to show us His will. GOD has preordained our lives. Many times Satan throws us off track by deception, innuendo and lies. He uses people and naysayers to hinder us from reaching our goals and plant seeds of fear and doubt in our minds. The best way to attack negative thoughts, deception and the workers of iniquity is the Words of GOD and prayer. Psalm 88:1-18 reads: "O LORD, GOD of my salvation, I have cried out day and night before You. Let my prayer come before You: Incline Your ear to my cry. For my soul is full of troubles, And my life draws near to the grave. I am counted with those who go down to the pit: I am like a man who has no strength, Adrift among the dead, Like the slain who lie in the grave, Whom You remember no more, And who are cut off from Your hand. You have laid me in the lowest pit, in darkness, in the depths. Your wrath lies heavy upon me, And You have afflicted me with all Your waves, Selah. You have put away my acquaintances far from me: You have made me an abomination to them: I am shut up, and I cannot get out: My eye wastes away because of affliction. LORD, I have called daily upon You: I have stretched out my hands to You. Will You work wonders for the dead? Shall the dead arise and praise You? Selah. Shall Your lovingkindness be declared in the grave? Or Your faithfulness in the place of destruction? Shall Your wonders be known in the dark? And Your righteousness in the land of forgetfulness? But to You I have cried out, O LORD, And in the morning my prayer comes before You. LORD, why do You cast off my soul? Why do You hide Your face from me? I have been afflicted and ready to die from my youth: I suffer Your terrors: I am distraught. Your fierce wrath has gone over me: Your terrors have cut me off. They came around me all day long like water: They engulfed me altogether. Loved one and friend You have put far from me, And my acquaintances into darkness." (NKJV)

When we forgive those who have hurt us, seek GOD's will and begin to praise GOD, He will make a way for us to succeed. Go ahead, thank GOD for your life today. Thank Him for the beautiful sunrise. Thank Him for past blessings and for restoring you, even if you don't see it yet. If you'll be faithful and choose integrity in the little things of life, GOD will pour abundant blessings on you as you honor Him all the days of your life.

Abraham Lincoln once remarked that people are just about as happy as they make up their minds to be. You can be unhappy if you want to be. It's the easiest thing in the world to accomplish. Just choose unhappiness. Happiness is determined by your thoughts. So you have to drive off negative thoughts that you have about people, places and things and replace them with happy thoughts about people, places and things. Proverbs 23:7 states, "As a person thinks in his heart, so is he." If you think you're unhappy, you become an unhappy person. But if you think you're happy, you become a happy person. Happy thoughts produce happy attitudes that become a happy life. Let's pray: Lord, thank you for Your hand of blessing in our lives. Thank you for the new opportunities You have allowed us to partake. Thank you for giving us Your Kingdom. Thank you for the happiness and joy you have provided us. We receive and claim joy and happiness by faith today and choose to follow Your Words in everything we do. Lord, You have been so merciful and allowed us to share Your abundance and we will forever give You the glory and honor, in Jesus' Name, Amen.

GOD promises so many good things for our lives. He wants us to step up and receive them. If we go to Him and claim the blessings and abundance He has offered, then our lives will be changed forever. GOD has all of the power necessary to restore broken families, replace lost trust, meet our financial needs and perform any miracle He chooses. All things are possible with GOD and when He is first in our lives, He will make us winners and empower us to be a blessing to others. Whatever battle you may be facing today, declare that you and GOD are stronger and you will win. Declare that you are an overcomer. Stand strong and declare you will experience GOD's victory and you will live in His abundance all the days of your life!

Matthew 6:33-39 reads, "But seek first his kingdom and his righteousness, and all these things will be given to you as well. Therefore do not worry about tomorrow, for tomorrow will worry about itself. Each day has enough trouble of its own." (NIV) Don't worry about tomorrow, seek GOD's kingdom today. GOD allows us to receive every good and perfect gift. Psalm 66:12 reads, "You let men ride over our heads: we went through fire and water, but you brought us to a place of abundance."

James 1:12-25 states, "Blessed is the man who perseveres under trial, because when he has stood the test, he will receive the crown of life that GOD has promised to those who love him. When tempted, no one should say, 'GOD is tempting me.' For GOD cannot be tempted by evil, nor does he tempt anyone: but each one is tempted when, by his own evil desire, he is dragged away and enticed. Then, after desire has conceived, it gives birth to sin: and sin, when it is full-grown, gives birth to death. Don't be deceived, my dear brothers. Every good and perfect gift is from above, coming down from the Father of the heavenly lights, who does not change like shifting shadows. He chose to give us birth through the word of truth that we might be a kind of first fruits of all he created. My dear brothers, take note of this: Everyone should be quick to listen, slow to speak and slow to become angry, for man's anger does not bring about the righteous life that GOD desires. Therefore, get rid of all moral filth and the evil that is so prevalent and humbly accept the word planted in you, which can save you. Do not merely listen to the word, and so deceive yourselves. Do what it says. Anyone who listens to the word but does not do what it says is like a man who looks at his face in a mirror and, after looking at himself, goes away and immediately forgets what he looks like. But the man who looks intently into the perfect law that gives freedom, and continues to do this, not forgetting what he has heard, but doing it—he will be blessed in what he does." (NIV)

Try to always allow GOD to fight your battles!! Don't let your enemies and adversity keep you from completing your divine assignment. GOD is always ready and available to rescue us in the time of trouble. The Bible gives many examples of GOD performing needed miracles for His children. "He is no respecter of persons." In the following scripture, King Jehoshaphat exclaimed to his people that, "The battle is not yours but the Lord." 2 Chronicles 20:18-29 states, "Jehoshaphat bowed with his face to the ground, and all the people of Judah and Jerusalem fell down in worship before the LORD. Then some Levites from the Kohathites and Korahites stood up and praised the LORD, the GOD of Israel, with very loud voice. Early in the morning they left for the Desert of Tekoa. As they set out, Jehoshaphat stood and said, 'Listen to me, Judah and people of Jerusalem! Have faith in the LORD your GOD and you will be upheld: have faith in his prophets and you will be successful.' After consulting the people, Jehoshaphat appointed men to sing to the LORD and to praise him for the splendor of his holiness as they went out at the head of the army, saying: 'Give thanks to the LORD, for his love endures forever.' As they began to sing and praise, the LORD set ambushes against the men of Ammon and Moab and Mount Seir who were invading Judah, and they were defeated. The men of Ammon and Moab rose up against the men from Mount Seir to destroy and annihilate them. After they finished slaughtering the men from Seir, they helped to destroy one another. When the men of Judah came to the place that overlooks the desert and looked toward the vast army, they saw only dead bodies lying on the ground: no one had escaped. So Jehoshaphat and his men went to carry off their plunder, and they found among them a great amount of equipment and clothing and also articles of value—more than they could take away. There was so much plunder that it took three days to collect it. On the fourth day they assembled in the Valley of Beracah, where they praised the LORD. This is why it is called the Valley of Beracah to this day. Then, led by Jehoshaphat, all the men of Judah and Jerusalem returned joyfully to Jerusalem, for the LORD had given them cause to rejoice over their enemies. They entered Jerusalem and went to the temple of the LORD with harps and lutes and trumpets. The fear of GOD came upon all the kingdoms of the countries when they heard how the LORD had fought against the enemies of Israel. And the kingdom of Jehoshaphat was at peace, for his GOD had given him rest on every side." (NIV)

CHAPTER ELEVEN
Two Cherished Letters

It's not a coincidence that throughout my life, I have been on the cutting edge of History in America. My early involvement in the Civil Rights Movement empowered me to take proactive positions and oppose unfair actions on the children of GOD. I still believe today, as Dr. King stressed throughout his lifetime that divine love is the only path to peace. It is imperative that we always fear GOD and not man. Our commitment to GOD and guide for His love is found in 1 John 4: 7 – 20, "Dear friends, let us love one another, for love comes from GOD. Everyone who loves has been born of GOD and knows GOD. Whoever does not love does not know GOD, because GOD is love. This is how GOD showed his love among us: He sent his one and only Son into the world that we might live through Him. This is love: not that we loved GOD, but that he loved us and sent his Son as an atoning sacrifice for our sins. Dear friends, since GOD so loved us, we also ought to love one another. No one has ever seen GOD: but if we love one another, GOD lives in us and his love is made complete in us. We know that we live in him and he in us, because he has given us of his Spirit. And we have seen and testify that the Father has sent his Son to be the Savior of the world. If anyone acknowledges that Jesus is the Son of GOD, GOD lives in him and he in GOD. And so we know and rely on the love GOD has for us. GOD is love. Whoever lives in love lives in GOD, and GOD in him. In this way, love is made complete among us so that we will have confidence on the day of judgment, because in this world we are like him. There is no fear in love. But perfect love drives out fear because fear has to do with punishment. The one who fears is not made perfect in love. We love because he first loved us. If anyone says, "I love GOD," yet hates his brother, he is a liar. For anyone who does not love his brother, whom he has seen, cannot love GOD, whom he has not seen."

No matter what is happening today, you can rise above your circumstances and feel GOD working out your situation for you. We all have times when people or circumstances come against us and there is disharmony. Sometimes there are days when we may feel cheated, confused or that someone has taken advantage of us. Maybe you're facing a difficulty today and you're not exactly sure how to handle it. If we look to GOD's Words, He'll give us what we need. He is always on time: He may wait to the last second but He's never late. It is written in Ecclesiastes 3: 1- 11, "To everything there is a season, and a time to every purpose under the heaven: A time to be born, and a time to die: a time to plant, and a time to pluck up that which is planted: A time to kill, and a time to heal: a time to break down, and a time to build up: A time to weep, and a time to laugh: a time to mourn, and a time to dance: A time to cast away stones, and a time to gather stones together: a time to embrace, and a time to refrain from embracing: A time to get, and a time to lose: a time to keep, and a time to cast away: A time to rend, and a time to sew: a time to keep silence, and a time to speak: A time to love, and a time to hate: a time of war, and a time of peace. What profit hath he that worketh in that wherein he laboureth? I have seen the travail, which GOD hath given to the sons of men to be exercised in it. He hath made everything beautiful in his time: also he hath set the world in their heart, so that no man can find out the work that GOD maketh from the beginning to the end."

Two of my most cherished letters appear below. These letters are from persons whose wisdom I deeply respect. One is from my first born child, Shanera and the other is from former President, Bill Clinton. They both came during times of tribulations in my life and from reading them, I was encouraged. They reads as follows:

17 April 1996 - Italy
Dear David,

I haven't forgotten you, I have just been rather busy. I don't know what the last thing that I told you about being here, so I'll just tell you what has been going on with me lately. First of all this was my first Christmas away from any family, (and by the way did I hear from you at Christmas time?) In January I went to visit Frankfurt and Heidelberg because I still have friends stationed in both places.

I really hated Italy at first because unlike Germany very few Italians speak English and the public transportation is not as good or as safe. I really didn't like the barracks here and I hate working with the Navy because they are so backwards compared to the Air Force and the Army.

Now things have changed, I bought a car (Alfa Romero) which is standard shift, (yes, I learned to drive a stick here!!). I moved out of the barracks and I have a roommate named —-. I am much happier now!! I forgot to tell you about my job. I am in NATO which means that every branch of service from almost every country is stationed here. It is kind of different and unique, but after a couple of months it seems normal and boring. I am basically a receptionist.

My home life is pretty unique too. My landlord lives downstairs with his family. One of his daughters and his wife live with him, but his other daughter, her husband, and their baby live on the other side. We have two bedrooms, two bathrooms, a den, a kitchen, a walk-in foyer and three balconies. Our landlord and his family speak very little English and we speak very little Italian. My roommate and I are learning to speak Italian while we teach them some English. My roomie is picking up Italian pretty fast because she is Puerto Rican and it is very similar to Spanish.

My boyfriend and I broke up because of the distance. He was sent to Johnston Island outside of Hawaii. We still keep in touch and he is visiting me next month. We plan to take a trip to Venice and I'll be on leave for a while.

How are things going for you? Even though you've forgotten me, I just wanted to send a brief synopsis of my life. If I hear from you I'll write back. If I don't hear from you, you'll get another synopsis in three to four months. See you and keep in touch.

Sincerely,
Shanera

The White House- Washington
August 10, 1999

Dear David:

Thank you for sharing your views and for the material you enclosed. I'm glad you took the time to tell me where you stand.

Knowing the thoughts and ideas of my fellow Americans is very important to me as we face the challenges ahead. I believe that our nation has made a great deal of progress since I took office. I am proud of what we have done to reduce the the deficit, expand our economy, improve educational opportunities, and empower hardworking Americans to make the most of their own lives.

As we work to protect our shared values, meet our common challenges, and ensure peace and security at home and abroad, I hope you will remain involved.

Sincerely,
Bill Clinton

These letters caused me to look up from whence cometh my help. The Words of GOD in Psalm121:1-8 reads, "I will lift up my eyes to the hills—from whence comes my help? My help comes from the LORD, Who made heaven and earth. He will not allow your foot to be moved: He who keeps you will not slumber. Behold, He who keeps Israel shall neither slumber nor sleep. The LORD *is* your keeper: The LORD *is* your shade at your right hand. The sun shall not strike you by day, Nor the moon by night. The LORD shall preserve you from all evil: He shall preserve your soul. The LORD shall preserve your going out and your coming in, from this time forth, and even forevermore." (NKJV)

Upon reflection, these letters helped me to realize that the health of the individual and that of the community are inseparable. I wrote in one of my graduate courses that, "In order for us to have a better world for all GOD's children, we must disengage the human spirit from neglecting the poor, deprived and hopeless citizens. I strongly believe that it is our personal mandate to help develop strong policies and programs to help the least of these." Although my daughter and I did not have a good relation, her letter created a feeling of love and compassion in me. It bridged our relationship and her words meant a lot to me. My grades in graduate school improved to two A's and two B's.

An unknown writer once wrote, "I asked GOD for strength that I might achieve. I was made weak that I might learn humbly to obey. I asked for health that I might do greater things. I was given infirmity that I might do better things. I asked for riches that I might be happy. I was given poverty that I might be wise. I asked for power that I might have the praise of men. I was given weakness that I might feel the need of GOD. I asked for all things that I might enjoy life. I was given life that I might enjoy all things. I got nothing that I asked for, but everything I hoped for. Almost despite myself, my unspoken prayers were answered. I am, among all men, most richly blessed." Yes, GOD is a peacemaker and He hears and always answers our prayers – His way and in His timing. All we are required to do is be patient and trust GOD.

CHAPTER TWELVE
Model Prayer: Senator John Kerry

When faced with dangerous or difficult situations, whispering a prayer to GOD helps. One of the most repeated prayers is the one often referred to as the "Model Prayer." It is found in Matthew 6:9-13 – "After this manner therefore pray ye: Our Father which art in heaven, Hallowed be thy name. Thy kingdom come, Thy will be done in earth, as it is in heaven. Give us this day our daily bread. And forgive us our debts, as we forgive our debtors. And lead us not into temptation, but deliver us from evil: For thine is the kingdom, and the power, and the glory, forever. Amen."

According to the Boston Globe, on Feb. 17, 1968, John Kerry received a telegram that said "Richard Pershing had died due to wounds received while on a combat mission when his unit came under hostile small-arms and rocket attack while searching for remains of a missing member of his unit. Kerry was devastated. The war was no longer an abstract policy issue. One of his best friends, bearing one of the most famous names in US military history, had died trying to find a fallen comrade." Kerry wrote the following letter to Pershing's parents, then to his own.

Dearest Mama and Papa,

What can I say? I am empty, bitter, angry and desperately lost with nothing but war, violence and more war around me. I just don't believe it was meant to be this cruel and senseless — that anyone could possibly get near to Persh to take his life. What a GOD damn total waste. Why?... I have never felt so void of feeling before.... With the loss of Persh something has gone out of me.

After losing his bid for President of the U.S. on November 2, 2004, I received the following letter from Senator John Kerry:

November 7, 2004

Dear Dave,

There is no way to hide the pain – and no point in trying. We poured our hearts and souls into winning this election. And there is no denying that it hurts to fall short of our goal. But, like you, I have lived my entire life believing that, as long as you fight hard for the things you believe in, you can never lose. I believe it more today than I ever have.

You and I have been part of a remarkable campaign together. No one can ever take that away from us. And no one can keep us from working with every ounce of energy we have to advance the values we cherish. Our campaign has come to an end. But our work together has just begun. You and I owe it to ourselves and to the millions of people who voted for us on November 2nd to play an active, spirited role in the political life of our nation.

I can't thank you enough for the role you played in our campaign and the passion you brought to our efforts and for how you stood by me every step of the way. For that, I will be forever grateful. I'm proud to have been your friend and colleague throughout our 2004 campaign and I'm looking forward to continuing our joint commitment to the values we share. We can only defend the values we cherish and advance policies that reflect those values by having the courage of our convictions. Let's keep standing up for what we believe in.

Sincerely,
John Kerry

The hard fought campaign in 2004 was lost by a closely contested vote count in Ohio. It was reported that there was substantial voter suppression and many voter machines were not working properly. Kerry stated in the Boston Globe, "The widespread irregularities make it impossible to know for certain that the Ohio outcome reflected the will of the voters." In the same article, former Democratic National Committee Chairman, Howard Dean said "I'm not confident that the election in Ohio was fairly decided." One of my highlights from Senator Kerry's campaign was meeting and taking a picture with Senator Ted Kennedy and Senator Kerry. Most loyal Black Democrats from the South heralded the Kennedys' as our heroes. Senator Kennedy passed on August 25, 2009. I was disgusted with the outcome of Senator Kerry's race but as usual I found solace in the Words of GOD. Isaiah 40:31 reads, "But they that wait upon the LORD shall renew their strength: they shall mount up with wings as eagles: they shall run, and not be weary: and they shall walk, and not faint."

As a believer in the Lord Jesus, I feel certain that in the end GOD's will always prevail. GOD always meet our needs and direct our paths. Despite all our trials and tribulations we face in our daily lives, keep holding on to GOD and He will lead us through our earthly journey and to His eternal home that awaits us. John 21:4-22 states, "But when the morning was now come, Jesus stood on the shore: but the disciples knew not that it was Jesus. Then Jesus saith unto them, Children, have ye any meat? They answered him, No. And he said unto them, Cast the net on the right side of the ship, and ye shall find. They cast therefore, and now they were not able to draw it for the multitude of fishes. Therefore that disciple whom Jesus loved saith unto Peter, It is the Lord. Now when Simon Peter heard that it was the Lord, he girt his fisher's coat unto him, (for he was naked,) and did cast himself into the sea. And the other disciples came in a little ship: (for they were not far from land, but as it were two hundred cubits,) dragging the net with fishes. As soon then as they were come to land, they saw a fire of coals there, and fish laid thereon, and bread. Jesus saith unto them, Bring of the fish which ye have now caught. Simon Peter went up, and drew the net to land full of great fishes, an hundred and fifty and three: and for all there were so many, yet was not the net broken. Jesus saith unto them, Come and dine. And none of the disciples durst ask him, Who art thou? knowing that it was the Lord. Jesus then cometh, and taketh bread, and giveth them, and fish likewise. This is now the third time that Jesus shewed himself to his disciples, after that he was risen from the dead. So when they had dined, Jesus saith to Simon Peter, Simon, son of Jonas, lovest thou me more than these? He saith unto him, Yea, Lord: thou knowest that I love thee. He saith unto him, Feed my lambs."

CHAPTER THIRTEEN
Rookie Diary

It is written in Luke 6:31-37: "And as ye would that men should do to you, do ye also to them likewise. For if ye love them which love you, what thank have ye? for sinners also love those that love them. And if ye do good to them which do good to you, what thank have ye? for sinners also do even the same. And if ye lend to them of whom ye hope to receive, what thank have ye? for sinners also lend to sinners, to receive as much again. But love ye your enemies, and do good, and lend, hoping for nothing again: and your reward shall be great, and ye shall be the children of the Highest: for he is kind unto the unthankful and to the evil. Be ye therefore merciful, as your Father also is merciful. Judge not, and ye shall not be judged: condemn not, and ye shall not be condemned: forgive, and ye shall be forgiven."

In Matthew 21:21-22 is found the following, "Jesus answered and said unto them, Verily I say unto you, If ye have faith, and doubt not, ye shall not only do this which is done to the fig tree, but also if ye shall say unto this mountain, Be thou removed, and be thou cast into the sea: it shall be done. And all things, whatsoever ye shall ask in prayer, believing, ye shall receive."

The following article appeared in the April 7, 1997, Detroit News in a column called, The Rookie Diary. It was a weekly column written by a former Detroit Pistons basketball player named Jerome Williams.

"FAN'S KIND LETTER IS GRATIFYING"

Two weeks ago, I asked you to write me and give your opinion on pro athletes from a fan's perspective. The response was gratifying, and the one letter that I chose to be the best was from David M. Williams (no relation).

David will receive a pair of my NBA knee-highs and my Pistons jersey. This is what he wrote: "I always believed athletes were millionaires who whined and destroyed their coaches when they couldn't have their way. I thought they lived in fenced-in mansions and cared nothing about everyday people.

After reading the Rookie Diary, I decided to volunteer to see what the Jerome Williams Rookie Camp and Mentor Program would contribute to the children of Detroit. My experience at this camp has given me a different perspective on pro athletes if Jerome is typical of his peers. To observe the children's love, respect and admiration of Jerome, and the pride they exhibit from being in this camp, has been a very emotional experience for me.

Few, if any, of these children's dreams of the NBA, NFL or NHL will ever become a reality, but Jerome's message will remain with them. That message emphasizes the importance of a quality education and will hopefully inspire many of these 7-12 year olds to proceed on to college. Thank you, Jerome Williams, for your commitment to make Detroit better. It is my wish that you are a Piston for a long time and you would continue to expand your program and ideas to other areas of our city. Thank you, David, for your kind letter."

A couple of local, concerned, motivational activists and I helped Jerome and his brother, Johnnie Williams originate "The Positive Shades of Black (PSB)." The PSB still are making positive contributions to Dr. King's "Beloved Community." Their vision statement from their website states, "Positive Shades of Black, inc., has a vision to dismantle negative stereotypes of the many ethnic groups making up our society. By finding a common ground, we may move forward together as "One Family." Our multi-cultural staff, family and board of trustees remain focused upon building bridges of understanding over man-made obstacles which separate us by social, economic and racial categories."

Philippians 4:8-13 states, "Finally, brethren, whatsoever things are true, whatsoever things are honest, whatsoever things are just, whatsoever things are pure, whatsoever things are lovely, whatsoever things are of good report: if there be any virtue, and if there be any praise, think on these things. Those things, which ye have both learned, and received, and heard, and seen in me, do and the GOD of peace shall be with you. But I rejoiced in the Lord greatly, that now at the last your care of me hath flourished again: wherein ye were also careful, but ye lacked opportunity. Not that I speak in respect of want: for I have learned, in whatsoever state I am, therewith to be content. I know both how to be abased, and I know how to abound: everywhere and in all things I am instructed both to be full and to be hungry, both to abound and to suffer need. I can do all things through Christ which strengtheneth me."

Pastor Rick Warren who wrote the, <u>Purpose Driven Life</u> said, "I used to think that life was hills and valleys - you go through a dark time, then you go to the mountaintop, back and forth. I don't believe that anymore. Rather than life being hills and valleys, I believe that it's kind of like two rails on a railroad track, and at all times you have something good and something bad in your life. No matter how good things are in your life, there is always something bad that needs to be worked on. And no matter how bad things are in your life, there is always something good you can thank GOD for. You can focus on your purposes, or you can focus on your problems: If you focus on your problems, you're going into self-centeredness, which is my problem, my issues, my pain.' But one of the easiest ways to get rid of pain is to get your focus off yourself and onto GOD and others. We discovered quickly that in spite of the prayers of hundreds of thousands of people, GOD was not going to heal Kay (his wife) or make it easy for her. It has been very difficult for her, and yet GOD has strengthened her character, given her a ministry of helping other people, given her a testimony, drawn her closer to Him and to people."

CHAPTER FOURTEEN
Blessing Plan

The 23rd Psalm reads as follow: "The LORD is my shepherd: I shall not want. He maketh me to lie down in green pastures: he leadeth me beside the still waters. He restoreth my soul: he leadeth me in the paths of righteousness for his name's sake. Yea, though I walk through the valley of the shadow of death, I will fear no evil: for thou art with me: thy rod and thy staff they comfort me. Thou preparest a table before me in the presence of mine enemies: thou anointest my head with oil: my cup runneth over. Surely goodness and mercy shall follow me all the days of my life: and I will dwell in the house of the LORD forever."

An unknown writer wrote the following story and I feel it is a great teaching moment to show GOD's love: "One day a while back, a man, his heart heavy with grief, was walking in the woods. As he thought about his life this day, he knew many things were not right. He thought about those who had lied about him back when he had a job. His thoughts turned to those who had stolen his things and cheated him. He remembered family who had passed on. His mind turned to the illness he had, that no one could cure. His very soul was filled with anger, resentment, and frustration. Standing there this day, searching for answers he could not find, knowing all else had failed him, he knelt at the base of an old oak tree to seek the one he knew would always be there. And with tears in his eyes, he prayed: 'Lord, You have done wonderful things for me in this life. You have told me to do many things for you, and I happily obeyed. Today, you have told me to forgive. I am sad, Lord, because I cannot. I don't know how. It is not fair Lord, I didn't deserve these wrongs that were done against me and I shouldn't have to forgive. As perfect as your way is Lord, this one thing I cannot do, for I don't know how to forgive. My anger is so deep Lord, I fear I may not hear you, but I pray you teach me to do the one thing I cannot do: Teach me to forgive.'

As he knelt there in the quiet shade of that old oak tree, he felt something fall onto his shoulder. He opened his eyes. Out of the corner of one eye, he saw something red on his shirt. He could not turn to see what it was because where the oak tree had been a large square piece of wood in the ground. He raised his head and saw two feet held to the wood with a large spike through them. He raised his head more, and tears came to his eyes as he saw Jesus hanging on a cross. He saw spikes in His hands, a gash in His side, a torn and battered body, deep thorns sunk into His head. Finally he saw the suffering and pain on His precious face. As their eyes met, the man's tears turned to sobbing, and Jesus began to speak. 'Have you ever told a lie?' He asked? The man answered, 'Yes, Lord'. 'Have you ever been given too much change and kept it?' The man answered, 'Yes, Lord.' And the man sobbed more and more.

'Have you ever taken something from work that wasn't yours?' Jesus asked? And the man answered, 'Yes, Lord.' 'Have you ever sworn, using my Father's name in vain?' The man, crying now, answered, 'Yes, Lord.' As Jesus asked many more times, 'Have you ever'? The man's crying became uncontrollable, for he could only answer, 'Yes, Lord'. Then Jesus turned His head from one side to the other, and the man felt something fall on his other shoulder He looked and saw that it was the blood of Jesus. When he looked back up, his eyes met those of Jesus, and there was a look of love the man had never seen or known before. Jesus said, 'I didn't deserve this either, but I forgive you.' It may be hard to see how you're going to get through something, but when you look back in life, you realize how true this statement is. Read the following first line slowly and let it sink in. If GOD brings you to it, He will bring you through it. When Jesus died on the cross, he was thinking of you!"

According to many ministers of GOD, His "Blessing Plan" is found in Deuteronomy 28: 1-13: It states, "And it shall come to pass, if thou shalt hearken diligently unto the voice of the LORD thy GOD, to observe and to do all his commandments which I command thee this day, that the LORD thy GOD will set thee on high above all nations of the earth: And all these blessings shall come on thee, and overtake thee, if thou shalt hearken unto the voice of the LORD thy GOD. Blessed shalt thou be in the city, and blessed shalt thou be in the field. Blessed shall be the fruit of thy body, and the fruit of thy ground, and the fruit of thy cattle, the increase of thy kine, and the flocks of thy sheep. Blessed shall be thy basket and thy store. Blessed shalt thou be when thou comest in, and blessed shalt thou be when thou goest out. The LORD shall cause thine enemies that rise up against thee to be smitten before thy face: they shall come out against thee one way, and flee before thee seven ways. The LORD shall command the blessing upon thee in thy storehouses, and in all that thou settest thine hand unto: and he shall bless thee in the land which the LORD thy GOD giveth thee. The LORD shall establish thee an holy people unto himself, as he hath sworn unto thee, if thou shalt keep the commandments of the LORD thy GOD, and walk in his ways. And all people of the earth shall see that thou art called by the name of the LORD: and they shall be afraid of thee. And the LORD shall make thee plenteous in goods, in the fruit of thy body, and in the fruit of thy cattle, and in the fruit of thy ground, in the land which the LORD sware unto thy fathers to give thee. The LORD shall open unto thee his good treasure, the heaven to give the rain unto thy land in his season, and to bless all the work of thine hand: and thou shalt lend unto many nations, and thou shalt not borrow. And the LORD shall make thee the head, and not the tail: and thou shalt be above only, and thou shalt not be beneath: if that thou hearken unto the commandments of the LORD thy GOD, which I command thee this day, to observe and to do them."

Chapter Fifteen
WGC

1 Corinthians 10:31 reads, "Whether therefore ye eat, or drink, or whatsoever ye do, do all to the glory of GOD." My current private venture is doing consultant work. The name of my company is Williams' Global Consultation (WGC). Its major focus is business and political consultation. The following is taken directly from my business brochure: "WGC assists potential entrepreneurs with: Start-up Strategies, Community Research, Demographic Data. WGC provides: Federal, State, Local Political Consultation. We assist with community organizing, we conduct polls and provide accurate trends, we help develop and research campaign issues. WGC assists with strategic planning to enable a candidate to be successful.

WGC assists with proposal writing and grant application upon request. We help our customers find a good fit between their ideas and needs with the necessary resources, both human and material, to enable their vision to become a reality.

WGC provides comprehensive and intensive therapy for children, adolescents and adults both individual and family. Many experts utilizing therapeutic interventions believe the effectiveness of any treatment program is determined by the ingenuity, intellect, talent and capacity for caring that a therapist demonstrates.

WGC spirit-filled interventions and holistic approach will help our customers reach realistic set goals within a short period of time. WGC offers medical assessment and referral as needed. Some customers will be provided with in-home assistance on a limited basis. You don't have to spend a lot of time on explaining or justifying underachievement and underdevelopment by allowing WGC to help you find a lasting solution to your need or your love one's need today.

Always remember!! Never give up on your dreams, ask for GOD's guidance: study and learn all you can: continue to stay focused and you will have "Success."

OUR MOTTO: "We Can Help Even You Have A Healthier and Happier Life"

A few months ago, the following e-mail was shared with my contacts:

"I Can"

There are days when we feel as though life is not going the way we want it. We feel like we are lost in a wilderness among the trees. The wilderness experience may be GOD's way to teach us to depend and rely on Him for our needs. When we trust GOD rather than react to circumstances, we will not be discouraged and GOD will provide us just what we need. He is never too busy and He will hear your cry. Philippian 4:13 states, 'I can do all things through Christ who strengthened me.' If you feel downcast today, I am prayerful this poem by Edgar A. Guest will bring you the same spiritual encouragement it gave me.

EQUIPMENT

Figure it out for yourself, my lad,
You've all that the greatest of men have had,
Two arms, two hands, two legs, two eyes,
And a brain to use if you would be wise.
With this equipment they all began,
So start for the top and say "I can."

Look them over, the wise and great,
They take their food from a common plate
And similar knives and forks they use,
With similar laces they tie their shoes,
The world considers them brave and smart.
But you've all they had when they made their start.

You can triumph and come to skill,
You can be great if only you will,
You're well equipped for what fight you choose,
You have legs and arms and a brain to use,
And the man who has risen, great deeds to do
Began his life with no more than you.
You are the handicap you must face,
You are the one who must choose your place,
You must say where you want to go.
How much you will study the truth to know,
GOD has equipped you for life, But He
Lets you decide what you want to be.
Courage must come from the soul within,
The man must furnish the will to win,
So figure it out for yourself, my lad,
You were born with all that the great have had,
With your equipment they all began.
Get hold of yourself, and say: "I can."

Hope is a very strong spiritual force that is activated by faith and trust in GOD. When a person has hope, they can positively believe that any goal they set for themselves is achievable: that job they have been tirelessly seeking is imminent: that nagging illness will be cured: that wayward child will return to the fold just as the prodigal son.

In Luke 15:11-32 is the parable of the prodigal son. It reads as follows: "Jesus continued: 'There was a man who had two sons. The younger one said to his father, 'Father, give me my share of the estate.' So he divided his property between them. Not long after that, the younger son got together all he had, set off for a distant country and there squandered his wealth in wild living. After he had spent everything, there was a severe famine in that whole country, and he began to be in need. So he went and hired himself out to a citizen of that country, who sent him to his fields to feed pigs. He longed to fill his stomach with the pods that the pigs were eating, but no one gave him anything. When he came to his senses, he said, 'How many of my father's hired men have food to spare, and here I am starving to death! I will set out and go back to my father and say to him: Father, I have sinned against heaven and against you. I am no longer worthy to be called your son: make me like one of your hired men.' So he got up and went to his father. But while he was still a long way off, his father saw him and was filled with compassion for him: he ran to his son, threw his arms around him and kissed him. The son said to him, 'Father, I have sinned against heaven and against you. I am no longer worthy to be called your son ' But the father said to his servants, 'Quick! Bring the best robe and put it on him. Put a ring on his finger and sandals on his feet. Bring the fattened calf and kill it. Let's have a feast and celebrate. For this son of mine was dead and is alive again: he was lost and is found.' So they began to celebrate. Meanwhile, the older son was in the field. When he came near the house, he heard music and dancing. So he called one of the servants and asked him what was going on. 'Your brother has come,' he replied, 'and your father has killed the fattened calf because he has him back safe and sound.' The older brother became angry and refused to go in. So his father went out and pleaded with him. But he answered his father, 'Look! All these years I've been slaving for you and never disobeyed your orders. Yet you never gave me even a young goat so I could celebrate with my friends. But when this son of yours who has squandered your property with prostitutes comes home, you kill the fattened calf for him!' 'My son,' the father said, 'you are always with me, and everything I have is yours. But we had to celebrate and be glad, because this brother of yours was dead and is alive again: he was lost and is found.' " (NIV)

As I am writing today, news reports state that there has been a tremendous response all over the world to the tragedy that occurred in Haiti on January 12, 2010. Many entertainers, sports personalities, churches, businesses, social organizations, and everyday citizens are sending support to the earthquake shattered island. Psalm 133:1states "How good and pleasant it is when brothers live together in unity!" (NIV)

Bishop Michael R. Cote of the Diocese of Norwich, Connecticut issued a letter immediately upon hearing of the tragedy. In it he said: "Our prayers tonight are with our brothers and sisters in Haiti who are in harm's way of the major earthquake that has hit close to Port au Prince. As we work to learn more through the night of their plight, we hope to make contact with our diocesan mission house, the Norwich Mission House in Tetionville and Hospice St. Joseph in Port au Prince: Our life lines to the Island. The Diocese has been on the ground in Haiti faithfully helping the good people of this impoverished Country for over 25 years. We care deeply about their struggle. We are a united family in that concern as we face this disaster. The people of

Haiti need our help...and the help of more and more people in our compassionate Country through this time and through the long road to recovery. May GOD watch over and bring strength to those suffering and those answering the call to help."

Pastor Joel Osteen said, "Churches should be honored to be working together with other believers all over the world to reach out to help the needy and bring hope to the hopeless. When you join your prayers and financial support with others, you are stepping into the place where GOD commands blessings for each of you. He promises that when we give, it shall be given back to us, pressed down, shaken together, and running over! He's our El Shaddai—the GOD of more than enough! Remember, working together in unity is something we should focus on every day with friends, family, and loved ones. What would happen in your home if you constantly looked for common ground with your family members? What would happen in your marriage if you focused on the things that brought you together instead of allowing differences to pull you apart? Today, focus on working together with the people in your life. Focus on finding things that unify you and bring you together. Be a peacemaker and step into the place where GOD commands the blessing!" Peace is a wonderful atmosphere in a home! There is such a calmness in a peace filled home and people share their unconditional love. It is our prayers that just as New Orleans is successfully recovering from hurricane Katrina, the people of Haiti will trust GOD for their healing and rebirth.

In John 11:28-44, we find these Words: " And after she had said this, she went back and called her sister Mary aside. 'The Teacher is here,' she said, 'and is asking for you.' When Mary heard this, she got up quickly and went to him. Now Jesus had not yet entered the village, but was still at the place where Martha had met him. When the Jews who had been with Mary in the house, comforting her, noticed how quickly she got up and went out, they followed her, supposing she was going to the tomb to mourn there. When Mary reached the place where Jesus was and saw him, she fell at his feet and said, 'Lord, if you had been here, my brother would not have died.' When Jesus saw her weeping, and the Jews who had come along with her also weeping, he was deeply moved in spirit and troubled. 'Where have you laid him?' he asked. 'Come and see, Lord,' they replied. Jesus wept. Then the Jews said, 'See how he loved him!' But some of them said, 'Could not he who opened the eyes of the blind man have kept this man from dying?' Jesus, once more deeply moved, came to the tomb. It was a cave with a stone laid across the entrance. 'Take away the stone,' he said. But, Lord,' said Martha, the sister of the dead man, 'by this time there is a bad odor, for he has been there four days.' Then Jesus said, 'Did I not tell you that if you believed, you would see the glory of GOD? So they took away the stone. Then Jesus looked up and said, Father, I thank you that you have heard me. I knew that you always hear me, but I said this for the benefit of the people standing here, that they may believe that you sent me.' When he had said this, Jesus called in a loud voice, 'Lazarus, come out!' The dead man came out, his hands and feet wrapped with strips of linen, and a cloth around his face. Jesus said to them, 'Take off the grave clothes and let him go.' " (NIV)

GOD can do anything but fail. When we trust and believe in Him, we will find solace and be redeemed. GOD is always on time! Although you may be wondering when He's coming or if He's aware of your circumstance, hold steadfast, GOD will deliver you from your unsettling situation.

CHAPTER SIXTEEN
President Ronald Reagan

I truly miss receiving letters from my deceased brother, Dr. Booker T. Williams Jr. His insight and profound wisdom always brought me an instant uplift when I read his letters.. Just knowing I met his approval in any task was most gratifying. All the way back to a political science course at Alabama State we took together, he was always there to help me reach for "Success." GOD told me to tell you, "Don't Hit Rock Bottom." This book gives you the prescription to "Success," it is easy to follow but the choice is yours. I declare, Isaiah 54:17 "No weapon that is formed against thee shall prosper: and every tongue that shall rise against thee in judgment thou shalt condemn. This is the heritage of the servants of the LORD, and their righteousness is of me, saith the LORD."

John 16:1-33 reads as follows: "All this I have told you so that you will not go astray. They will put you out of the synagogue: in fact, a time is coming when anyone who kills you will think he is offering a service to GOD. They will do such things because they have not known the Father or me. I have told you this, so that when the time comes you will remember that I warned you. I did not tell you this at first because I was with you. Now I am going to him who sent me, yet none of you asks me, 'Where are you going?' Because I have said these things, you are filled with grief. But I tell you the truth: It is for your good that I am going away. Unless I go away, the Counselor will not come to you: but if I go, I will send him to you. When he comes, he will convict the world of guilt in regard to sin and righteousness and judgment: in regard to sin, because men do not believe in me: in regard to righteousness, because I am going to the Father, where you can see me no longer: and in regard to judgment, because the prince of this world now stands condemned. I have much more to say to you, more than you can now bear. But when he, the Spirit of truth, comes, he will guide you into all truth. He will not speak on his own: he will speak only what he hears, and he will tell you what is yet to come. He will bring glory to me by taking from what is mine and making it known to you. All that belongs to the Father is mine. That is why I said the Spirit will take from what is mine and make it known to you. In a little while you will see me no more, and then after a little while you will see me. Some of his disciples said to one another, 'What does he mean by saying,' 'In a little while you will see me no more, and then after a little while you will see me,' and 'Because I am going to the Father'? They kept asking, 'What does he mean by a little while'? 'We don't understand what he is saying.' Jesus saw that they wanted to ask him about this, so he said to them, 'Are you asking one another what I meant when I said, in a little while you will see me no more, and then after a little while you will see me'? 'I tell you the truth, you will weep and mourn while the world rejoices. You will grieve, but your grief will turn to joy. A woman giving birth to a child has pain because her time has come: but when her baby is born she forgets the anguish because of her joy that a child is born into the world. So with you: Now is your time of grief, but I will see you again and you will rejoice, and no one will take away your joy. In that day you will no longer ask me anything. I tell you the truth, my Father will give you whatever you ask in my name. Until now you have not asked for anything in my name. Ask and you will receive, and your joy will be complete. Though I have been speaking figuratively, a time is coming when I will no longer use this kind of language but will tell you plainly about my Father. In that day you will ask in my name. I am not saying that I will ask the Father on your behalf. No, the Father himself loves you because you have loved me and have believed that I came from GOD. I came from the Father and entered the world: now I am leaving the world and going back to the Father.' Then Jesus' disciples said, 'Now you are speaking clearly and without figures of speech. Now we can see that you know all things and that you do not even need to have anyone ask you questions. This makes us believe that you came from GOD.' 'You believe at last!' Jesus answered. 'But a time is coming, and has come, when you will be scattered, each to his own home. You will leave me all alone. Yet I am not alone, for my Father is with me. I have told you these things, so that in me you may have peace. In this world you will have trouble. But take heart! I have overcome the world' "

John 17:1-5 states: "After Jesus said this, he looked toward heaven and prayed: Father, the time has come. Glorify your Son, that your Son may glorify you. For you granted him authority over all people that he might give eternal life to all those you have given him. Now this is eternal life: that they may know you, the only true GOD, and Jesus Christ, whom you have sent. I have brought you glory on earth by completing the work you gave me to do. And now, Father, glorify me in your presence with the glory I had with you before the world began." (NIV)

The third verse of James Weldon Johnson's hymn, "Lift Every Voice and Sing" (The Black National Anthem) is, "GOD of our weary years, GOD of our silent tears, Thou Who hast brought us thus far on the way: Thou Who hast by Thy might, led us into the light, Keep us forever in the path, we pray. Lest our feet stray from the places, our GOD, where we met Thee. Lest our hearts, drunk with the wine of the world, we forget Thee. Shadowed beneath Thy hand, may we forever stand, True to our GOD, true to our native land." Yes, GOD has brought us this far and He will not leave us. When you follow GOD's Words and do things according to His will, "Success is imminent."

A National Holiday to honor Dr. Martin Luther King Jr. was signed into law in 1983 by President Ronald Reagan. At first, some states resented observing a holiday for Dr. King. I worked with the NAACP to get signatures for this Holiday. My many experiences growing up in Montgomery, Alabama during the Civil Rights Movement and the lessons learned while serving in the US Army have made Politics my passion. I feel it is my obligation to fight for and help empower those citizens who feel hopeless and left out of the American Dream. One of the most emotional feelings of my life evolved from a correspondence I received from the Office of President Ronald Reagan, a Republican. His letter stated:

The White House
Washington
March 21, 1983

Dear Mr. Williams:

On the behalf of President Reagan, I want to thank you for your expression of interest in the establishment of a special day commemorating Dr. Martin Luther King, Jr. His memory is a source of inspiration to millions of Americans.

To establish a holiday in honor of Dr. King, Congress and the legislatures of the states choosing to honor him would have to enact appropriate legislation. Should Congress adopt such legislation, I assure you it would receive the President's most careful consideration.

As you may know, the President devoted his radio address to the nation on January 15, 1983, to the life and vision of Dr. King. I am enclosing a copy of this address which I am sure you'll enjoy reading.

With the President's best wishes,

Sincerely,
Anne Higgins, Special Assistant to the President and Director of Correspondence

Enclosure
President Reagan's Radio Address to the Nation on the Anniversary of the Birth of Martin Luther King, Jr.

January 15, 1983

"My fellow Americans: A few hours from now in the East Room of the White House, I'll be hosting a reception honoring the memory of a man who played a truly historic role in expanding the freedom we enjoy in America. Dr. Martin Luther King, Jr., was born into a world where bigotry and racism still held sway. Before he died, he had touched the conscience of a nation and had contributed immeasurably to the human rights of black Americans. He was a man of character and a man of courage.

Early in his life, Martin Luther King learned the meaning of discrimination. He and his father — a distinguished minister in a large Baptist church — went to a shoe store and were told that they would have to go to the back of the store. To his credit, the father took his son and walked out, vowing as he went to fight against such racism and discrimination. As Martin Luther King grew older, following his father's example, he studied, earned a college degree, and was ordained into the ministry. Racism was still widespread in the world in those days. In this country, which served in so many ways as an example of liberty, racial discrimination remained a tragic taint. Injustice held black Americans in a vice-like grip, making it harder for them to build a better life. Black Americans were forced into separate facilities, as they were bused past nearby schools to be put into segregated and sometimes inferior schools miles away. No matter how qualified for a job, they often knew they need not apply because their skin color, rather than their skills, might determine who filled the position. Roughly one-tenth of our people were forced to endure humiliating and degrading conditions. One such rule in one city required all blacks to sit in the back section of public buses.

But sometimes a single human act of courage can change the world. In 1955 a brave woman named Rosa Parks refused to give up her seat and move to the back of the bus. She was arrested. When the bus company refused to change the rule, a young minister in a local Baptist church, Martin Luther King, Jr., helped organize a boycott that captured the attention of the country. In 6 months, the courts had ruled the segregation of public transportation to be unconstitutional. It was the first real test of Dr. King's nonviolent philosophy. He advocated nonviolence because he believed that with hard work and good will, people's hearts can be touched and progress can be made. Yet, progress is not easy. In his book, ``The Strength To Love,'' Dr. King wrote, ``Nothing pains some people more than having to think.''

Well, during the years following the bus boycott, Dr. King, with tremendous courage and resourcefulness, got a lot of Americans thinking. He was instrumental in getting passage of legislation that provided Federal protection for the crown jewel of American liberty — every American's right to vote. That legacy still lives. Last year I signed into law the longest extension of the Voting Rights Act since its passage — a measure that will protect the right to vote for many years to come. In 1964 Dr. King was awarded the Nobel Peace Prize — the youngest man ever to earn that high award. Through his actions, his teachings, and his deep dedication to nonviolence, he opened the eyes of his fellow citizens. Civil rights legislation was passed, but perhaps even more important, he awakened the moral sense of an entire nation. He appealed to the good that is in our people.

In 1968 Martin Luther King was brutally murdered, shot down by a cowardly assassin. He had remained true to his principles to the end, never succumbing to the hatred that had destroyed the effectiveness of lesser men. On the steps of the Lincoln Memorial, he had held a great and peaceful civil rights rally. He spoke there of a dream — his dream for an America where there would be no place for hatred. His words are now a moving part of our history. Had he lived, the man we honor on this day would be only 54 years old. He cannot be with us. But today in Atlanta, Vice President Bush is attending a gathering honoring his 83-year-old father who did so much to start his son on the road to achievement and martyrdom.

In honoring them both, we should look to the future as well as the past. Yes, we should be proud of the progress we've made. But we also must face the fact that 15 years after Martin Luther King's death, traces of bigotry and injustice still remain. So, let the anniversary of this courageous American's birth be for us both a time of thanksgiving and a time of renewal. Let us be grateful for the providence that sends among us men and women with the courage and vision to stand peacefully but unyieldingly for what is right. But let us also make this a time when we rededicate ourselves, young and old, black and white to carry on the work of justice and to totally reject the words and actions of hate embodied in groups like the Ku Klux Klan.

Martin Luther King, Jr., showed us how much good a single life, well led, can accomplish. His death proved how much harm a single hand, intent on evil, can inflict. Let each of us honor his memory by pledging in our own lives to do everything we can to make America a place where his dream of freedom and brotherhood will grow and flourish from sea to shining sea. If we do this, then his sacrifice will not have been in vain, and we will have helped to make our country the special place we all know in our hearts that it was meant to be.

Thank you for listening. GOD bless you."

Serenity Prayer: GOD grant me the serenity to accept the things I cannot change, the courage to change the things I can, and the wisdom to know the difference.

CHAPTER SEVENTEEN
Mayor Dave Bing

"Arise, shine, for your light has come, and the glory of the LORD rises upon you." (Isaiah 60:1-NIV) Sometimes, many people feel that all politicians are untrustworthy and corrupt. Many of them are said to have the propensity to talk out of both sides of their mouth. While working as a volunteer in the campaign of then Senator Barack Obama, I went to the opening of the Dave Bing for Mayor campaign rally in Detroit, Michigan. After hearing Mr. Bing speech and reflecting on his long career history in Detroit, I decided he was my choice. Subsequently, I sent the sentiments below to the Detroit Free Press "Letter To Editor."

"DAVE BING IS BEST EQUIPPED"

Can the potential candidates for mayor of Detroit make their talk match their walk? Many people believe that past behavior is a great indicator of future behavior. Our next mayor must have some discernible accomplishments and have a good grasp of the issues that face Detroit. It is imperative that the next mayor of Detroit be a person we can trust to bring economic stability and deliver good city services to all the citizens of Detroit! We need someone who will have the public interest foremost on their agenda and helping Detroit become a model city in the days ahead.

As a veteran of the Vietnam War, I have noticed that some of Detroit's communities are becoming just like a war zone. Too many of our children and young minds are being killed or injured by this culture of violence. Our next mayor must provide aggressive leadership to target and alleviate this violence. Our schools are deplorable and our drop-out rate is too high. Our youths must be redirected to obtaining a good education in a safe, uncrowded environment. Dilapidated schools and deteriorating neighborhoods must be addressed. Our senior citizens must not continue to live in fear and be shown disrespect. Our roads and infrastructure must be properly maintained.

One of the best known and respected mayors of Detroit was Coleman Alexander Young. He was born in Tuscaloosa, Alabama and migrated to Detroit with his parents and four younger siblings to escape the racial injustices and the Klan in the south. Some people are trying to label Dave Bing a carpetbagger. In his announcement speech I witnessed on 10-16-08 Bing said, 'Contrary to what some folks may say, Detroit is not a stranger to me, and I am not a stranger to Detroit. For the past 42 years I've lived in and around Detroit. I raised my family here. I started my business here. I've expanded my business here, and I will continue to operate right here in the city of Detroit.' Bing went on to say that, 'Detroit needs a leader who will end corruption and reestablish trust in city government. We need a mayor with integrity and a person who has no hidden agendas. Our next mayor must have a proven record of making tough decisions during tough times. We need a fighter who will stand up for our city and our people. The opposition talks about things that they are going to do, but I can show you the things I've already done for the city. I've proven my commitment to the city of Detroit.'

This is a moment in Detroit's history where we all need to come together as one city — young and old, rich and poor, black and white, inner city and suburbs to transform this town. Dave Bing has a track record that displays a steadiness of achievements, an intellectual curiosity to be proactive on tasks that need to be done and the depth of knowledge to solve the myriad of problems that face Detroit. Without equivocation, I believe Dave Bing is best equipped to lead Detroit's comeback most effectively."

While striving to reach your goals, you may encounter great opposition and fall many times before you become a "Success." Keep on trying and always rely on the Words of GOD. In 1 John 4:4 are found these Words: "Ye are of GOD, little children, and have overcome them: because greater is he that is in you, than he that is in the world." On May 6, 2009, I sent the following to my e-mail contacts:

"It's Over"

Dave Bing is the new Mayor of Detroit. Detroit needs a fresh start and Bing begins the housecleaning at City Hall. Bing has the right skills, temperament and vision to lead Detroit's revival. Let's support Him wholeheartedly and pray for his 'Success.'

Asked by Erica Hill on The CBS Early Show Saturday Edition about people who get discouraged and frustrated when they don't see material gains even though they're trying their best, Pastor Joel Osteen replied, 'You know... prosperity is being blessed in your health, in your relationships, and of course, in your finances, too. We have to have money. But we encourage people that, no matter what comes your way, GOD's gonna give you strength to make it through. So don't get negative. Don't get bitter. Don't start blaming people, blaming your employer and things. We just have to take what life deals us with an attitude of faith. And we believe that, if you keep doing your best and keep believing, GOD will open up new doors.'

2 Chronicles 7:14 exclaims, "If my people, who are called by my name, will humble themselves and pray and seek my face and turn from their wicked ways, then will I hear from heaven and will forgive their sin and will heal their land."

We need leaders to help direct our African- American youths in order for them to get out of this gang and violence mentality. Recent research indicates that Black youths make up 50% of the incarcerated youths although being only 6% of the population. It is mandatory that these youths be redirected so they will realize that getting an education is critical for their future success. These role models or leaders for our youths must convey their stories by the kind of lives they are living and through example, seek to inspire our youths. People who do not practice what they preach are hypocrites and hypocrisy is easily recognized by our street smart youths.

In one of my graduate courses, I wrote a paper that listed some of the traits of effective leaders. It stated, "The rarest type of leader is the visionary. The visionary is not content to relate a current story but creates a new story or has an idea of a different approach not known to most individuals. Good leaders always have a vision. The scripture states, 'Without a vision the people perish.'

The ability to develop and articulate a vision is a defining leadership characteristic. A second requirement of a good leader is they must be creative change agents. It is the leader's job in an organization to shape things up, to create environments where continuous improvements and change are norms. A third leadership mandate is the ability to motivate. People have to believe in the vision, idea and strategy for it to be a "Success." Leaders must radiate a continuous self- confident that rallies team members to relentless pursue the goals of the organization. Finally leaders must have courage. They have the inner strength to carry their ideas forward regardless of what others may believe or say. Effective leaders must be results oriented in order to persuade others that their vision will be a 'Success' and is achievable."

GOD's Words make His will for us very clear. GOD knows we will not always make the right decisions so He allows for repentance. As a child coming humbly to a parent when they have done wrong, GOD wants us to come to Him. He is a forgiving GOD. His grace and mercy help us to have a good life and gives us peace. If we continue to obey His Words, GOD will always work out our problems and fulfill our deepest needs.

I say again, never, never, give up!! Keep trusting GOD and in His perfect timing, He will remove all obstacles and bring you through any adversity. Keep your soul anchored in the Words of GOD. Feed your faith daily and when those trials and tribulations appear to have you surrounded, all you have to do is remain steadfast and immovable. GOD has your back!! 1 Corinthians 15:58 states, "Therefore, my beloved brethren, be firm (steadfast), immovable, always abounding in the work of the Lord [always being superior, excelling, doing more than enough in the service of the Lord], knowing and being continually aware that your labor in the Lord is not futile." (AMP)

You can go ahead and shout now, GOD said, "Victory over life's injustice is imminent for you. I have heard your knock and your cry. You will be a 'Success.' I am with you and I will meet all your needs." The 100th Psalm exclaims: "Make a joyful noise to the Lord, all you lands! Serve the Lord with gladness! Come before His presence with singing! Know (perceive, recognize, and understand with approval) that the Lord is GOD! It is He Who has made us, not we ourselves [and we are His]! We are His people and the sheep of His pasture. Enter into His gates with thanksgiving and a thank offering and into His courts with praise! Be thankful and say so to Him, bless and affectionately praise His name!

For the Lord is good: His mercy and loving-kindness are everlasting, His faith-fulness and truth endure to all generations." (AMP) Let's pray, "Lord, I ask You right now to give me more patience and the faith to follow You until the end of this journey. Lord, I thank you for being my refuge in the time of my trials and tribulations. I resolve again today to trust and depend on You forever, Amen."

As President Barack Obama likes to exclaim, "Winning the White house is what we have done! Solving the jobless problems, rebuilding our economy, passing the Health Care Bill, and getting our troops home are things that need expedient work. This victory alone is not the change we seek. It is only the chance for us to make that change." One supporter said, "To ensure that President Obama succeeds in fulfilling the promise of change, we must act together. We can overcome the obstacles that for too long have prevented real change on the critical issues that Americans face day in and day out. Now is the time to leave behind the status quo and build support for real solutions."

On November 3, 2009 Dave Bing won the General Election and will serve the next four years as the Mayor of Detroit. In September, 2008, the sentiments below were e-mailed to my contacts. I believe these sentiments are more relevant today and citizens of Detroit need to rally behind Mayor Bing to help heal our city.

My e-mailed stated:

It's A Time For Healing

Hope can be defined as, 'the happy anticipation of good things.' We all daily trust and hope for the best to happen for us and our loved ones. Everything in life is a process in motion. Sometimes we wonder whether we are doing the right thing or moving in the right directions. GOD created each of us to be a goal-oriented visionary. He will direct our footsteps and lead us to our preordained destination. I believe the epitome of having a successful life is following your heart and doing those things that not only bring you satisfaction but help GOD's children. When we extend a hand to give back to our community, we have helped the least of these and fulfilled our spiritual mission. Without equivocation, **it's a time for healing** in Detroit and just as David came forth for Israel, David Bing will lead Detroit to our best days ever!!!

I first met Dave Bing in 1968 when I came to Detroit to work to earn money to attend college in Alabama. He worked at the NBD Bank at Grand River and Grand Boulevard. He also honed his basketball skills at the Fisher YMCA where some other college students and I lived. Bing opened up my first savings account and encouraged us to save our money and do well in school. He impressed me as a gentleman and good role model.

One sports writer stated, 'NBA All Star and successful, Detroit business-man, David Bing is known as an unassuming, quiet leader who thinks long term and has consistently made an effort to improve the Detroit com-munity. Bing was born and raised in Washington, D.C., where he hung out with pal Marvin Gaye and played both basketball and baseball in high school. He eventually played basketball for Syracuse University, where he studied economics and business and earned a B.A. He married his college sweetheart and had three daughters, who are currently working in various capacities in the Bing Group, climbing their way up the corporate ladder.

Bing's basketball career spanned over a decade and he was rated as one of the 50 greatest players in NBA history. From 1966 to 1975 he played for the Pistons, serving as captain. Bing was considered a quiet leader and well-rounded player, who excelled at feeding the ball to his teammates. He even played through an eye injury that threatened his vision, parlaying the potential handicap into an asset by working even harder on other as-pects of his game: free throws. The result was that Bing's overall game im-proved rather than degenerated after the injury.

Bing often read on the road. Planning for a future after basketball and supplementing a more modest 1970s basketball income, Bing worked at the National Bank of Detroit during the Piston's off season. He also at-tended a car-dealer training program and then took a PR job with a small steel company, where he apparently found his niche because, after retiring from basketball, he took his savings and started his own steel company.

Bing Steel was founded in 1980. Bing considered Detroit to be in rebuilding mode following the 1967 riots and saw nothing but opportunity as a result. Through acquisitions, the cultivation of relationships and collaboration, Bing parlayed Bing Steel into a manufacturing conglomerate: The Bing Group. The Bing Group consists of a diversified group of manufacturing companies that, among other things, supply parts to the big-three car companies. Bing also has interests in construction and money-management companies. Most of the companies making up The Bing Group are located in Detroit, near the Highland Park and Hamtramck borders, and are certified as minority-owned businesses. Bing considers it a priority to employ city residents and has worked to re-develop residential neighborhoods adjacent to The Bing Group's headquarters. Bing is also involved in a project to redevelop areas along the Detroit River waterfront, including luxury condos.

Bing is consistently involved in the Detroit community. When the Detroit public schools were going to cancel sports, he got involved, fundraising to support the program. He has also worked to reform Highland Park and create 15 charter schools in the city.

He is also active on several boards of directors, including the Detroit Renaissance, Michigan Business Development Council, National Association of Black Automotive Suppliers, Trustee McGregor Fund, Junior Achievement of Southeastern Michigan, inc., Downtown Detroit Partnership and the Detroit Investment Fund.

Bing spearheaded the Next Detroit Neighborhood Initiative that selected six neighborhoods for targeted renewal. The five-year plan for each neighborhood sought to target city resources and nonprofit contributions toward the reduction of crime, economic renovation, beautification and renovation.'

While Bing has been twirling his hat with an eye to the mayoral ring in 2008, this is not the first time his name has been mentioned as a possible mayoral candidate. Back in 1993, outgoing Mayor Coleman Young tried to convince Bing to run for mayor. The 64-year-old Bing says Detroit needs a mayor 'with a clean, fresh outlook.' Bing told the Detroit Free Press columnist Rochelle Riley he'll enter the nonpartisan Feb. 24 primary election. The top two finishers face off in a May 5 special election to choose a permanent replacement for mayor.

I am hopeful you will concur with the preceding sentiments and govern yourselves accordingly.

Dave

Proverbs 18:21, 22 read: "The tongue has the power of life and death, and those who love it will eat its fruit. He who finds a wife finds what is good and receives favor from the LORD."

As a Believer in Christ, you can speak things into existence. Romans 4:17 empowers us to, "Calls things that are not as though they were." Words we speak can do good work and help focus our children to positive and creative activities: or they may be evil or destructive causing hatred between relatives and friends. Harmony or disaster are determined daily in nations of the world by words either written or spoken. Good leaders must be cognizant of what they say and do. I believe that good spiritual leaders should possess the eight (8) qualities that follow:

1. **Creativity** - Creativity is a mental and social process involving the discovery of new ideas or concepts, or new associations of the creative mind between existing ideas or concepts. Creativity is fueled by the process of either conscious or unconscious insight.

2. **Character** - Moral character or character is an evaluation of a particular individual's moral qualities. The concept of character can imply a variety of attributes including the existence or lack of virtues such as integrity, courage, fortitude, honesty, and loyalty, or of good behaviors or habits. Moral character primarily refers to the assemblage of qualities that distinguish one individual from another.

3. **Confidence** - Confidence is generally described as a state of being certain either that a hypothesis or prediction is correct or that a chosen course of action is the best or most effective. Self-confidence is having confidence in oneself.

4. **Competence** - Competence is the ability to perform a specific task, action or function successfully.

5. **Collaborative** - Collaborative is a recursive process where two or more people or organizations work together in an intersection of common goals — for example, an intellectual endeavor that is creative in nature—by sharing knowledge, learning and building consensus.

6. **Complete excellence always their goal** - Excellence is the state or quality of excelling. Particularly in the field of business and organiza-

tions, excellence is considered to be an important value, and a goal to be pursued.

7. **Continuous independent intellectual visionary** - Defined narrowly, a visionary is one who purportedly experiences a vision or apparition connected to the supernatural. At times this involves seeing into the future. Visionaries are independent, rational thinkers.

8. **Christ-like Spirit** – According to one writer, the initial change one must make to become Christ-like is renewing your mind. Philippians 2:5 states, "Let this mind be in you which was also in Christ Jesus." (NKJV) The main characteristics of Christ are: love, patience, kindness, servant, healer, friend to all. When we get into the will of GOD, He gives us His Spirit.

John 14:26 states: "But the Helper, the Holy Spirit, whom the Father will send in My name, He will teach you all things, and bring to your remembrance all things that I said to you." John 15:3-17 states: "You are already clean because of the word which I have spoken to you. Abide in Me, and I in you. As the branch cannot bear fruit of itself, unless it abides in the vine, neither can you, unless you abide in Me. I am the vine, you are the branches. He who abides in Me, and I in him, bears much fruit: for without Me you can do nothing. If anyone does not abide in Me, he is cast out as a branch and is withered: and they gather them and throw them into the fire, and they are burned. If you abide in Me, and My words abide in you, you will ask what you desire, and it shall be done for you. By this My Father is glorified, that you bear much fruit: so you will be My disciples. As the Father loved Me, I also have loved you: abide in My love. If you keep My commandments, you will abide in My love, just as I have kept My Father's commandments and abide in His love. These things I have spoken to you, that My joy may remain in you, and that your joy may be full. This is My commandment, that you love one another as I have loved you. Greater love has no one than this, than to lay down one's life for his friends. You are My friends if you do whatever I command you. No longer do I call you servants, for a servant does not know what his master is doing: but I have called you friends, for all things that I heard from My Father I have made known to you. You did not choose Me, but I chose you and appointed you that you should go and bear fruit, and that your fruit should remain, that whatever you ask the Father in My name He may give you. These things I command you, that you love one another." (NKJV)

The Holy Spirit is sincere and many call the love giving personality of the Trinity (Father, Son and Holy Spirit). The Holy Spirit is always available to each of us. If we invite the Holy Spirit in today, It will make your life an immediate "Success!!" Ecclesiastes 9:11-12a states, "I have seen something else under the sun: The race is not to the swift or the battle to the strong, nor does food come to the wise or wealth to the brilliant or favor to the learned: but time and chance happen to them all. Moreover, no man knows when his hour will come:" (NIV) Hope can be defined as, "the happy anticipation of good things." We all daily trust and hope for the best to happen for us and our loved ones. Everything in life is a process in motion. Sometimes we wonder whether we are doing the right thing or moving in the right directions. GOD created each of us to be a goal-oriented visionary. He will direct our footsteps and lead us to our preordained destination. I believe the epitome of having a successful life is following your heart and doing those things that not only bring you satisfaction but help GOD's children. When we extend a hand to give back to our community, we have helped the least of these and fulfilled our spiritual mission.

Let's pray: Thank you Lord for sharing your love, peace, joy and mercy with us to empower us to bless others. Thank you for giving us Your Words to guide us throughout this earthly journey. Lord, help us to learn more of You through Your words and be all that You want us to be, in Jesus Name, Amen. As I look back over my life, I thank GOD again for His grace and mercy. When I had doubt, He said, "Have faith, I am in control and I am working it out for your good." If GOD said it, that settles it! A verse and the chorus of one of the great hymns of Mahalia Jackson, "If I Can Help Somebody" follows:

"If I can help somebody, as I pass along,
If I can cheer somebody, with a word or song,
If I can show somebody, how they're travelling wrong,
Then my living shall not be in vain.

Chorus:
My living shall not be in vain,
Then my living shall not be in vain
If I can help somebody, as I pass along,
Then my living shall not be in vain."

Yes, we are our brothers' and sisters' keeper. In order for the citizens, "We the People" to turn America in the right directions, we all must play our role. When we get involved in the activities of our block, community, city, state and nation, we all will benefit and help make the needed improvements. Lou Holtz, the famous football coach said, "When I die, my accomplishments will eventually be forgotten. But what I've invested in my players will continue to live on." Pastor Joel Osteen said, "The best legacy is not what we leave for people. It's what we leave in people. We all have things that we've learned: skills, talents, life experiences, wisdom. You have a wealth of knowledge that GOD has entrusted you with. You are not supposed to keep that to yourself. You should be passing that on to somebody else. We have a responsibility to transfer what we know to the next generation. Are you taking time to invest in your children? And if you don't have any children, how about your nieces and nephews? Your neighbors? The kid down the street? You and I have an opportunity to leave a mark that cannot be erased. Yes, eventually we're all going to die, but when you invest in somebody else, you will continue to live on. Your life can have influence for generations to come if you will take time to invest in people."

When we share GOD'S Words with our contacts and people we meet, the love of GOD is noticed in us. Our lives are daily being examined by others without our knowledge. So when you feel the Holy Spirit urging you to help someone by prayer, kind words or even financially, (if you are able) do it hastily. GOD uses us to be a blessing to others. As the law of Karma goes, "Every act done, no matter how insignificant, will eventually return to the doer with equal impact. Good will be returned with good: evil with evil."

Psalms 37:23-26 states, "The steps of a good man are ordered by the Lord, and he delighteth in his way. Though he fall, he shall not be utterly cast down, for the Lord upholdeth him with His hand. I have been young and am now old, yet I have not seen the righteous forsaken nor his seed begging bread. He is ever merciful and lendeth and his seed is blessed." GOD wants to lead us each step on this journey of life. When you are in GOD's will, He directs your path and He will never lead you astray. GOD wants us to have "Success." He wants us to learn him better through His Words. Once we get in His will, we will obtain infinite "Success." Thank you Lord for allowing me to be Your vessel to impart these Words You have given me. Bless each reader in a mighty manner and help us to continue to stretch our faith to save other lost souls, Amen.

There is nothing that gives a parent more satisfaction than the love and achievements of their children. All parents want to have good bonding with their child/children. They try to provide the love, warmth, and comfort that the child wants and needs in every phase of their development. It makes them quite proud to see their children finish high school and college. When our children start working, and living independent of us, we feel sometimes lonely in our empty nest. There is no better feeling than to hear from them and know they are doing good and making a success of their lives. The following was expressed to my brother Bill, by his daughter Ashley; "No matter how you slice the pie, I am amazed by you. Thank you for all that you do and have done. This man has made sacrifices beyond belief to show me unconditional, everlasting love from the day of my existence. Words cannot touch how important my Daddy is to me. I am so blessed to have you in my life, and I thank God every day for you. May He continue to bless you with a healthy, happy life. Love you always."

Sam Cook

Cook helps Dr. Martin Luther King Jr. through a crowd. 1963

Niece Ashley and Speaker of the House Nancy Pelosi.

Brother Bill and Mary Williams

ASHLEY & DAJUAN

JUNE 10 - 12, 2022

TEMECULA, CALIFORNIA

"Love is an action word."

Ashley M. Williams; 5/11/13 "The Mecca" Howard University, DC

CHAPTER EIGHTEEN
Let GOD Fight Your Battle

GOD is always available and ready to meet the needs of His children. He is never too busy and He is with you every second throughout each day. He loves hearing your voice and being the center of your activities. When you pray, He hears your cry and knows how to provide your need. So don't hesitate, cast all your problems, circumstances, concerns and desires on Him, He can bear all your loads!!

I believe each of GOD's children has an angel who watches over us, cares/protects and intercede on our behalf. Exodus 23:20-23 confirms, "See, I am sending an angel ahead of you to guard you along the way and to bring you to the place I have prepared. Pay attention to him and listen to what he says. Do not rebel against him: he will not forgive your rebellion, since my Name is in him. If you listen carefully to what he says and do all that I say, I will be an enemy to your enemies and will oppose those who oppose you. My angel will go ahead of you and bring you into the land of the Amorites, Hittites, Perizzites, Canaanites, Hivites and Jebusites, and I will wipe them out." (NIV) GOD's angels always prepare the way for us to navigate our daily tasks. We should be grateful to GOD for His assigned angel. These angels may be humans that insure our safety and respond to our smallest need.

Psalm 56 reads, "Be merciful to me, O GOD, for men hotly pursue me: all day long they press their attack. My slanderers pursue me all day long: many are attacking me in their pride. When I am afraid, I will trust in you. In GOD, whose word I praise, in GOD I trust: I will not be afraid. What can mortal man do to me? All day long they twist my words: they are always plotting to harm me. They conspire, they lurk, they watch my steps, eager to take my life. On no account let them escape: in your anger, O GOD, bring down the nations. Record my lament: list my tears on your scroll are they not in your record? Then my enemies will turn back when I call for help. By this I will know that GOD is for me. In GOD, whose word I praise, in the LORD, whose word I praise-in GOD I trust: I will not be afraid. What can man do to me? I am under vows to you, O GOD: I will present my thank offerings to you. For you have delivered me from death and my feet from stumbling, that I may walk before GOD in the light of life."

Job 1:1 reads, "In the land of Uz there lived a man whose name was Job. This man was blameless and upright: he feared GOD and shunned evil. He had seven sons and three daughters, and he owned seven thousand sheep, three thousand camels, five hundred yoke of oxen and five hundred donkeys, and had a large number of servants. He was the greatest man among all the people of the East." (NIV)

In the Book of Job, GOD allowed Satan to test Job and try to make him become an evil man. Satan told GOD that if GOD took away all his riches and his family, Job would curse GOD to His face. GOD allowed Satan to take away all that Job had but told Satan not to harm his body at all. Job lost his children and cattle. Job had a painful disease and sores were all over his body. Job's wife saw him suffering and said that his faith was of no value. She told him to curse GOD and die. Job held on in spite of the torment by his friends and relatives. GOD saw that Job understood the power and greatness of GOD. He reversed Job's curse and gave him double for his trouble. Job 42:10-17 reads as follows:

"After Job had prayed for his friends, the LORD made him prosperous again and gave him twice as much as he had before. All his brothers and sisters and everyone who had known him before came and ate with him in his house. They comforted and consoled him over all the trouble the LORD had brought upon him, and each one gave him a piece of silver and a gold ring. The LORD blessed the latter part of Job's life more than the first. He had fourteen thousand sheep, six thousand camels, a thousand yoke of oxen and a thousand donkeys. And he also had seven sons and three daughters. The first daughter he named Jemimah, the second Keziah and the third Keren-Happuch. Nowhere in all the land were there found women as beautiful as Job's daughters, and their father granted them an inheritance along with their brothers. After this, Job lived a hundred and forty years: he saw his children and their children to the fourth generation. And so he died, old and full of years." (NIV)

In his poem below, Langston Hughes writes about a mother speaking to her son about her life's experiences, it states:

> "Well, son, I'll tell you:
> Life for me ain't been no crystal stair.
> It's had tacks in it,
> And splinters,
> And boards torn up,
> And places with no carpet on the floor —
> Bare.
> But all the time
> I'se been a-climbin' on,
> And reachin' landin's,
> And turnin' corners,
> And sometimes goin' in the dark
> Where there ain't been no light.
> So boy, don't you turn back.
> Don't you set down on the steps
> 'Cause you finds it's kinder hard.
> Don't you fall now —
> For I'se still goin', honey,
> I'se still climbin',
> And life for me ain't been no crystal stair."

Isaiah 61:3 states, "And provide for those who grieve in Zion, to bestow on them a crown of beauty instead of ashes, the oil of gladness instead of mourning, and a garment of praise instead of a spirit of despair. They will be called oaks of righteousness, a planting of the LORD for the display of his splendor." Don't let no one or nothing steal your joy. Faith in GOD helps us believe, in spite of our current problems or circumstances, better days are ahead. GOD's favor can instantly change our situation. We should always expect good things to happen in our lives. When we have done all we could to overcome an issue, GOD will meet us at the level of our expectation and propel us to "Success." When we maintain the right attitude and get out of our negative mentality, GOD will help us overcome any adversity. Jesus endured the burdens of the cross because He had to save mankind and do the will of GOD. When we show we are determined to oppose the wiles of the devil, GOD rewards us. A change in our attitude and our heart let the enemy know, we will resist his attacks and that we are GOD's children. We are full of faith and courage and will be victors and not victims. GOD knows our circumstances and also knows our hearts. Again I say, when we make efforts to alleviate our situation, GOD will step in and at His timing, meet our need. An example of GOD stepping in to help one of His children in need is found in John 5:6-10, it exclaims: "When Jesus saw him lying there and learned that he had been in this condition for a long time, he asked him, 'Do you want to get well?' 'Sir,' the invalid replied, 'I have no one to help me into the pool when the water is stirred. While I am trying to get in, someone else goes down ahead of me.' Then Jesus said to him, 'Get up! Pick up your mat and walk.' At once the man was cured: he picked up his mat and walked." (NIV)

Mother Teresa said, **DO IT ANYWAY**.

> "People are often unreasonable, illogical and self-centered: Forgive them anyway.
>
> If you are kind, people may accuse you of selfish ulterior motives: Be kind anyway.
>
> If you are successful, you will win some false friends and true enemies: Succeed anyway.
>
> If you are honest and frank, people may cheat you: Be honest anyway. What you spend years building, someone could destroy overnight: Build anyway. If you find serenity and happiness,
>
> they may be jealous: Be happy anyway. The good you do today, people will often forget tomorrow: Do good anyway. Give the world the best you have, and it may never be enough:
>
> Give the world the best you've got anyway. You see, in the final analysis, it is between you and GOD: It was never between you and them anyway."

In your hours of trials and tribulations, hold on and let GOD fight your battles. Galatians 6:9 reads: "Let us not become weary in doing good, for at the proper time we will reap a harvest if we do not give up." Workers of evil are always looking to attack those who they think will give up on their faith.

When your enemies see that you are going to stand firm on the Words of GOD and that you are determined to outlast their wickedness, they will surrender. They know they are no match for GOD and cannot win. So don't ever give up or lose hope in your faith, because GOD will never give up on you. Stay strong and move forward despite trouble or adversity in your path, GOD is fighting your battle.

Let's pray: Holy Spirit, thank you for this day. At this moment, I feel Your anointing during the stillness and silence of this early hour. I hear Your voice encouraging me to be not afraid and telling me to go on in your name. Almighty GOD, thank you for dying for our sins. Thank you for raising Yourself up from the grave to show the world that You have all power. Thank you for saving my lost soul. Lord we know You can do anything but fail. Right now, we ask You to keep us moving forward, constantly defeating the wiles of the devil. Lord, I thank you for the Words You allowed Your servant to write. By me reading these Words, I declare, I will turn my life around. With Your help, I believe I will have eternal "Success." We ask these requests, in Jesus' Name, Amen.

Before you speak, ask yourself three questions: Is it kind? Is it true? Is it necessary? If you can answer yes to all three, it's okay to say it!!! The golden rule, "Do unto others as you want them to do unto you," can be said in many ways: "It is not fair to ask of others what you are unwilling to do yourself." (Anna Eleanor Roosevelt) "We should bear ourselves toward others as we would desire they should bear themselves toward us." (Aristotle) "What you would avoid suffering yourself, seek not to impose on others." (Epictetus, circa 100 CE) "You should always ask yourself what would happen if everyone did what you are doing." (Jean-Paul Sartre) "May I do to others as I would that they should do unto me." (Plato) "Each man takes care that his neighbor shall not cheat him. But a day comes when he begins to care that he does not cheat his neighbor. Then all goes well - he has changed his market-cart into a chariot of the sun." (Ralph Waldo Emerson) "One of the most potent of the weapons of influence around us is the rule for reciprocation. The rule says that we should try to repay, in kind, what another person has provided us." (Robert B Cialdini)

Psalm 24:1-10 reads as follows: "The earth is the LORD's, and everything in it, the world, and all who live in it: for he founded it upon the seas and established it upon the waters. Who may ascend the hill of the LORD? Who may stand in his holy place? He who has clean hands and a pure heart, who does not lift up his soul to an idol or swear by what is false. He will receive blessing from the LORD and vindication from GOD his Savior. Such is the generation of those who seek him, who seek your face, O GOD of Jacob, Selah. Lift up your heads, O you gates: be lifted up, you ancient doors, that the King of glory may come in. Who is this King of glory? The LORD strong and mighty, the LORD mighty in battle. Lift up your heads, O you gates: lift them up, you ancient doors, that the King of glory may come in. Who is he, this King of glory? The LORD Almighty — he is the King of glory. Selah" (NIV)

When each of us was birthed to this earth, GOD was in charge. When we have our ups and downs during our life span, GOD is in charge. When we depart for Heaven or Hell, GOD is in charge. The Great I Am is Alpha and Omega and He is always in charge.

CHAPTER NINETEEN
Success

Romans 2:11-14 state: "For there is no respect of persons with GOD. For as many as have sinned without law shall also perish without law: and as many as have sinned in the law shall be judged by the law: For not the hearers of the law are just before GOD, but the doers of the law shall be justified." This means that each of us as children of GOD are treated in the same manner and given GOD's unconditional love. It doesn't matter if your name is one of the persons we talked about in this book: King, Wallace, Obama, Clinton, Keith, Kennedy, Reagan, Siegelman or Dave Williams: GOD is your Father and He wants you to do His will and become a "Success." GOD does not limit or judge us because of color, gender, culture or any other personal trait. When you study and obey GOD's Words, pray unceasingly, offer GOD regular praise and worship and strive to do His will, GOD will see your heart and He will bless you and make you a "Success."

Romans 8:1-28 read: "There is therefore now no condemnation to them which are in Christ Jesus, who walk not after the flesh, but after the Spirit. For the law of the Spirit of life in Christ Jesus hath made me free from the law of sin and death. For what the law could not do, in that it was weak through the flesh, GOD sending his own Son in the likeness of sinful flesh, and for sin, condemned sin in the flesh: That the righteousness of the law might be fulfilled in us, who walk not after the flesh, but after the Spirit. For they that are after the flesh do mind the things of the flesh: but they that are after the Spirit the things of the Spirit. For to be carnally minded is death: but to be spiritually minded is life and peace. Because the carnal mind is enmity against GOD: for it is not subject to the law of GOD, neither indeed can be. So then they that are in the flesh cannot please GOD. But ye are not in the flesh, but in the Spirit, if so be that the Spirit of GOD dwell in you. Now if any man have not the Spirit of Christ, he is none of his. And if Christ be in you, the body is dead because of sin: but the Spirit is life because of righteousness. But if the Spirit of him that raised up Jesus from the dead dwell in you, he that raised up Christ from the dead shall also quicken your mortal bodies by his Spirit that dwelleth in you. Therefore, brethren, we are debtors, not to the flesh, to live after the flesh. For if ye live after the flesh, ye shall die: but if ye through the Spirit do mortify the deeds of the body, ye shall live. For as many as are led by the Spirit of GOD, they are the sons of GOD. For ye have not received the spirit of bondage again to fear: but ye have received the Spirit of adoption, whereby we cry, Abba, Father. The Spirit itself beareth witness with our spirit, that we are the children of GOD: And if children, then heirs: heirs of GOD, and joint-heirs with Christ: if so be that we suffer with him, that we may be also glorified together. For I reckon that the sufferings of this present time are not worthy to be compared with the glory which shall be revealed in us. For the earnest expectation of the creature waiteth for the manifestation of the sons of GOD. For the creature was made subject to vanity, not willingly, but by reason of him who hath subjected the same in hope, Because the creature itself also shall be delivered from the bondage of corruption into the glorious liberty of the children of GOD. For we know that the whole creation groaneth and travaileth in pain together until now. And not only they, but ourselves also, which have the first fruits of the Spirit, even we ourselves groan within ourselves, waiting for the adoption, to wit, the redemption of our body. For we are saved by hope: but hope that is seen is not hope: for what a man seeth, why doth he yet hope for? But if we hope for that we see not, then do we with patience wait for it. Likewise the Spirit also helpeth our infirmities: for we know not what we should pray for as we ought: but the Spirit itself maketh intercession for us with groanings which cannot be uttered. And he that searcheth the hearts knoweth what is the mind of the Spirit, because he maketh intercession for the saints according to the will of GOD. And we know that all things work together for good to them that love GOD, to them who are the called according to his purpose."

"Success" comes to those who follow the instructions from GOD's Words. Hopefully, statements from some of these Americans written in this discourse are beneficial to you and help lead you to Christ. Without question, what He has done for others He'll do for you. An old revival song called, "It Is No Secret (What GOD Can Do)" stated it this way:

"The chimes of time ring out the news, another day is through.

Someone slipped and fell, was that someone you?

You may have longed for added strength your courage to renew.

Do not be disheartened, I have news for you.

It is no secret what GOD can do, what he's done for others he'll do for you.

With arms wide open, he'll pardon you, it is no secret what GOD can do.

There is no night for in his light you'll never walk alone.

Always feel at home, wherever you may roam.

There is no power can conquer you while GOD is on your side.

Just take him at his promise, don't run away and hide.

It is no secret what GOD can do, what he's done for others he'll do for you.

With arms wide open he'll pardon you, it is no secret what GOD can do."

James 1:25 puts it this way, "But the man who looks intently into the perfect law that gives freedom, and continues to do this, not forgetting what he has heard, but doing it—he will be blessed in what he does. If anyone considers himself religious and yet does not keep a tight rein on his tongue, he deceives himself and his religion is worthless. Religion that GOD our Father accepts as pure and faultless is this: to look after orphans and widows in their distress and to keep oneself from being polluted by the world." (NIV)

If you want to be a "Success" and receive GOD's favor, it is possible when you begin to understand and act out Colossians 3:23-24. "Whatever you do, do it heartily, as to the Lord and not to men, knowing that from the Lord you will receive the reward."

We should practice not working just for our boss or for a paycheck. Instead we should be performing our tasks as if we are working for GOD. Pastor Joel Osteen says, "When you love your family and show true friendship and kindness to others, it's as if you are doing that for Jesus too! When your focus is on GOD in whatever you do, you are living out His exciting purpose for you. That's why GOD wants you to put your whole heart into everything you do... every day. And when you give your best effort for GOD, He promises to reward you. Your life can be transformed by practicing this very basic principle of seeking to please and honor GOD in all you do." GOD is always fair and He will reward you with favor and abundance when you obey His Words and follow His Spirit.

Let's pray: Lord, I thank you for being with us each step of this journey and showering Your blessings upon us. We thank and praise You for current blessings and those on the way. Lord, continue to lead and order our footsteps. Our Creator and Provider, we come to You right now to say thank you for giving us Your Words. Thank you for bringing us safely through this journey to this day. GOD, help us to become the person who, through Your power, chooses to live our best life now and refuse to settle for second best. We declare, we will be a "Success" in Your Name. Thank you for being so generous and merciful to us. We ask Your continuous protection and guidance as we move forth today. We will continue to trust You and will forever give You the honor and praise. We ask it all, in Jesus' Mighty Name, Amen.

One of the most important ingredients for "Success" is the internal belief that you will succeed. "Success" begins with your beliefs and thoughts. You can't change your life until you change your mind. It's always the thought that precedes the action. The changes that you need to make in order to succeed begins with your mental outlook. Always try to think positive thoughts. It's okay to declare it right now, "I'm blessed and highly favored and from this day forward, with GOD's help, I will be a "Success!!!" GOD will never turn away from His children. If you cast all your anxieties and cares on GOD, He will help you to get up, shake loose from your problems and be a "Success." Psalm 118:5 reads, "Out of my distress I called upon the Lord: the Lord answered me and set me free."

Psalm 1:1-6 declares, "Blessed is the man that walketh not in the counsel of the ungodly, nor standeth in the way of sinners, nor sitteth in the seat of the scornful. But his delight is in the law of the LORD: and in his law doth he meditate day and night. And he shall be like a tree planted by the rivers of water, that bringeth forth his fruit in his season: his leaf also shall not wither: and whatsoever he doeth shall prosper. The ungodly are not so: but are like the chaff which the wind driveth away. Therefore the ungodly shall not stand in the judgment, nor sinners in the congregation of the righteous. For the LORD knoweth the way of the righteous: but the way of the un-GODly shall perish."

Psalm 121:2 says, "My help comes from the LORD, Who made heaven and earth."

GOD is available to each of us not only when our backs are against the wall, He will help us with even our smallest need. GOD's Words say, "He is an ever present help in time of need. GOD wants to be our source for all things. Be encouraged, GOD is getting ready to give you His favor and move you up the ladder of "Success!" Wait upon the Lord for His blessings and increase. Move yourself out of the way! Be patient and wait on GOD to give you "Success" and work out your circumstances for you. He will exceed all of your expectations and diligently reward all those who seek Him.

1 Thessalonians 5:11-19 reads, "Wherefore comfort yourselves together, and edify one another, even as also ye do. And we beseech you, brethren, to know them which labour among you, and are over you in the Lord, and admonish you: And to esteem them very highly in love for their work's sake. And be at peace among yourselves. Now we exhort you, brethren, warn them that are unruly, comfort the feebleminded, support the weak, be patient toward all men. See that none render evil for evil unto any man: but ever follow that which is good, both among yourselves, and to all men. Rejoice evermore. Pray without ceasing. In everything give thanks: for this is the will of GOD in Christ Jesus concerning you. Quench not the Spirit."

1 Thessalonians 5:23 states, "And the very GOD of peace sanctify you wholly: and *I pray GOD* your whole spirit and soul and body be preserved blameless unto the coming of our Lord Jesus Christ."

One writer wrote, "We're always sowing seeds in life by everything we do and say, so let's make sure the fruit we reap comes from the good we do each day. The seeds we sow today determine the kind of fruit we'll reap tomorrow." Galatians 6:7 says, "Be not deceived: GOD is not mocked: for whatsoever a man soweth, that shall he also reap." Psalm 34:3 "O magnify the LORD with me, and let us exalt his name together." A portion of one of my favorite old Hymns is below:

"I MUST TELL JESUS"

I must tell Jesus all of my trials:
I cannot bear these burdens alone:
In my distress He kindly will help me:
He ever loves and cares for His own.
I must tell Jesus all of my troubles:
He is a kind, compassionate Friend:
If I but ask Him, He will deliver,
And in my griefs with me He will blend.
Tempted and tried I need a great Savior,
One who can help my burdens to bear:
I must tell Jesus, I must tell Jesus:
He all my cares and sorrows will share,
Chorus: I must tell Jesus! I must tell Jesus!
I cannot bear my burdens alone:
I must tell Jesus! I must tell Jesus!
Jesus can help me, Jesus alone."

Jeremiah 29:11 reads, "For I know the thoughts that I think toward you, saith the LORD, thoughts of peace, and not of evil, to give you an expected end." Expect to be blessed and a "Success." GOD's favor is on you and as Luke 1:37 declares, "For With GOD, Nothing Shall Be Impossible."

CHAPTER TWENTY
I Pledge Myself

Romans 5:1-21 reads: "Therefore, having been justified by faith, we have peace with GOD through our Lord Jesus Christ, through whom also we have access by faith into this grace in which we stand, and rejoice in hope of the glory of GOD. And not only that, but we also glory in tribulations, knowing that tribulation produces perseverance: and perseverance, character: and character, hope. Now hope does not disappoint, because the love of GOD has been poured out in our hearts by the Holy Spirit who was given to us. For when we were still without strength, in due time Christ died for the unGODly. For scarcely for a righteous man will one die: yet perhaps for a good man someone would even dare to die. But GOD demonstrates His own love toward us, in that while we were still sinners, Christ died for us. Much more then, having now been justified by His blood, we shall be saved from wrath through Him. For if when we were enemies we were reconciled to GOD through the death of His Son, much more, having been reconciled, we shall be saved by His life. And not only that, but we also rejoice in GOD through our Lord Jesus Christ, through whom we have now received the reconciliation. Therefore, just as through one man sin entered the world, and death through sin, and thus death spread to all men, because all sinned (For until the law sin was in the world, but sin is not imputed when there is no law. Nevertheless death reigned from Adam to Moses, even over those who had not sinned according to the likeness of the transgression of Adam, who is a type of Him who was to come. But the free gift is not like the offense. For if by the one man's offense many died, much more the grace of GOD and the gift by the grace of the one Man, Jesus

Christ, abounded to many. And the gift is not like that which came through the one who sinned. For the judgment which came from one offense resulted in condemnation, but the free gift which came from many offenses resulted in justification. For if by the one man's offense death reigned through the one, much more those who receive abundance of grace and of the gift of righteousness will reign in life through the One, Jesus Christ.) Therefore, as through one man's offense judgment came to all men, resulting in condemnation, even so through one Man's righteous act the free gift came to all men, resulting in justification of life. For as by one man's disobedience many were made sinners, so also by one Man's obedience many will be made righteous. Moreover the law entered that the offense might abound. But where sin abounded, grace abounded much more, so that as sin reigned in death, even so grace might reign through righteousness to eternal life through Jesus Christ our Lord." (NKJV)

Fed up with all the violence frequently occurring all over Detroit neighborhoods as well as the US, I met with the community relations' person for the Sheriff Department here in Detroit on January 13, 2005. I provided him a plan to help our families intervene and prayerfully alleviate some of the violence here in Detroit. One of the documents I shared was the pledge below which I suggested be distributed to leaders in the churches, schools, neighborhood centers and other targeted areas utilized by our youths. I was hopeful this pledge would be read and discussed with our youths to help redirect their negative behavior. The pledge which was adapted from the Million Man March Pledge states:

I PLEDGE MYSELF

"I pledge that, from this day forward, I will strive to treat everyone as I wish to be treated. I, from this day forward, will strive to improve myself spiritually, morally, mentally, socially, politically and economically for the benefit of myself, my family, my church and community. I pledge that I will do my best in all endeavors. I will develop my talents to the fullest potential and help reshape our world in a positive manner. I pledge that from this day forward, I will never raise my hand with a knife, gun, or any weapon to beat, cut, or shoot any human being except in self-defense. I pledge from this day forward that I will respect and get along better with all individuals. I will walk away from circumstances that may cause me trouble or create bad feelings. I pledge from this day forward that I will not poison my body with drugs or that which is destructive to my health and my well-being. I pledge that I will help make this world better by being a right-thinking person and doing those actions that will have a positive result. I solemnly swear I will do my best to keep all of this pledge."

We live in a world where violence and discord seem to dominate many communities throughout America. In spite of such adverse situations and the great turmoil, GOD is still in control. He wants us to display the fruit of the spirit that is spelled out in Galatian5:22,23: "But the fruit of the Spirit is love, joy, peace, longsuffering, gentleness, goodness, faith, meekness, temperance: against such there is no law."

In particular, teenage violence is causing great problems and much tragedy throughout our nation. Many people are fed up with drive by shootings, gang wars, robberies, murders, rapes and daily violence where weapons are causing enormous injuries and often death. This violence and criminal activity is not confined to any particular group, but youths between the ages of 15 and 24 commit more violent crimes than people in any other age group. In a survey published a few years ago, the Center for Disease Control and Prevention said that one in ten high school students carried a weapon on school property. Violence in the schools is a major problem for teens. Teachers can't teach and children can't learn in an atmosphere of fear. Too many funerals are being held for people killed with handguns. Getting guns, drugs and violence out of our schools must be everyone's top priority.

The killing of Derrion Albert in Chicago has caused national attention to be given to this violence. US Justice Department officials said in October, 2009 that most children in the United States are exposed to violence in their daily lives, which Attorney General Eric Holder called "staggering." More than 60 percent of children surveyed were exposed to violence within the past year, either directly or indirectly, according to data compiled by the department. The survey's compilers defined exposure to violence as being a victim, or having witnessed violence, or learning about violence against a relative, friend, or hearing about a threat to their school or home. "Those numbers are astonishing, and they are unacceptable," Holder said in Chicago, where he was meeting with local officials to discuss the disturbing beating death of a high school student by other teens. "We simply cannot stand for an epidemic of violence that robs our youth of their childhood and perpetuates a cycle in which today's victims become tomorrow's criminals," Holder said. The results were based on telephone interviews of 4,549 children and adolescents aged 17 and younger between January and May of 2008. For children ages 9 and younger, a parent or guardian answered the questions. The National Survey of Children's Exposure to Violence was sponsored by the Justice Department's Office of Juvenile Justice and Delinquency Prevention, with help from the Centers for Disease Control. It was conducted by university researchers.

The attorney general went to Chicago in October, 2009 to meet with local officials, parents, and students to discuss the vicious beating of a 16-year-old high school student who was killed on September 24, 2009. This student's beating was captured on a cell phone video. Derrion Albert, an honor roll student at Christian Fenger Academy High School, was attacked when he got caught up in a mob of teens about six blocks from school. Video showed him curled up on the sidewalk as fellow teens kick him and hit him with splintered railroad ties. So far, four teens have been charged in his death. "What kind of person, what kind of individual, has such rage and such anger and such madness?" the Rev. Michael Pfleger of Chicago said. "We've got to get to the hearts of our children, because nothing, nothing, excuses or justifies the actions of an individual who would beat another individual. Nothing justifies that in this society.

Each day GOD feeds the birds and gives them shelter. GOD provides abundantly for the birds and we are far more important to GOD than birds. We were made in His image! GOD loves each one of us unconditionally and He will meet all our needs. You are GOD's child and He wants you to be the best and have the best!!! GOD led me to write this book! GOD can present you with a challenge to undertake to give Him some glory and you some fulfillment. GOD said, "It's time out for all this violence and negative behaviors."

We often hear politicians say, "Our children are our future." If we believe this is true, the importance of early education and training cannot be overestimated. The foundation for a child's language ability, ethics, morals and value systems is developed early in a child's life. Mahatma Gandhi said, "I am convinced that for the proper upbringing of children the parents ought to have a general knowledge of the care and nursing of babies. We labor under a sort of superstition that the child has nothing to learn during the first five years of its life. On the contrary, the fact is that the child never learns in after life what it does in its first five years. The education of a child begins with conception."

Many experts believe and research document that crime prevention/alleviation lies in helping our children to learn proper behavior and good manners before they enter the first grade. We must refocus and place more emphasis on early childhood development. Children are like seeds we plant in a garden,: with proper watering/nurturing they grow into great and meaningful citizens. So be careful what you plant now, it will determine what you reap tomorrow.

Someone once said, "If you plant honesty, you will reap trust. If you plant goodness, you will reap friends. If you plant humility, you will reap greatness. If you plant perseverance, you will reap victory. If you plant consideration, you will reap harmony. If you plant hard work, you will reap success. If you plant forgiveness, you will reap reconciliation. If you plant openness, you will reap intimacy. If you plant patience, you will reap improvements. If you plant faith, you will reap miracles." Yes, the seeds you now scatter will make life worse or better. Someday, you will enjoy the fruits or you will pay for the choices you plant today. "Train up a child in the way he should go and when he is old, he will not depart from it." Proverbs 22:6

Let's pray: O Lord, how excellent is thy name in all the earth. We ask a special blessing upon our children today. Show our children Your will. Help their faith to grow stronger and sweeter as the days go by, Amen

Parents must take the major responsibility for redirecting their children behavior. Parents must teach and demonstrate good behavior to their children. Being a good example shows GOD that you are after His heart and He will help you. GOD wants you to be a "Success." 1 Timothy 4:12-16 states, "Don't let anyone look down on you because you are young, but set an example for the believers in speech, in life, in love, in faith and in purity. Until I come, devote yourself to the public reading of Scripture, to preaching and to teaching. Do not neglect your gift, which was given you through a prophetic message when the body of elders laid their hands on you. Be diligent in these matters: give yourself wholly to them, so that everyone may see your progress. Watch your life and doctrine closely. Persevere in them, because if you do, you will save both yourself and your hearers." Romans 8:28 reads, "And we know that in all things GOD works for the good of those who love him, who have been called according to his purpose." (NIV) Soon and very soon will be the day of reckoning: Will you be ready?" GOD wants to lead you to "Success" and now is the time.

CHAPTER TWENTY-ONE
Blessed

It often is said that in the Beatitudes that this sermon is connected with the upcoming Kingdom of GOD which I believe is closer than we think. This sermon gives the character of GOD and those suitable for entry into His Kingdom. In the Beatitudes found in the Book of Matthew, Jesus names a group of people normally thought to be unblessed and exclaims that they are blessed. GOD's kingdom will be available to everyone, regardless of their status, race, gender or condition. The Beatitudes are blessings from GOD recorded in the Sermon on the Mount, Matthew 5:1-15 states, "Now when he saw the crowds, he went up on a mountainside and sat down. His disciples came to him, and he began to teach them saying: Blessed are the poor in spirit, for theirs is the kingdom of heaven. Blessed are those who mourn, for they will be comforted. Blessed are the meek, for they will inherit the earth. Blessed are those who hunger and thirst for righteousness, for they will be filled. Blessed are the merciful, for they will be shown mercy. Blessed are the pure in heart, for they will see GOD. Blessed are the peacemakers, For they will be called sons of GOD. Blessed are those who are persecuted because of righteousness, for theirs is the kingdom of heaven. Blessed are you when people insult you, persecute you and falsely say all kinds of evil against you because of me. Rejoice and be glad, because great is your reward in heaven, for in the same way they persecuted the prophets who were before you. You are the salt of the earth. But if the salt loses its saltiness, how can it be made salty again? It is no longer good for anything, except to be thrown out and trampled by men. You are the light of the world. A city on a hill cannot be hidden. Neither do people light a lamp and put it under a bowl. Instead they put it on its stand, and it gives light to every-one in the house." (NIV)

When you know GOD and dwell in His will, the criticisms and opinions of other people to create discord will not matter to you. Try to ignore but if you can't, a good response to workers of iniquity should always be: "I am anointed and appointed by GOD to perform my divine assignment. I will let nothing or no one hinder me from completing my assignment. I believe in GOD's Words and He has promised that those who trust and obey Him will He guide, protect and comfort." Proverbs 3:13-26 state: "Blessed is the man who finds wisdom, the man who gains understanding, for she is more profit-able than silver and yields better returns than gold. She is more precious than rubies: nothing you desire can compare with her. Long life is in her right hand: in her left hand are riches and honor. Her ways are pleasant ways, and all her paths are peace. She is a tree of life to those who embrace her: those who lay hold of her will be blessed. By wisdom the LORD laid the earth's foundations, by understanding he set the heavens in place: by his knowledge the deeps were divided, and the clouds let drop the dew. My son, preserve sound judgment and discernment, do not let them out of your sight: they will be life for you, an ornament to grace your neck. Then you will go on your way in safety, and your foot will not stumble: when you lie down, you will not be afraid: when you lie down, your sleep will be sweet. Have no fear of sudden disaster or of the ruin that overtakes the wicked, for the LORD will be your confidence and will keep your foot from being snared." (NIV)

The Apostles' Creed is believed to be a formula containing statements of the fundamental tenets of Christian belief, and having for its authors, accord-ing to tradition, the Twelve Apostles. Many Christians believe that this Creed is the spiritual seal of our heart's meditation, an ever-present guardian and the treasure of our soul. It reads as follows:

THE APOSTLES' CREED

"I believe in GOD the Father, Almighty, Maker of heaven and earth: And in Jesus Christ, his only begotten Son, our Lord: Who was conceived by the Holy Ghost, born of the Virgin Mary: Suffered under Pontius Pilate: was crucified, dead and buried: He descended into hell: The third day he rose again from the dead: He ascended into heaven, and sits at the right hand of GOD the Father Almighty: From thence he shall come to judge the quick and the dead: I believe in the Holy Ghost: I believe in the Church Universal: the communion of saints: The forgiveness of sins: The resurrection of the body: And the life everlasting. Amen"

We please GOD by showing kindness to His children. GOD looks at our heart and He knows our motives when we perform an action. We are made in the image of GOD and He wants us to be holy. Following GOD's Words always pays us dividends, breeds "Success" and prepares us for eternity. Leviticus 11:44-45 states: "I am the LORD your GOD: consecrate yourselves and be holy, because I am holy. Do not make yourselves unclean by any creature that moves about on the ground. I am the LORD who brought you up out of Egypt to be your GOD: therefore be holy, because I am holy." Matthew 6:1-4 reads: "Be careful not to do your 'acts of righteousness' before men, to be seen by them. If you do, you will have no reward from your Father in heaven. So when you give to the needy, do not announce it with trumpets, as the hypocrites do in the synagogues and on the streets, to be honored by men. I tell you the truth, they have received their reward in full. But when you give to the needy, do not let your left hand know what your right hand is doing, so that your giving may be in secret. Then your Father, who sees what is done in secret, will reward you." Matthew 5:43-48 states: "You have heard that it was said, Love your neighbor and hate your enemy. But I tell you: Love your enemies and pray for those who persecute you, that you may be sons of your Father in heaven. He causes his sun to rise on the evil and the good, and sends rain on the righteous and the unrighteous. If you love those who love you, what reward will you get? Are not even the tax collectors doing that? And if you greet only your brothers, what are you doing more than others? Do not even pagans do that? Be perfect, therefore, as your heavenly Father is perfect." Psalm 62:5-10 states: "Find rest, O my soul, in GOD alone: my hope comes from him. He alone is my rock and my salvation: he is my fortress, I will not be shaken. My salvation and my honor depend on GOD: he is my mighty rock, my refuge. Trust in him at all times, O people: pour out your hearts to him, for GOD is our refuge, Selah." (NIV)

CHAPTER TWENTY-TWO
Recovery

A story goes, "While shopping at a local Wal-Mart, a woman spotted a man with an acronym on his shirt that had B.A.D. Being the person that she was (curious), she stopped the man and asked, 'What does B.A.D. stand for?' And trust me: you'll be amazed at what his response was. He replied B.A.D. stands for: 'Blessed And Delivered.' That thought stuck with her as she finished doing her shopping that day. So she came up with a little advice for you today.

1. When the enemy tries to attack you, be B.A.D.
2. When things don't seem to be going right on your job, be B.A.D.
3. When things are not looking good in your marriage, be B.A.D.
4. When folks scandalize your name, just be B.A.D.

Get with somebody who you know that you can be B.A.D. With!!!
May GOD Bless You And Have A B.A.D. Day!

Psalm 24:1-10 reads as follows: "The earth is the LORD's, and everything in it, the world, and all who live in it: for he founded it upon the seas and established it upon the waters. Who may ascend the hill of the LORD? Who may stand in his holy place? He who has clean hands and a pure heart, who does not lift up his soul to an idol or swear by what is false. He will receive blessing from the LORD and vindication from GOD his Savior. Such is the generation of those who seek him, who seek your face, O GOD of Jacob, Selah. Lift up your heads, O you gates: be lifted up, you ancient doors, that the King of glory may come in. Who is this King of glory? The LORD strong and mighty, the LORD mighty in battle. Lift up your heads, O you gates: lift them up, you ancient doors, that the King of glory may come in. Who is he, this King of glory? The LORD Almighty — he is the King of glory. Selah" (NIV)

When each of us was birthed to this earth, GOD was in charge. When we have our ups and downs during our life span, GOD is in charge. When we depart for Heaven or Hell, GOD is in charge. The Great I Am is Alpha and Omega and He is always in charge.

One writer said, "At some point in our lives, every one of us has missed out on GOD-given opportunities, we have come short of the glory of GOD. Maybe you can think of a few right now. If so, I want to encourage you: Don't live in regret. Don't let lost opportunities make you feel disappointed and discouraged. GOD is bigger than your lost opportunities. No matter what has happened in your past, He can still get your life back on track! It's sort of like using one of those GPS systems in your car. You set the location to where you want to go and the GPS calculates the best route. You can be driving along and get distracted and completely miss the street where the GPS instructed you to turn, but that doesn't mean you'll never reach your destination. You wouldn't just pull off to the side of the road crying, 'Now I'm stuck here. I'll never get where I need to go, all because I missed my turn!' No, there's always another way to get there. In fact, that GPS system will instantly re-calculate the route to your destination based on your present location.

Well, GOD works in a similar way. He is constantly giving us direction, speaking to our hearts, leading us by granting peace or unrest in our spirits, but even when we miss His instructions—and we all do from time to time—He will recalculate our route and get us back where we need to be. I love what the Apostle Paul said in Philippians 13: 'One thing I do: Forgetting what is behind and straining toward what is ahead…' He was saying, we must turn our thoughts toward the future and keep looking for the new opportunities. GOD is a restorer and He loves to restore opportunities. It may not always happen the way you think, but keep your heart open to Him. He'll get you back on track towards the wonderful destiny He has prepared for you!" Let's pray: Thank you Lord for new opportunities. Forgive us of our sins, restore Your righteous spirit within us and allow us to live for You forever, Amen.

Pastor Joel Osteen said, "So many people are dealing with burdens brought on by the economic downturn on top of the everyday challenges in their families, careers, relationships, and health. The enemy would love nothing more than to make you feel isolated, hopeless, and forgotten. But I want to remind you that you are not forgotten. You are not alone, and you do have hope! GOD Almighty has promised to be with you on the mountain and in the valley. He is as close to you as the air you breathe. He is there to walk with you and guide you even in the dark, difficult times." The e-mail below is a letter that I received from Pastor Joel Osteen:

3-19-10

David, Did you know that GOD can use a single moment to transform your life for the better? GOD is always working, even when we have no idea what He's doing. He loves to bless us with His amazing, awe-inspiring goodness, even when we least expect it or when things don't seem to be going the right way. Romans 8:28 is a popular verse but never gets old. To me, it's one of the most encouraging verses in the entire Bible. "And we know that GOD causes everything to work together for the good of those who love GOD and are called according to his purpose for them" (NLT). I love the word "everything" in this verse. We tend to think of bad things and difficult seasons, but "everything" includes more. It includes the good things as well as the things that we are indifferent about. GOD takes all of those things and works them out for our good. He wants you to be the kind of person who thinks about His promises all the time, who believes the best, and who keeps hoping when others just give up. If you live this way, I believe you'll be amazed at how GOD works in your life. You'll experience His favor in what I call a "GOD-ordained moment." A GOD-ordained moment is an incredible, supernatural event that GOD's been setting up, working behind the scenes so that you can experience His goodness at just the right time. These GOD-ordained moments don't come on our schedule, but when they come, all we can say is: "Wow!" Victoria and I want to remind you not to allow discouragement, a busy schedule or the hurts from your past to cause you to miss what GOD is doing in your life. Most importantly, don't give up on being blown away by GOD's favor. Because of how big our GOD is and how much He loves us, I believe that we can experience "Wow" moments on a continual basis, as long as we continue to love

Him and obey His Word. Victoria and I want to say thank you for supporting this ministry and helping us share the message of HOPE in Jesus Christ around the world. We are believing with you for a year filled with GOD-or-dained moments in your life!Joel Osteen'"For whoever finds me finds life, And obtains favor from the LORD." Proverbs 8:35 The following was discreetly given to a group of young men who were serving time in the juvenile justice system. The aim of this booklet was to help them learn to read and hopefully would bring them daily encouragement/success as they completed their incarceration period.*Comeback...10 Days To Recovery* by Dave Williams Introduction GOD Promises Life and its circumstances may sometimes make you feel fearful and uncertain about how to resolve things you are confronted with on a day-to-day basis. You must learn how to deal with situations and face your fears. Don't be so hard on yourself because of the disorder and confusion that may enter your life. You can learn how to battle it and overcome it. I believe you should not deprive yourself from what life has to offer. There is a special purpose for each and every individual on this earth. When feeling disgusted and discouraged, just remember, you are GOD's child, He cares for you and wants you to enjoy the fullness of His land. Sometimes we may wish that we could just fly away from this problem, issue or situation that we may be facing and never see or deal with it again. How many of you have headed for bed with a cry on your lips at one time or another, that you could just fly away from the miseries of this world? Mothers shut in with their children all day, businessmen trapped in the pressures of making crucial decisions, and fathers/mothers working two jobs so that their families can survive are among those who wish they could run away at times and never come back. Even David dreamed of escape when he sang to the Lord: "Oh, that I had the wings of a dove! I would fly away and be at rest – I would flee far away and stay in the desert: I would hurry to my place of shelter, far from the tempest and storm" (Psalm 55:6-8, NIV). David returned to reality and took active steps to resolve the dilemma which made him want to "fly away" in the first place. He didn't "desert the ship." David decided to cast the whole depressing situation on the Lord. He concluded his song by saying, "I trust in you" (verse 2). If you're in a "fly away" mood, don't do anything foolish! Don't physically run away. Go to the Lord instead. Give up the burden to Him first. It's hard to fly like a dove with a weight around your neck! One minister put it this way, "GOD promises that He will draw close to us when we draw closer to Him - which leads us to ask the question: How can we draw closer to GOD? You can accomplish this by doing your part to communicate to GOD and giving your heart to Him. This can be as simple as reading your Bible, praying or even choosing to live a healthy lifestyle. The closer you become to GOD, the more you will experience His love and blessings." **Our Prayer** Lord, thank you for Your grace and mercy You have extended me throughout my life. GOD, thank you for drawing close to me even when I didn't draw close to You. Continue to give me the strength to serve You and walk closer to You this day and for the rest of my life. We ask these and other blessings, in Jesus' Name, Amen. *Day 1* From the 1955 Montgomery Bus Boycott, the combat struggles of Vietnam, rigors of graduate school and the ongoing daily challenges of life, the Lord has been by my side and I offer Him gratitude and honor daily. When I thought about giving up, He assured me that He would make a way and told me not to quit. Pastor Joel Osteen is one of the world's new generation of spiritual leaders. I enjoy his books and his television ministry immensely. Pastor Osteen said, "It's easy to get discouraged when you look at what's going on in the world around us. Maybe you have even been hit with recent personal struggles that you just don't know how to handle. Every setback in life is GOD's setup for a comeback. Well, GOD has something better in store for you. So start giving GOD praise all through the day! … Thank Him that your new season is on its way. …Thank Him that your set time for favor is here. …Thank Him that your hour of deliverance has come. When you start praising and thanking Him, you will see the wind of GOD's blessings and favor blow in your life in a greater way. You'll rise out of mediocrity. You'll defeat the enemy, overcome obstacles and live that life of victory GOD has in store for you." "Provide for those who grieve…a garment of praise instead of a spirit of despair. They will be called oaks of righteousness, a planting of the Lord for the display of his splendor" (Isaiah 61:3 NIV). Do you need a new garment today? I'm not talking about a physical garment. I'm talking about what's covering your mind and emotions. Are you clothed with despair and disappointment? Are you wearing "heaviness"? If you've gone through a hurtful situation, the Bible says there is a time to grieve, and it's important to release that hurt to the Lord. But the Bible also tells us that GOD wants to give you a garment of praise instead of a spirit of despair. You can put on a garment of praise instead of a heavy, burdened spirit. What's holding you back today? Are the garments of yesterday weighing you down and holding you back? The garment of praise is light and filled with peace and joy. Don't carry those heavy burdens around anymore! Today is the day for new garments! Forgive those who have hurt you and begin to praise Him! Thank GOD for life today. Thank Him for the beautiful sunrise. Thank him for restoring you, even if you don't see it yet. And this verse says, you will be called an oak of righteousness, strong and secure, and you will display the splendor of the Lord all the days of your life! **Our Prayer** Lord thank you for Your provisions from my early existence until now. Lord You have been so good to me and on this day I want to praise You and say I'm much obliged. Heavenly Father, I come to You today and ask that You take off my old, heavy garments of despair and heaviness. Make me new today. Give me a garment of praise so that I can be a display of Your glory and splendor, in Jesus' Name, Amen. *Day 2* Your Destiny "A good name is rather to be chosen than great riches…" (Proverbs 22:1). What do people think when they hear your name? Do they think, "Oh that person is always so trustworthy and faithful: they always do the right thing." Or do they think, "Watch out for that person. You never know what they're going to do." You might say, "Oh I'm a pretty good person. I do the right thing most of the time." But understand: it's the little foxes that spoil the vine. You can veer off course just a little bit, and before you know it, you're miles away from your destination. Don't allow the little things to keep you from your destiny. Choose integrity—even when no one is looking. For instance, you might need some paper at home, but you shouldn't take supplies from the office. Or you might be running into a store for just a minute, but don't park in the handicap parking spot unless you're supposed to. Sure, you might need a few extra bucks this week, but if the check-out clerk makes a mistake and gives you back too much money, that's not GOD's provision, that's a test of integrity. If you'll be faithful and choose integrity in the little things, it will be a great treasure in your life. GOD will pour out His blessing on you as you honor Him all the days of your life. **Our Prayer** Father GOD, today I commit to live a life of integrity. I choose a life of excellence and ask for Your hand of favor. Show me any area that is not pleasing to You so that I can continue to grow and increase in You. Lord strengthen me where I am weak and help me to do and give my best as Your servant, in Jesus' Name, Amen. *Day 3* Be Happy "It is the Father's good pleasure to give you the Kingdom." (Luke 12:32) Our GOD is an extravagant GOD. He loves to do exceedingly beyond anything we can hope for or imagine! It gives Him pleasure to pour out His abundance and goodness in our life. It gives Him pleasure to give us His Kingdom. What is the Kingdom of GOD? It's simply GOD's operating system, or His way of doing things. Throughout the Word of GOD, He reveals His principles and precepts for living the abundant life He has in store. When you follow His Word, when you do things GOD's way, you get GOD's results: you get His success and blessing. Choose GOD's Kingdom today by following the Word of GOD. Romans chapter 14 tells us that the Kingdom of GOD is righteousness, peace, and joy in the Holy Spirit. Do you need more joy and peace in your life? Follow the Word of GOD in everything you do and open your heart to His Kingdom. As you do things GOD's way, you will get His results and walk in victory and blessing all the days of your life. Who decides whether you will like a place or don't like a place? You do! Who decides whether you will be happy or unhappy? You do! Who decides whether you will like co-workers or don't like co-workers? You do! Who decides whether you will be enthusiastic or unenthusiastic? You do! Who decides whether you will accept people or reject people? You do! Who decides whether you will like a situation or don't like a situation? You do! Who decides whether you will give your best or not give your best? You do! Did you notice who decides? You do! Every day you make decisions about how your brain will process thoughts into attitudes that become actions. Abraham Lincoln remarked that people are just about as happy as they make up their minds to be. You can be unhappy if you want to be. It's the easiest thing in the world to accomplish. Just choose unhappiness. Go around telling yourself that things aren't going well, that nothing is satisfactory, I don't like this place, I don't like my co-workers, I don't want anything to do with these people, I'm better than everybody else, and you can be quite sure of being unhappy. But say to yourself," things are going well. I have favor with my clients, customers, co-workers, and supervisor. People want to do good things for me. I like the people, and they like me. Life is good. I choose happiness," and you can be quite certain of having your choice. To become a happy person, have happy thoughts toward others, see the best in others, have a child's heart, and a simple faith. Most of the time, we manufacture our own unhappiness. By our own thoughts and attitudes, we determine whether we will be happy or unhappy. Choosing to be happy or unhappy is only a two-step process. First you make a simple decision to be happy: secondly, you replace unhappy thoughts with happy thoughts. Happiness is determined by your thoughts. So you have to drive off negative thoughts you have about people, places and things and replace them with happy thoughts about people, places and things. "As a person thinks in his heart, so is he." Proverbs 23:7. If you think you're unhappy, you become an unhappy person. But if you think you're happy, you become a happy person. Happy thoughts produce happy attitudes that become a happy life. **Our Prayer** Heavenly Father, thank you for Your hand of blessing in my life. Thank you for the new opportunities You allow me to partake. Thank you for giving me Your Kingdom. Thank you for the happiness and joy you have provided me. I receive it by faith today and choose to follow Your Word in everything I do. Lord, You have been so merciful and allowed me to share Your abundance and I will forever give You the glory, in Jesus' Name, Amen. *Day 4* Fulfill Your Dreams Everyone should strive to treat others as we want to be treated. To do this we must see each other as family. That old guy over there he's like your dad, that young guy is like your brother, that older woman is like your mother, and that young woman is like your sister. There's a unity and a bond in a healthy family that is different than every other relationship. There is strength and refuge in a healthy family. There is productivity and a common sense of purpose in a healthy family. As family we've got to treat each other right and we all will enjoy GOD's abundant world together in peace, love and with Christ understanding. "Therefore encourage one another and build each other up..." (I Thessalonians 5:11). GOD designed us to live in relationship with others. He wants us to help each other grow. None of us will reach our highest potential by ourselves. We need people in our lives to encourage us, and we need to encourage the people in our lives and help them reach their potential. The word "encourage" means to "urge forward." Many times you can see things in other people that they don't see themselves. You can see their strengths and talents. You can see that GOD has a special plan for them even though they may be going through a difficult time. Don't assume that people see what you see in them. Take a moment and encourage them either with a kind word or a simple note. There might be a special gift you can give that will remind them of their goal or dream. In whatever way you can, urge the people in your life to keep moving forward. If you'll be a people builder and help others fulfill their dreams, GOD will help you fulfill your dreams also, and you'll live in blessing all the days of your life. **Our Prayer** O Lord have mercy on us and help us to do Your will. Father in heaven, thank you for the people You have placed in my life. Help me to be of encouragement to others even when things aren't going the way I want them to be going. Help me build others up and find creative ways to urge them forward to Your glory, in Jesus' Name, Amen. *Day 5* Eternal Life But now since you have been set free from sin…you have your present reward in holiness and its end is eternal life." (Romans 6:22) How can I make it to heaven? If you ask most people this question, they will say something like, "If you do more good things than bad things, GOD will probably let you into heaven." You need faith in the blood of Jesus. There are no good deeds that you can do on your own that will erase the sins that you have committed. Jesus shed blood for you sins. He came to save you from the guilt of past sins and the power of sin over your life. Holiness is a powerful force in our lives. It leads us to eternal life. Holiness simply means being "set apart." You are set apart when you accept Jesus as your Lord and Savior. He makes His home in you, and His holiness lives on the inside of you, too. The Bible tells us that without holiness, no one can see GOD. GOD sets us apart and calls us His own, but it's up to us to continue living a life that is set apart from sin and destructive influences. We have to set ourselves apart from our old ways, old behaviors, and old mindsets. Remember, GOD chose to set you apart for Himself because He loves you. He doesn't want anything to keep you from His promises and blessings. Make the decision to let go of anything that would hold you back today. Remember, you are set apart for GOD's purposes. Let that sink down into your heart today and fill you with hope. As you embrace holiness and live a life that is set apart, you will see GOD and you will have the eternal life He has ordained for you! **Our Prayer** Father in heaven, thank you for setting me apart and making me holy in Your sight. I want to live a life that is set apart and pleasing to You. Fill me with Your Holy Spirit right now and enable me to have Your peace and power today. Help me to receive those blessings you want me to have and do those things you want me to do. I will forever give You the honor and praise, in Jesus' Name, Amen. *Day 6* Rise Higher Honoring the experiences we have in our lives is an invaluable way to communicate with life, our greatest teacher. We do this when we take time at night to say what we are thankful for about our day through prayer. This act involves consciously acknowledging the events of our lives to GOD. This is important because it brings us into closer connection with life and GOD's will for our life. Only when we acknowledge what's happening to us can we truly benefit from life's teachings and grow closer to our Creator. GOD promises so many good things for our lives. He wants us to step up and receive them. If we go to Him and claim the blessings and abundance He has offered, then our lives will be changed forever. GOD has all of the power necessary to restore broken families, replace lost trust, meet our financial needs and perform any miracle He chooses. All things are possible with GOD and when He is first in our lives, He will make us winners and empower us to be a blessing to others. Pastor Joel Osteen once said, "You are a child of the Most High GOD. You have been crowned with GOD's glory and honor. You can do all things through Christ. You are full of potential. You are overflowing with creativity. There's nothing in your heart that you cannot accomplish. You have courage, strength and ability. The favor of GOD surrounds you wherever you go. Whatever you touch is going to prosper and succeed. You are blessed and cannot be cursed." I believe that you become a better you by keeping GODly thoughts in your mind. I fervently believe we are endowed with greatness by GOD. "I have set before you life and death, the blessing and the curse. So choose life in order that you may live…" (Deuteronomy 30:19) GOD desires that you live in blessing in every area of your life. He's given promises in His Word and has established a plan for you to live in total victory. He promises to give you the answers, but you have to be the one to decide to obey His voice. You have the final choice, so choose life and blessing! Every time you choose to obey the Word of GOD, you are choosing blessing. When you put GOD first in your life: when you walk in love towards others even when it's difficult, you are choosing blessing. When you turn away from ungodly influences and when you give to others, GOD will pour out His blessing on you in return. Start today and do what you know to do. Obey His word and His blessing will overtake you! You'll rise higher and higher and live the abundant life He has for you. **Our Prayer** Thank you Lord for this day. You have walked beside me and led me in all my endeavors today. Lord I pray that you will continue to manifest Your goodness in my life. Father in heaven, today I choose life. I choose blessing by obeying Your Word. Keep me close to You so that I can honor You in all I say and do, in Jesus' Name, Amen. *Day 7* He

Will Deliver For many of us, Mother's Day is a painful reminder of what we never had or what we no longer have. My mother passed in 1980 and as I celebrate her memory on this day and give thanks for the years I had with her, I remember the life lessons that are still imprinted throughout my being. If, on the other hand, you will be seeing your mom on this Mother's Day, I suggest you enjoy every moment, hug her often, and make sure you tell her that you love her. "Many are the afflictions of the righteous, but the LORD delivers him out of them all" (Psalm 34:19). We often think and believe in the here and now. Most of us want instant gratification. If we trust GOD, we will believe His timing is always perfect for everything in our lives. We may not know how or when GOD will do something regarding our situation but rest assured He is an "On-time GOD." Everyone goes through seasons of difficulty and challenge in our lives. One of the enemy's traps is to isolate you and make you feel that you won't make it. GOD promises that He will deliver the righteous out of all of their afflictions. You are righteous because of your relationship with GOD through Christ Jesus. You are righteous simply by having faith in Him, His goodness, and the promises in His Word. If you're going through a tough time today, keep an attitude of faith and expectancy. Declare His promises over your life. You are more than a conqueror through Him! The joy of the Lord is your strength! As you continue to stand, even during the difficult times, you can be assured that victory is on the way. It might be today…it might be next week…next month, or next year, but GOD is faithful! Through faith and patience, you will inherit the promise. You will get beyond your difficulty, and you'll increase in wisdom, strength and live the abundant life GOD has promised for you! **Our Prayer** Heavenly Father, thank you for Your promise of victory in every area of our lives. Thank you for bringing us from our early existence until now. When we had doubt and fear, You made a way. We choose to trust You for the rest of our life. We know that You will continue to work behind the scenes on our behalf and allow us to receive those blessings You want us to have, in Jesus' Name, Amen. *Day 8* Test Into A Testimony Pastor Joel Osteen said, "Every person goes through adversities or times of difficulty. Maybe you didn't get a promotion you deserved, or you lost a loved one, a friend betrayed you. It's easy to get negative and bitter and lose your enthusiasm for life, but understand today, you are not defined by your past, you are prepared by your past. Every challenge you've been through, every adversity you've faced, GOD has deposited something on the inside of you. Your character was being developed. Strength was being increased. Your vision was being enlarged. With every difficulty, you can experience a new level of GOD's goodness! You may have had unfair things happen, but remember, all things work together for good when you love the Lord! It doesn't say that all things are good, but GOD will turn your test into a testimony. No matter what challenge you may be facing now, no matter what you've experienced in your past, if you'll stay in faith GOD will turn it around for your good! Choose to have a resurrection mentality—you may have gone through an emotional death, and burial but it's time for you to rise again. GOD wants to give you His beauty for ashes, and joy for mourning. He wants to bring you out stronger, happier, healthier, better off than you were before!" When the storms of life come, what do you do? Where do you go for comfort and safety? Some people find it easy to turn to their friends, their job, happy hour or even a bowl of ice-cream! There's nothing wrong with any of those things per se, but GOD the Father wants us to turn to Him first. He wants us to take refuge in Him. He longs to protect us and defend us and give us His strength. We serve a good GOD, and when we take refuge in Him, He will pour out His abundant blessing in our lives. I ask the Lord to bless you, as I pray for you today: to guide you and protect you, as you go along your way. GOD's love is always with you, GOD's promises are true. When you give GOD all your cares, you know GOD will see you through. GOD determines who walks into your life... it's up to you to decide who you let walk away, who you let stay, and who you refuse to let go. When there is nothing left but GOD that is when you find out that GOD is all you need. **Our Prayer**Oh Merciful Master, Our Father, GOD, My Lord and Savior, bless all my love ones, each reader and their contacts in whatever it is that You know they may need this day! May their life be full of your peace, prosperity, and power as they seek to have a closer relationship with you. Thank you Lord for being our refuge in the time of storm. We ask these blessings, in Jesus' Name, Amen. . *Day 9* Every New Day Is An Opportunity This is the day the Lord has made, we will rejoice and be glad in it" (Psalm 118:24). Whatever battle you may be facing today, declare that you are free. Declare that you are an overcomer. Celebrate the victory that is on its way! As you stand strong and declare your freedom, you will experience His victory and you will live in true freedom all the days of your life! An unknown author said, "Slaves live with **fear**...Independent people live with **confidence!!!**" You can declare your independence when: You love and respect yourself. You are able not only to forgive others but forget what had happened. You start seeing the beauty in everyone and everything. You are able to appreciate solitude as much as your best company. You really are your best friend. **Our Prayer** Almighty GOD, thank you for this day and for every opportunity that You've given me to bless and praise You. Thank you for those persons You placed in my life to help me to navigate my daily earthly journey. Lord, keep me in Your will. I give You everything I am today and always, in Jesus' Name, Amen. *Day 10* You Are Blessed And Highly FavoredOne of the most important ingredients in the formula for "Success" is the heartfelt belief that you can succeed. You must believe this because "Success" is absolutely within your ability. It all begins, however, with your beliefs and your thoughts. You can't change your life until you change your mind. It's always the thought that precedes the action. The changes that you need to make in order to succeed and make your life better are found from the neck up. Think positive thoughts, make healthier choices and your body will change – it can't help it. Declare it right now, "I'm blessed and highly favored. I repent of my past sins and from this day forward I claim GOD's abundance!!" We may fall down but GOD will help us get up. We enjoy many freedoms in the United States but unless you are freed by GOD Almighty, you still are enslaved. You are captive to your wrongs, failures and regrets. Even if you have fallen and everyone else has rejected you, GOD will not turn away from you. Only you can cast all your anxieties and concerns on the One who cares for you and will help you to get up and succeed. "Out of my distress I called upon the Lord: the Lord answered me and set me free." Psalm 118:5**Our Prayer** Lord, I know that when I have done all I can, You will step in and do what I couldn't. I am confident that this problem or situation is not going to defeat me or steal my joy. I am determined, with GOD's help, to overcome all adversity I face and live a life of abundance. My Divine Assignment will be completed and I know my best days are ahead. Lord I thank you for being with me each step of this journey and blessing me. I thank and praise You for those blessings on the way. Lord, continue to lead and order my footsteps, in Jesus' Name, Amen.

CHAPTER TWENTY-THREE
Epilogue

Excerpts from an e-mail I received from President Barack Obama on the night of the passage of the health care bill contained the following:

3-21-10

Dave —

For the first time in our nation's history, Congress has passed comprehensive health care reform. America waited a hundred years and fought for decades to reach this moment. Tonight, thanks to you, we are finally here. **Because of you, every American will finally be guaranteed high quality, affordable health care coverage.**

My gratitude tonight is profound. I am thankful for those in past generations whose heroic efforts brought this great goal within reach for our times. I am thankful for the members of Congress whose months of effort and brave votes made it possible to take this final step. But most of all, I am thankful for you.

This day is not the end of this journey. Much hard work remains, and we have a solemn responsibility to do it right. But we can face that work together with the confidence of those who have moved mountains.

Our journey began three years ago, driven by a shared belief that fundamental change is indeed still possible. We have worked hard together every day since to deliver on that belief. We have shared moments of tremendous hope, and we've faced setbacks and doubt. We have all been forced to ask if our politics had simply become too polarized and too short-sighted to meet the pressing challenges of our time. **This struggle became a test of whether the American people could still rally together when the cause was right** — and actually create the change we believe in. **Tonight, thanks to your mighty efforts, the answer is indisputable: Yes we can.**" Pat's and my favorite poem follows:

"MY DEAREST DARLING (2-14-93)

There's no one like you in this whole wide world. You make each day a pleasure.
Of all the things I love or possess, you are my dearest treasure.
Through happy days or sad days, good time or bad…
I will continue to be the very best friend and lover you have ever had.
I thank GOD with each passing day,
for allowing your sweet love to come my way.
As I write these heartfelt words this day,
I want you to know you are my one and only love and I'm here to stay.
My Dearest Darling, I will forever honor, love and respect thee: even beyond the day the good Lord decides to call me home for eternity.
I love you, my pearl, more than anything in this world."

1 Corinthians13:1-13 states, "If I speak in the tongues of men and of angels, but have not love, I am only a resounding gong or a clanging cymbal. If I have the gift of prophecy and can fathom all mysteries and all knowledge, and if I have a faith that can move mountains, but have not love, I am nothing. If I give all I possess to the poor and surrender my body to the flames, but have not love, I gain nothing. Love is patient, love is kind. It does not envy, it does not boast, it is not proud. It is not rude, it is not self-seeking, it is not easily angered, it keeps no record of wrongs. Love does not delight in evil but rejoices with the truth. It always protects, always trusts, always hopes, always perseveres. Love never fails. But where there are prophecies, they will cease: where there are tongues, they will be stilled: where there is knowledge, it will pass away. For we know in part and we prophesy in part, but when perfection comes, the imperfect disappears. When I was a child, I talked like a child, I

thought like a child, I reasoned like a child. When I became a man, I put childish ways behind me. Now we see but a poor reflection as in a mirror: then we shall see face to face. Now I know in part: then I shall know fully, even as I am fully known. And now these three remain: faith, hope and love. But the greatest of these is love." (NIV)

When I ran for the Alabama House of Representatives in 1985, one of my favorite campaign letters included the following: "Over the years I have learned it is imperative to be governed by the five P's: Prudent planning prevents poor performance. Grassroots organization is my top priority at this time. I am constantly meeting with residents, business leaders, organizations and ministers throughout the District forming the network that is required for victory. Thomas Huxley, a nineteenth century English biologist stated, 'the most valuable result of all education is the ability to make yourself do the thing you have to do, when it ought to be done.' I want to help Alabama become a place we all can be proud of calling home. I believe it is time for people with integrity, foresight and wisdom to get involved in my campaign. With your help, I am certain we can make the needed changes to help Alabama make progress in areas that desperately need to move forward. Our future is at stake. Please immediately join with me to do what must be done now! I trust the following by an unknown author drives my message home:

"THE BUILDER"

A builder built a temple.
He wrought it with grace and skill:
Pillars and groins and arches
All fashioned to work his will.
Men said, as they saw its beauty,
'It shall never know decay.
Great is thy skill, O Builder!
Thy fame shall endure for aye.'

A teacher built a temple
With loving and infinite care,
Planning each arch with patience,
Laying each stone with prayer.
None praised her unceasing efforts.

None knew of her wondrous plan,
For the temple the teacher builded
Was unseen by the eyes of man.

Gone is the builder's temple,
Crumbled into the dust.
Low lies each stately pillar,
Food for consuming rust.
But the temple the teacher builded
Will last while the ages roll,
For that beautiful unseen temple
Was a child's immortal soul.

From the bottom of my heart, I want to thank you for your support in this crusade.

Dave Williams, Next State Representative, District 78

The shepherd (GOD) knows His sheep and they know His voice. John 10:27 says, "My sheep hear My voice, and I know them, and they follow Me. "Psalms 23:1-2, "The LORD is my shepherd: I shall not want. He makes me to lie down in green pastures: He leads me beside the still waters." John 10:3, 14,16: "To him the doorkeeper opens, and the sheep hear his voice: and he calls his own sheep by name and leads them out......I am the good shepherd: and I know My sheep, and am known by My own....And other sheep I have which are not of this fold: them also I must bring, and they will hear My voice: and there will be one flock and one shepherd."

Wikipedia defines conscience as, "An ability or a faculty that distinguishes whether one's actions are right or wrong. It leads to feelings of remorse when one does things that go against his/her moral values and to feelings of rectitude or integrity when one's actions conform to our moral values." Many people believe that our conscience is the voice of GOD. It is GOD's way of communicating to us and directing us along the right path. Some people refers to this still, small voice of GOD as the Holy Spirit. The Holy Spirit is our guide, teacher, comforter and it instructs us on whether an action is right or wrong. The Holy Spirit directs our mind and gives us peace and wisdom. GOD loves each of His children and wants us to do His will. The Bible reads in 1 Corinthians 3:16:"Know ye not that ye are the temple of GOD, and that the Spirit of GOD dwelleth in you?"

Let's pray: GOD, You are our bridge over troubled waters. I AM Your Temple. Right now, I feel overwhelmed by the issues that are confronting me.

Help me today to hold on a little while longer. I feel You are working out my situations and resolving those issues at this moment. Lord, help us to be a friend to the friendless and be bridge builders to help save lost souls. Thank you Lord for sharing Your love, peace, joy and mercy with us to empower us to bless others, Amen.

As I look back to the beginning of my life growing up in Alabama, I recollect when just going downtown and being Black, brought you scorn and dishonor. I remember many days having to run from rocks being hurled at me by White youths on my way to H.L. Green, a downtown supermarket, known for having discounted meats. These meats were often not fresh but most shoppers bought anyway due to it being sold at reduced prices. President Kennedy's efforts for Civil Rights and his commitment to end segregation changed Alabama, the South and other parts of America. The Kennedys' have always been a family I have much admired. While I was doing all I could to help get Dr. King's birthday to be a national holiday, I decided to write Senator Ted Kennedy a letter. He sent the following letter to me:

Edward M. Kennedy
March 21, 1985
Dave Williams
559 South Court Street
Apartment # D-2
Montgomery, Alabama 36104

Dear Dave:

Many thanks for your recent and thoughtful letter. It is always a pleasure to hear from concerned and informed people like yourself on the major issues facing our country and our Party. Once again, many thanks for taking the time to write.

With best wishes,

Sincerely,
Ted Kennedy

This letter meant a lot to me as I was struggling to do my part to honor Dr. King, my hero. This letter confirmed my belief that Senator Kennedy and his brothers have always invited Blacks to sit at the table of brotherhood. They have always been proactive in trying to ensure all Americans receive fair and equal justice. They have been on the forefront leading other right-thinking Americans to work toward actualizing Dr. King's "Beloved Community." Senator Kennedy's letter encouraged me and increased my interest/participation in national Politics.

Although Senator Kennedy expired on August 25, 2009, his words and deeds will never be forgotten. His contributions are forever etched in America's History. Senator Kennedy was a GOD-fearing man and GOD made him a "Success." In my opinion, one of the most memorable orations of Senator Kennedy is as follows:

"All of my life, the teachings of my faith have provided solace and hope, as have the wonders of nature, especially the sea: where religion and spirituality meet the physical. This faith has been as meaningful to me as breathing or loving my family. It's all intertwined. My faith and the love of following its rituals, has always been my foundation and my inspiration. These foundations have been shaken at times by tragedy and misfortune, but faith remains fixed in my heart, as it has been since my childhood days. It is the most positive force in my life and the cause of my eternal optimism. I have fallen short in my life, but my faith has always brought me home. Life can be violent and grim, but I think of the Resurrection and I feel a sense of hope. I believe if you have a warm and embracing heart, faith can have a powerful impact on your outlook."

As I have mentioned previously, my first contact with Senator Edward Moore (Ted) Kennedy came from the letter I shared above during the early struggle to make Dr. Martin Luther King's birthday, a national holiday. Senator Kennedy was one of the leading advocates on Capitol Hill for this holiday. My first face-to-face contact with Senator Kennedy came during the 2004 presidential elections. He was in Detroit campaigning with Senator John Kerry in his bid for President. Senator Kennedy allowed me to take a picture with him and shared some words of encouragement with me and some of my VFW comrades. Senator Kennedy was the epitome of showing that, "Success is in the doing not the getting: in the trying not the triumph." Thanks, Senator Kennedy for using your GOD-given talents and trying to lead us to a fair and equal society. You fought a good fight, we salute you and I'm certain, GOD is rewarding you graciously.

From September 1992 until now, I have worshipped at the Christland Missionary Baptist Church. Our Pastor name is Allen Odell Langford. He has served as a GOD-Fearing leader since becoming Pastor. I joined Christland and was ordained a deacon under our former Pastor, Rev. Charles L. Branch who is deceased. Pastor Branch brought Christland and this community much encouragement during his illustrious career. It was written in his "Homegoing" program that, "After ministering to the community for 40 years, on Friday, April 28, 2000, Pastor Branch simply 'Exchanged' his earthly responsibilities for heavenly rewards."

Pastor Langford was elected on April 16, 2005. A letter to the congregation at his installation services read in part:

August 30, 2005
Christland Missionary Baptist Church
Detroit, MI 48227

To my Beloved Members:

I am writing to you today to express how excited I am about the possibilities that lay ahead for us as we move together in God's Will. For the past three months we have had the opportunity to begin the healing process and grow closer as a family. I want you to know that my family and I have come to love you all in the short time we have been here and you have shown us love in return.

I thank God for Christland and for guiding you through the process that brought us together as pastor and people. I pray God will continue to draw us closer to Him and closer together as we, 'Go ye therefore, and teach all nations, baptizing them in the name of the Father, and of the Son, and of the Holy ghost: Teaching them to observe all things whatsoever I have commanded you: and lo, I am with you always, even unto the end of the world.' (Matthew28:19-20.)

Praying for you,
Pastor Allen O. Langford

We began this journey in the Prologue with John 3:16, "For GOD so loved the world, that he gave his only begotten Son, that whosoever believeth in him should not perish, but have everlasting life." Yes, every day of my existence, GOD has been so good to me. From that Sunday when I tore my "church suit" running from police officers on horses in a Civil-Rights protest in 1963, to my flight out of Vietnam combat in 1970, to this last season of my life, GOD has never let me down. Sometimes we get anxious and feel uneasy but hang on in there. Continue to trust GOD and He always will make a way.

During the current depressed economy of 2010, although the unemployment rate is quite high and causing many social ills in America, GOD is still in control. He has His timing set to change our circumstances when He sees fit. GOD never makes a mistake and He will always deliver our blessings in our time of need.

One of America's great leaders is Dr. Julius R. Scruggs, president of the National Baptist Convention, USA, inc. (NBC). He was elected to serve as president of NBC from 2009 – 2014. Dr. Scruggs said in a message to "Fellow Pastors and Board Members: I am most grateful for the support and confidence entrusted to me as you elected me your seventeenth (17th) president of NBC. I promised to you in September, 2009 that I would do all that is in my power, by the help of GOD, to live up to your trust and I am striving to do just that. The work of our Convention is challenging, but GOD will give each of us the strength, wisdom and grace to execute His will for our global, national, state, and local ministries."

Through the grace of GOD, I have completed this book assignment and I thank GOD. It was a humbling experience to fulfill GOD's mission for me. This work is fact-based and I am certain has essential historical value. The Words of GOD will always help you complete your destiny. Let's pray: Lord, we thank you daily for showing us Your love and demanding that we love one another. Lord, I will continue to serve You until the end of this journey, Amen. 2 Timothy 4: 7 states, "I have fought the good fight, I have finished the race, I have kept the faith."

CHAPTER TWENTY-FOUR
Reflections: A Convoy Across The Finishing Line!!!

GOD knows the secret petitions of our heart. He knows every hidden dream He's placed within us. He knows the things that you haven't told anyone about. Maybe you thought they would never come to pass, or maybe you buried them because they didn't happen on your timetable. Maybe, in the natural, you have every reason to give up on those dreams. Be encouraged today — GOD is still working behind the scenes for you! He still has a plan to bring those dreams to pass. Let's pray: Lord it's me, standing in the need of prayer. Forgive me of my sins. I repent and turn to Your path for me. I come now Lord asking You to hear and answer my prayer. Thank you Lord for always being there to meet all of my needs. Father, You said the path of the righteous gets brighter and brighter. You said no good thing will You withhold because I walk uprightly before You. You said because I delight myself in You, You will give me the secret petitions of my heart. Thank you Lord for being in control of my life. Thank you for all Your blessings from birth to this day. I give You thanks for the good things You have in store for my future, in Jesus' Name, I pray, Amen.

Some things are worth repeating!!! God often repeated Scriptures throughout the Bible to allow readers to obtain more information and insights they may have previous missed!!! Mother Teresa said in her poem, Do It Anyway: "People are often unreasonable, illogical and self-centered: Forgive them anyway. If you are kind, people may accuse you of selfish ulterior motives: Be kind anyway. If you are successful, you will win some false friends and true enemies: Succeed anyway. If you are honest and frank, people may cheat you: Be honest anyway. What you spend years building, someone could destroy overnight: Build anyway. If you find serenity and happiness, they may be jealous: Be happy anyway. The good you do today, people will often forget tomorrow: Do good anyway. Give the world the best you have, and it may never be enough: Give the world the best you've got anyway. You see, in the final analysis, it is between you and GOD: It was never between you and them anyway." Without a shadow of doubt my brothers and sisters, I believe, "It's Time For The Favor Of GOD To Shine Abundantly On You!!!"

Being drafted to serve in Vietnam was one of the lowest periods (Rock Bottom) of my life due to my disagreement with this war. In Vietnam and other wars, a convoy was a group of fighter jets, vehicles or ships, traveling together for mutual support and protection of soldiers changing locations. Often, a convoy is organized with armed defensive support. Convoys provided route security for troops moving to other areas of Vietnam to engage the enemies. They normally had sufficient troops and equipment to cope with any enemy attacks during a movement. I felt as though, during this protracted battle with the Veterans Affairs Department mentioned in the last chapter, I had a convoy of guardian angels assigned to protect and guide me to a successful ending against the VA injustice. Even during my down time or desolate moments when VA were filibustering, angels provided my needs and assured me that GOD still had me in "The Palm of His Hand." Matthew 24:13 states, "But he that shall endure unto the end, the same shall be saved." By daily studying and obeying GOD's Words, He will guide you by His light and He will fill you with His peace each day on this earthly journey. Yes, faith in GOD is the key to "Success." Faith will enable us to enjoy GOD's blessings and help us to overcome our trials and adversities when they come our way. The many messages via emails, phone calls, legal assistance and letters sustained me greatly during my convoy across the "Finishing Line." These communications brought me needed comfort. I am a firm witness that, "Trusting and obeying GOD will bring big dividends!!!" I believe that happiness is not a destination. It is a way of life and often leads to "Success!!!"

One of the main lessons I learned from the Civil Rights Movement, having grown up in Alabama, was that these mostly poor African Americans, marched for non-negotiable dignity and respect as citizens. They were tired of being denied the rights that every non-Black citizen was innately given. No matter what hinderances got in their way, those marchers kept singing, "Ain't gonna let nobody turn me around! Turn me Around! Turn me Around! Gonna keep on walking, keep on talking, marching up to freedom land!" They fervently believed that GOD was on their side. They were determined that they would work and fight through their pain, fear, and insecurities to reach their goal of emotional freedom and justice for all!

In today's sports jargon, it is often said that certain professional athletes have "SWAG." This usually means that they are focused on winning, play with confidence and always bring their "A- game." It's okay to have "SWAG" as many of our young people say among their peers. I must confess, I agree with them as long as they mean: S – Safe: W – With: A – Almighty: G – GOD! This spiritual SWAG is unbeatable!!! So always remember, don't just look at things in the natural but also look spiritually at the greatness of GOD and believe He can do anything but fail. Stay focused and embrace all GOD has done and will do for you! In Hebrews 12:1-2, we find these Words, "Therefore we also, since we are surrounded by so great a cloud of witnesses, let us lay aside every weight, and the sin which so easily ensnares us, and let us run with endurance the race that is set before us, looking unto Jesus, the author and finisher of our faith, who for the joy that was set before Him endured the cross, despising the shame, and has sat down at the right hand of the throne of GOD."

Yes, the Holy Spirit leads, speak to us and always comforts us. The Holy Spirit often brings us timely encouragement from our earthly relatives, friends and contacts. On May 17, 2014 the following letter of inspiration was received from one of my spiritual contacts:

Dear Dave:

GOD is up to something special. From time to time, I sense in my spirit that He is about to do a new work. When that happens, I want to share with you what I think He is about to do. Why you? Because you are the target of His affections. You are the target of His goodness, mercy and grace. GOD is radically in love with you and He is about to do something really special. That's why I am writing to you today. I see it happening in people lives and in our own personal lives. Today, I am putting my faith in Christ that this word is for you too.

What is this work He is doing? GOD is positioning you for something new, and something great - New levels of favor: New levels of blessings: New levels of joy, New levels of creativity: New levels of influence. The dictionary defines position as "a particular way in which someone or something is placed or arranged." When someone is positioned it's not random or haphazard, they are carefully and strategically placed for success.

Imagine an army general. He is going to position his troops under his command in a tactical position to succeed. Or imagine the director of a Broadway musical. The director is going to position each actor in the right spot on stage so their lines can be successfully delivered. No detail is overlooked. No technicality is left up to chance. Each person is positioned to succeed. Dave, that's what GOD is doing in your life. GOD is not a random, haphazard GOD. The Creator of the Universe is working behind the scenes to carefully and strategically position you for new levels of favor and influence. Everything you've been through – every challenge you're facing GOD is using it all to position you for something new.

This letter again confirmed to me that even during our time of distress and uncertainty, GOD cares for His children. No matter what the naysayers may say, GOD wants you to achieve your preordained destiny. GOD wants you to be a "Success!"

Thank you Lord for Your Holy Spirit leading and overseeing my thoughts this day. As the old Vietnam Veteran said, "I am hurting but I'm here!" This is truly the times that try people souls and they are perplexed about which way to go. Most investments are made to produce wealth and increase material goods. A spiritual investment produces peace, GOD's favor and eternal life. So always trust GOD, pray often, have a determined faith and daily read GOD's Words. You will be abundantly blessed and He will take you from, "Rock Bottom To Success!!!" James 1:12 reads, "Blessed is the man that endureth temptation: for when he is tried, he shall receive the crown of life, which the Lord hath promised to them that love him." Your healing from GOD comes from your reading and hearing the Words of GOD for He loves His children and wants us to be saved. Let's pray: Thank you Lord right now for allowing Your Holy Spirit to speak to us and making clear Your vision and plans for our lives this day. Help us to hold on to Your hand as we invest in You and we wait on You to meet all our needs. We pray in Jesus' Name, Amen.

When we have to wait on something longer than we thought it would take, we often get disgusted and sometimes angry. But always remember that GOD's timing is always perfect. He is never late and He has your best plan in His hand. Continue to trust GOD and realize that He is working behind the scenes for your good. "Success" is not always measured in dollars and cents but the difference you make in your community to help others is of great value. "Success" to GOD means we are helping His children who are hurting, sometimes referred to as the least of these. Matthew 25:40 reads, "Truly I tell you, whatever you did for one of the least of these brothers and sisters of mine, you did for me." Each of us has a role to play in making our world better. It is always invaluable to learn from the past. Sharing your experiences and helpful life lessons with others can encourage your contacts to become outstanding future leaders. Helping GOD's children to develop their lives to fullest potential is a rich, powerful and enjoyable endeavor. Leading lost souls to GOD's will, yield tremendous benefits and is the epitome of "Success."

Reflections sum up how this author used prayers, an unwavering faith in GOD and personal applications of the Bible in his daily life to overcome trials and tribulations. My frequent recount and references to Scriptures will hopefully encourage readers to seek GOD daily by reading and obeying His Words and praying unceasingly. Again I say, GOD is no respecter of persons, if He did it for me He will gladly do it for you!!! Continue to hold on to GOD's hand my brothers and sisters, "Your Success Is Imminent!!!" GOD will always bless us and answer our prayers when we seek Him and obey His Words. 1 John 3:22 states, "And whatever we ask we receive from Him, because we keep His commandments and do those things that are pleasing in His sight."

As I write today on Memorial Day, May 26, 2014, I'm giving a loud shout-out in memory of our ancestors who fought the good fight of faith against discrimination and injustice. They stood proudly and had "GOD's Favor" on their lives. I reflect with special thanks and homage to my deceased parents and my brother, Dr. Booker T. Williams Jr.. Our ancestors are the giants whose shoulders we now stand and enjoy many freedoms they did not have. "To GOD Always Goes The Glory!!!" Psalm 57:1-3 read, "Be merciful unto me, O GOD, be merciful unto me: for my soul trusteth in thee: yea, in the shadow of thy wings will I make my refuge, until these calamities be overpast. I will cry unto GOD most high: unto GOD that performeth all things for me. He shall send from heaven, and save me from the reproach of him that would swallow me up. Selah. GOD shall send forth his mercy and his truth." Let's pray: Lord, thank you for those who fought to make this world better for Your children to live as equals. We know that You have no respect of persons and You want us to treat our brothers and sisters with love. Help us to keep You first in our lives and daily study Your Words. Right now, we vow that no matter what may happen from day to day, we will obey and trust You Lord. We know the battle belongs to You. We believe You will give us total victory over every situation we may face on this earthly journey. Give us Your favor and keep us in the palm of Your hand. In Jesus' Name we offer this prayer, Amen.

I believe that chess is a game similar to fighting a war or enduring the trials and tribulations of your journey on earth. I view life as a game of chess and you do your best each day to avoid dangers or being put in checkmate (king is captured to end the game). In chess you have the opening stage of the game in which players develop their pieces, get their king to safety, and attempt to control the center. It switches to the middle stage when players begin to attack and defend each other. The endgame is when most of the pieces are off of the board. There is no definite number of pieces, but it's usually a safe bet to call it the endgame when each player has three or four pieces (knights, bishops, rooks, queens, pawns) or less. To me, your life is similar: your birth is your opening stage, middle stage is from youth to adult and your endgame is adult to senior citizen and eternity. As in chess, there are many challenges and with GOD's help, we will stay observant, focused and achieve our preordained destiny before our life ends or we are checkmated. Ecclesiastes 3:1 exclaims, "To everything there is a season, and a time to every purpose under the heaven."

GOD's timing is already in our future at birth and He only knows what will occur and when it will happen!! Don't let the negative thoughts and the evil talk distress you. The way you know that you're really believing in GOD's timing is when you have peace on the inside. You feel calm during your storm and know the answer is on the way. You trust that GOD is working things out and His grace and favor is about to overwhelm you! Someone once said, "When we accept that we always exist in a state of grace, we are able to live our lives more graciously. Knowing we have GOD's grace gives us hope, makes us more generous, and allows us to trust that we are taken care of even when we are going through difficult times. Grace is our benevolence of heart, and our generosity of spirit. Grace gives us unconditional love and the beauty that is our humanity. When we know that we are blessed with grace, we can't help but want to live our lives in harmony and offer peace with other children of GOD." 2 Corinthians 12:9 reads, "My grace is sufficient for you, for my power is made perfect in weakness." (NIV) Thank you Lord for Your grace and peace as I daily keep my mind stayed on You. GOD's grace is sufficient. Expressing thanks to GOD for the blessings He has allowed into our lives is the starting place for an attitude of gratitude. Philippians 4:6 reads, "Be anxious for nothing, but in everything by prayer and supplication with thanksgiving, let your requests be made known to GOD." Be thankful for the talents GOD has given you and do your best each day to be a blessing to others. As one football coach said, "Leave it all on the field, don't have to regret that you did not give your all and you may have caused the defeat instead of victory." I fervently believe that when you give your best efforts, and with GOD's help, you always will have "Success!!!"

I consider the best part of your life to be at this moment. Enjoy it and as believers, we should thank GOD for waking us up this morning having a sound mind and reasonably good health. Put on your "Reflections" lens and give honor and praise to GOD for bringing you a long, long way! Psalm 31:14 reads, "But I trusted in thee, O Lord: I said, Thou art my GOD." As one saint in church use to exclaim in her testimony, "When I think of the goodness of Jesus and all He has done for me, my soul cries Hallelujah, thank GOD for saving me!!!"

THE BEGINNING OF THE END

Sometimes, before GOD takes us to a new level, He allows trials and difficulties to come our way. This is when you have to really trust GOD, you have to relentlessly resist Satan and then, enjoy watching him flee. Don't be a weakling but put on your warrior mentality, dig in and fight with your all. Always decree that GOD and I can win any battle!!! As GOD helped David kill Goliath and as GOD helped Moses lead the Israelites out of bondage, it's still true today, GOD will always defend His children in their time of struggle. Yes, when you need a breakthrough or need a transformation in your life, the Holy Spirit can step in to guide you and meet all your needs. It behooves us to read and digest the Words of GOD each day to fight the twists and turns we encounter on this journey of life. One writer said it this way, "Many books can inform you but only one book can transform you. GOD's Words give us good food for life!" Deuteronomy 6:4-9 read, "Hear O Israel: The Lord our GOD, the Lord is one! You shall love the Lord your GOD with all your heart, with all your soul, and with all your strength. And these words which I command you today shall be in your heart. You shall teach them diligently to your children, and shall talk of them when you sit in your house, when you walk by the way, when you lie down, and when you rise up. You shall bind them as a sign on your hand, and they shall be as frontlets between your eyes. You shall write them on the doorposts of your house and on your gates."

When we abide in GOD's Words, victory is imminent. A psychologist once said, "Prayer is the best medicine for our spiritual and physical needs. When we give GOD thanksgiving and offer Him prayers, our aches and pains throughout our bodies are relieved. Prayers also help alleviate many of our emotional and mental health issues that may come our way. In His timing, GOD always provides favor and positive actions when we ask His intervention!!!" Let's pray: Thank you Lord for breathing on us right now. Lord, doubt keeps pressing us but I know You have us in Your hand and I feel Your favor. Without reservation, I know my victory is on the way. Right now, give me the strength to fight on in Your Name, Amen.

We all have times when people or circumstances come against us and there is disharmony. Often there may be days when we may feel angry, disgusted or that someone has misused us. Maybe you're facing a difficulty today and you're not exactly sure how to handle it. If we look to GOD's Words, He'll give us what we need. He is always on time: He may wait to the last second but He's never late. It is written in Ecclesiastes 3: 1- 11, "To everything there is a season, and a time to every purpose under the heaven: A time to be born, and a time to die: a time to plant, and a time to pluck up that which is planted: A time to kill, and a time to heal: a time to break down, and a time to build up: A time to weep, and a time to laugh: a time to mourn, and a time to dance: A time to cast away stones, and a time to gather stones together: a time to embrace, and a time to refrain from embracing: A time to get, and a time to lose: a time to keep, and a time to cast away: A time to rend, and a time to sew: a time to keep silence, and a time to speak: A time to love, and a time to hate: a time of war, and a time of peace. What profit hath he that worketh in that wherein he laboureth? I have seen the travail, which GOD hath given to the sons of men to be exercised in it. He hath made everything beautiful in his time: also he hath set the world in their heart, so that no man can find out the work that GOD maketh from the beginning to the end."

The following Words of GOD found in Psalm121:1-8, always will bring you comfort and let you know GOD is always near: "I will lift up my eyes to the hills—from whence comes my help? My help comes from the LORD, Who made heaven and earth. He will not allow your foot to be moved: He who keeps you will not slumber. Behold, He who keeps Israel shall neither slumber nor sleep. The LORD is your keeper: The LORD is your shade at your right hand. The sun shall not strike you by day, Nor the moon by night. The LORD shall preserve you from all evil: He shall preserve your soul. The LORD shall preserve your going out and your coming in, from this time forth, and even forevermore."

Always remember the words of the writer who said, "I asked GOD for strength that I might achieve. I was made weak that I might learn humbly to obey. I asked for health that I might do greater things. I was given infirmity that I might do better things. I asked for riches that I might be happy. I was given poverty that I might be wise. I asked for power that I might have the praise of men. I was given weakness that I might feel the need of GOD. I asked for all things that I might enjoy life. I was given life that I might enjoy all things. I got nothing that I asked for, but everything I hoped for. Almost despite myself, my unspoken prayers were answered. I am, among all men, most richly blessed." I truly believe GOD has me in the palm of His hand. He has that abundant blessing that I had been seeking ready for me in His timing! Throughout the Bible it is apparent that suffering is a prerequisite for believers to receive their breakthrough.

Yes, GOD is a peacemaker and He hears and always answers our prayers – His way and in His timing. He's never a second late. So when things aren't going the way you want them to go, it's ok to go ahead and declare, "I will be patient and trust GOD for I know His angels are overseeing me!!! I will be victorious and successfully cross the finishing line."

The ongoing battle with the VA regarding benefits I thought I deserved often was quite irritable but kept me intellectually stimulated. It also kept me depending on GOD's mercy and my spiritual contacts for prayers and encouragement. An e-mail from one of my spiritual contacts decreed:

Grace and Peace,

Thank you for entrusting us with your heartfelt prayer request. It is our endeavor to see you walk in the freedom wherewith Christ has made you free. The intercessors and I will take your request to the Lord. We look forward to the praise report. "The effectual prayer of a righteous man availeth much." James 5:16

Thank you for giving us the opportunity to touch and agree with you in prayer for healing, family salvation, restoration, marriage, financial breakthrough, or whatever is nearest your heart. For we know the power of prayer is real! "But we will give ourselves continually to prayer, and to the ministry of the word." Acts 6:4

Christ Servant

This message, along with the following one received by US Mail from Pastor Joel Osteen brought me great spiritual revelation and a needed uplift in a time of despair!! A handwritten post-it note attached to his letter stated, "GOD wants you to fulfill the dream He's given you! Keep believing and expecting big things today." Pastor Osteen's letter read:

9-12-13

Dear Dave:

If you've heard me speak at least once, I'm pretty confident that you know how much I believe in GOD's power to do the impossible. And today, I write knowing He wants to do the impossible for You. It doesn't matter where you were born or what life circumstances you've been through,

GOD wants to do amazing things in you and for you. GOD has a unique dream and destiny for all of us! When I use the word "dream," perhaps you may just associate it with some specific event. You may want to go on a dream vacation, or you want to be able to send your kids to their dream college, or start your own dream company. But I want to take it a step further. A dream is that thing you have on the inside that keeps coming back.

You can tell it's more than just a desire, it's more than a wish, but rather you sense it was put there by GOD. You sense it's tied to your destiny – or even the destiny and purpose of a son or daughter or other loved one. I realize that most dreams GOD puts in our hearts look impossible. But Dave, what seems impossible with man is completely possible with GOD (see Matthew 19:26)!

Maybe you're believing for a dream relationship, but it hasn't happened yet. Or you want to get out of debt, but your bills are piling up. Freedom from an addiction can be a dream. Healing is a dream. Having a friend that is closer than a brother is a dream. I can verify in my own life – so many times over – that I've seen GOD work, especially when at first it didn't seem possible. I saw Him build a church out of a basketball arena that people said was impossible. I saw him heal my mother of cancer when the doctors told her she had three weeks to live. The stories go on and on.

That's what GOD wants to do for you. The dream that is in your heart – that breakthrough you want to see happen – can happen for you. So are you ready for it? Inside this letter you'll find a small index card. I've enclosed it for you because I want you to write down your dream, no matter how big or small, and send it back to us. I trust you know I am still dreaming… to encourage and inspire faith and hope in as many people as possible through all of our ministry efforts.

I've shared this before, but it's something I've seen happen so many times. Many believers finally realize their own dream shortly after they reached out to someone in need. It's a supernatural thing. GOD cares about people, and when we get outside of ourselves and love others like He loves us, amazing things start to happen! This is your time to lay hold of the dream in your heart. Take a step today. I can assure you that it is totally worth it!"

Pastor Joel Osteen

Wow, this was a powerful letter from Pastor Osteen and it gave me the tenacity to fight harder in my struggle with the VA. After reading this letter, I wrote down the following Scriptures which I read daily during my Bible study:

> Proverbs 3:5-6, "Trust in the Lord with all thine heart: and lean not unto thine own understanding. In all thy ways acknowledge him, and he shall direct thy paths."
>
> Proverbs 18:21, "Death and life are in the power of the tongue: and they that love it shall eat the fruit thereof."
>
> 1 John 4:4, "Greater is He who is in me than he that is in the world."
>
> Isaiah 54:17, "No weapon formed against me shall prosper."
>
> 2 Corinthians 2:14, "GOD always causes me to triumph."
>
> Proverbs 8:35, "Whoever finds me finds life, and obtains favor from the Lord."
>
> Psalm 37:23-24, "The steps of a good man are ordered by the Lord: and he delighteth in his way. Though he fall, he shall not be utterly cast down: for the Lord upholdeth him with his hand."
>
> 2 Timothy1:7, "GOD has not given us a spirit of fear but of power, of love and a sound mind."
>
> Luke 1:37, "For with GOD nothing shall be impossible."
>
> Philippians 4:19, "But my GOD shall supply all your need according to his riches in glory by Christ Jesus."
>
> Psalm 51:10, "Create in me a clean heart, O GOD: and renew a right spirit within me."
>
> Isaiah 40:31, "But they that wait upon the Lord shall renew their strength: they shall mount up with wings as eagles: they shall run, and not be weary: and they shall walk, and not faint."

I found additional strength after reading 2 Corinthians 4:15 -18 which state, "For all things are for your sakes, that the abundant grace might through the thanksgiving of many redound to the glory of GOD. For which cause we faint not: but though our outward man perish, yet the inward man is renewed day by day. For our light affliction, which is but for a moment, worketh for us a far more exceeding and eternal weight of glory: While we look not at the things which are seen, but at the things which are not seen: for the things which are seen are temporal: but the things which are not seen are eternal."

* (Indicates e-mails I received or sent to encourage my contacts and most of them also brought me inspiration and spiritual enlightenment.)

*—An excerpt from a letter from First Lady Michelle Obama reads:

Dear Mr. Williams:

I'm not writing to you today just because we support one extraordinary man – although I'll admit I'm a little biased, because I think our President is awesome. And it's not just because we want to win an election. I'm writing because of values we believe in and the vision for this country that we share. We want our children to have a good education – schools that push them and inspire them, prepare them for good jobs. We want our parents and grandparents to retire with dignity, because we believe that after a lifetime of hard work, they should enjoy their golden years. We want to restore that basic middle-class security for our families, because we believe that folks shouldn't go bankrupt because they get sick. They shouldn't lose their home because someone loses a job. We believe that responsibility should be rewarded and hard work should pay off. Dave, I am not going to kid you. This journey is going to be long. And it is going to be hard. But we know that is how change always happen in this country. And if we keep showing up, if we keep fighting the good fight, then eventually we'll get there. We always do… maybe not in our lifetimes, but maybe in our children's lifetimes, maybe in our grandchildren's lifetimes –because in the end, that's what this is all about.

Michelle Obama

* Someone said that, "Attaining success and happiness is not for a small privileged elite, it is for everyone. It is achieved by having a positive belief system. You cannot blame anyone or anything for your present life. You have created your own reality. If you want to change your life, you must first look at your present beliefs for they have created you as you are now." Karma may be defined as a comeback. The Law of Karma was mentioned thousands of years ago in a famous verse taken from the Old Testament in The Holy Bible: Psalm 126:5-6, "They who sow in tears shall reap in joy and singing. He who goes forth bearing seed and weeping [at needing his precious supply of grain for sowing] shall doubtless come again with rejoicing, bringing his sheaves with him." (Amp) Galatians 6:7 states, "Whatsoever a man soweth, that shall he also reap."

In today's usage, Karma means, "whatever you do or think will be returned to you." If for example, you are full of hate and treat others poorly, then you can be certain that others will treat you the same way. Mean and nasty people live in a mean and nasty world—a world that they have created by their own thoughts and actions. The Law of Karma can impose a very heavy burden upon you, particularly if you're ignorant of its existence. The Law of Karma underpins most of our actions: for, in essence you build your "world" in your mind first, then demonstrate with your actions what is in your thoughts (what kind of "world" you have created). You are the master of your fate, each and every day, whether you want to acknowledge it or not. In Ephesians 1:19 we find, "And [so that you can know and understand] what is the immeasurable and unlimited and surpassing greatness of His power in and for us who believe." (AMP)

The Law of Unlimited Supply is based on the belief that mankind has access to an unlimited supply of love, happiness, and wealth from GOD. Poverty of any kind is unnatural—it is a man-made condition. The belief that only a few people can be wealthy or enjoy good health and happiness is not true. The only limit placed on GOD is the limit we artificially create. Someone once said, "If I had a thousand gallons of water to give you but you only had a one-gallon container, you wouldn't be able to receive what I had for you. The problem would not be with the supply. It would be with your ability to receive. If you would get rid of the small container and get something larger, I could give you so much more. It's the same way with GOD. We might have a tendency to think that because the economy is down, I could never afford that house I really want. My business will never expand. I don't have the funding. I don't have the people behind me. All you have to do is get rid of that one-gallon bucket. Get rid of that small idea or dream. The GOD we serve is a big GOD! He has an unlimited supply." Jesus said in Matthew 9:29, "According to your faith it will be done unto you." GOD has all the power, all the resources in the world. It's according to what we believe. Today, increase your capacity to receive. Enlarge your thinking by meditating on the Word of GOD. Praise Him and magnify Him because with GOD all things are possible, and He has an unlimited supply!

GOD promises so many good things for our lives. He wants us to step up and receive them. If we go to Him and claim the blessings and abundance He has offered, then our lives will be changed forever. GOD has all of the power necessary to heal any physical impairment, restore broken families, replace lost trust, meet our financial needs and perform any miracle He chooses. All things are possible with GOD and when He is first in our lives, He will make us winners and empower us to be a blessing to others. Whatever battle you may be facing today, declare that you and GOD are stronger and you will win. Declare that you are an overcomer. Declare you will be the head and not the tail. Stand strong and declare you will experience GOD's victory and you will live in His abundance all the days of your life! Matthew 6:33-39 read, "But seek first his kingdom and his righteousness, and all these things will be given to you as well. Therefore do not worry about tomorrow, for tomorrow will worry about itself. Each day has enough trouble of its own." (NIV)

Always remember, "Through faith your achievement of your dream or 'Success' is assured! Regardless of your trials and tribulations you may face on this journey of life, continuously stay in an attitude of faith. Seek GOD's Words and never doubt that the favor of GOD is around you. The Bible coaches us that if we meet our battles with peace and respond to the challenges in life with peace, we will experience the victory GOD has preordained for us."

Ephesians 6:10-20 read, "Finally, be strong in the Lord and in his mighty power. Put on the full armor of GOD, so that you can take your stand against the devil's schemes. For our struggle is not against flesh and blood, but against the rulers, against the authorities, against the powers of this dark world and against the spiritual forces of evil in the heavenly realms. Therefore put on the full armor of GOD, so that when the day of evil comes, you may be able to stand your ground, and after you have done everything, to stand. Stand firm then, with the belt of truth buckled around your waist, with the breastplate of righteousness in place, and with your feet fitted with the readiness that comes from the gospel of peace. In addition to all this, take up the shield of faith, with which you can extinguish all the flaming arrows of the evil one. Take the helmet of salvation and the sword of the Spirit, which is the word of GOD. And pray in the Spirit on all occasions with all kinds of prayers and requests. With this in mind, be alert and always keep on praying for all the Lord's people. Pray also for me, that whenever I speak, words may be given me so that I will fearlessly make known the mystery of the gospel, for which I am an ambassador in chains. Pray that I may declare it fearlessly, as I should."

OUR PRAYER

Oh Merciful Father, bless President Obama and his family. Lead him to victory on November 6, 2012. Help him to be a blessing to Your children here in the U.S. and abroad. Father, thank you for Your unlimited supply of everything we need in this life. We open our hearts to You and we choose to take the limits off. Increase our faith so that we can receive every blessing You have in store for us. Lord, thank you for Your hand of blessing in our lives. Thank you for the new opportunities You have allowed us to partake. Thank you for giving us Your Kingdom. Thank you for the happiness and joy You have provided us. We receive and claim joy and happiness by faith today and choose to follow Your Words in everything we do. Lord, You have been so merciful and allowed us to share Your abundance and we will forever give You the glory and honor, in Jesus' Name, Amen. My spiritual mantra to my contacts is, "I Did It!!! You Can Do It To!!! (What Doesn't Make Sense To You Is Often GOD Leading You To Your Divine Destiny.)"

    *A recent e-mail sent to my contacts read, "I Declare Today That GOD Has A New Chapter For Me. When you have done all you can do, it's time to turn it over to GOD to supernaturally perform what you can't!!! A song by Donny Hathaway entitled, We Need You Right Now states, 'There's no one else to turn to but You, yeah—You're the only answer to the situation that we've gotten ourselves into, So Master, won't You please come down and give us a helping hand, cause we need You: We need You, right now.'

A story is told about a young lady who hoped to attend Yale or Harvard, prestigious colleges on the U.S. east coast. She was filling out her application and feeling rather good about her GPA and her entrance scores when her heart sank as she came to one question. It asked simply, 'Are you a leader.' Being both honest and very conscientious she wrote simply, 'No'. As she sent off the application she expected the worst. Schools are always looking for leaders, she thought, but I couldn't honestly claim to be one. Weeks went by and the young lady had given up even faint hope of acceptance when an envelope arrived from one of the universities. She opened it fully expecting a rejection notice. Instead she discovered a brief note which read: 'Dear applicant: a review of our applications reveals that this year our incoming freshmen class will have 1,452 eager leaders. We are accepting you because we feel it important that they have at least one follower.'

It is often said that the world needs leaders, but it also needs followers. We need great men and women of GOD who can share the gospel to many people. But we also need quiet saints who share the love of Christ, one person at a time, in a doctor's office, at the lunch table at school, by e-mail or on the telephone to friends and contacts. We need believers that in their neighborhoods and groceries stores, share the love of Christ in word and deed. But we also need devoted parents who will lead their children and grandchildren to faith by constant example and compassionate witnessing.

Only GOD knows what mission and plans He has preordained for you. But I believe GOD is calling you now to move swiftly to do His will. Yes, GOD is calling and if you get quiet and listen, You will hear His voice. There is an old spiritual, the repeated chorus of which goes, 'Hush, hush, somebody is calling my name. Hush, hush, somebody is calling my name. Hush, hush, somebody is calling my name. Oh my Lord, Oh my Lord, what shall I do, what shall I do.'

Noted novelist, C.S. Lewis wrote that there are two kinds of people in the world, those who respond to GOD saying, 'Thy will be done,' and those to whom GOD says, 'All right then, have it your way.' Listen, GOD is calling your name. What will you do? Will you open your ears, your eyes and your heart? Will you listen carefully for His voice? Will you then answer, 'Speak Lord, for I am listening.' Will you respond, 'Thy will be done?'

2 Timothy 1:7 proclaims, 'For GOD hath not given us the spirit of fear: but of power, and of love, and of a sound mind.' (KJV) Get ready for a new chapter in your life and GOD's plans for your future are about to be made a reality. Sometimes, in order to move forward into the blessing GOD has for you, you have to be willing to let go of the old. The things that are behind you are not nearly as important as what is out in front of you. It's time to get ready for the new! You may have had some unfair things happen, things that you don't understand: but let me tell you that you have come too far to stop now. Instead of allowing those things to hold you back, why don't you let go and take a step of faith into the new? It's time to get a new, bigger vision: it's time to get a new, fresher outlook: it's time to rise up with a new attitude! Instead of settling where you are, pick up and move forward. Have an attitude that says, 'I may not understand it: it may not have been fair, but I am not getting stuck on this page.' I declare today that GOD has a new chapter for me — a chapter filled with blessings, favor, peace, prosperity and victory. I am now letting go and I turn all over to GOD!!!"

OUR PRAYER

Almighty GOD, My Lord and Savior, today, I ask forgiveness of my sins. Lord, I have heard Your voice and I accept Your plans for me. Help me to do Your will and obey Your Words. I know we are called to serve humanity and for kingdom building, help me to walk in Your way. Father, thank you for Your faithfulness in my life and for Your favor. Today, I choose to trust You with my past, present and future. Give me wisdom to discern the season of my life and teach me to embrace the new things You want me to do. Father in heaven, thank you for this new day. Thank you for the opportunity to begin afresh in Your love and led by Your Holy Spirit. I choose to press forward and keep believing for the dreams and desires You've placed in my heart. I trust You today with everything that I am and what I will become. Right now I turn everything over to You! I offer this request In Jesus' Name, Amen.

*"GOD Is Always On Time. Always believe that GOD is near and always ready to hear your call. No matter what may be happening in your life and how bad your situation may appear, hold on to your faith!!! GOD's Word is the key weapon in bringing down mental strongholds and adversity we face in our daily lives. GOD is in control, even when life seems out of control. Sometimes when trouble comes into our lives, it's hard to believe that statement in your gut, no matter what you say aloud. Most of us struggle to truly trust that GOD always takes good care of His people. Life experience with GOD can help us trust Him and help us to believe He will help us on time. It's also helpful to read in the Bible how perfectly GOD has guided events to care for His people in the past.

The story of Moses in Exodus 2:1-10 is a good example. It reads as follow, "Now a man of the tribe of Levi married a Levite woman, and she became pregnant and gave birth to a son. When she saw that he was a fine child, she hid him for three months. But when she could hide him no longer, she got a papyrus basket for him and coated it with tar and pitch. Then she placed the child in it and put it among the reeds along the bank of the Nile. His sister stood at a distance to see what would happen to him. Then Pharaoh's daughter went down to the Nile to bathe, and her attendants were walking along the riverbank. She saw the basket among the reeds and sent her female slave to get it. She opened it and saw the baby. He was crying, and she felt sorry for him. 'This is one of the Hebrew babies,' she said. Then his sister asked Pharaoh's daughter, 'Shall I go and get one of the Hebrew women to nurse the baby for you?' 'Yes, go,' she answered. So the girl went and got the baby's mother. Pharaoh's daughter said to her, 'Take this baby and nurse him for me, and I will pay you.' So the woman took the baby and nursed him. When the child grew older, she took him to Pharaoh's daughter and he became her son. She named him Moses, saying, I drew him out of the water." (NIV)

Through divine providence, midwives managed to help with Moses birth and when he was three months old and hard to hide, his mother concealed him in a basket among reeds in the Nile River, appointing his big sister to keep watch. Soon, none other than Pharaoh's daughter came to the river and found the basket. So Moses first grew up safe in his own family, where he could learn about GOD. Later he was adopted into Pharaoh's family with all the training and privileges that entailed. Everything was perfect and Moses was ideally pre-pared to confront Pharaoh and lead GOD's people out of slavery.

It's great that the people in Exodus had GOD controlling things so good for them, but can we be sure that He will do the same for us. Yes, we can!!! When you make Jesus the Lord of your life, GOD puts within you an eternal well that will never run dry. You have an unlimited supply of good things inside you which should be continually bubbling out of you. A minister told his con-gregation that, "Satan doesn't want your joy, happiness, and existence to flow freely. So he comes along and throws a stone worry into your well. You may think, that's just one little stone. It's not hurting anything. The water is still flowing pretty well. But Satan will be back soon with another stone, whether it's fear, self-pity, or hopelessness. If you haven't dealt individually with each of these stones and gotten rid of them, your nice, free-flowing well of good things will become clogged. But you can still unclog it with a major dose of prayer and reading of GOD's words. No matter what is happening today, you can rise above your circumstances and feel GOD working out your sit-uation for you."

We all have times when people or circumstances come against us and there is fear and uncertainty. Sometimes there are days when we may feel mistreated, confused or that something is not going as we hoped. Maybe you're facing a problem today and you're not exactly sure how to handle it. If we read GOD's Words and pray, He'll give us what we need in His timing. GOD's timetable may appear to move slowly, but it does move surely. GOD is always on time. He may wait to the last second but He's never late and He will meet all your needs and those desires He wants you to have!!! Psalm 30:5 reads, "His favor is for life: Weeping may endure for a night, But joy comes in the morning." (NKJ)

OUR PRAYER

I come to thee Oh Lord to give Praise and Honor to Your Mighty Name. As I travel this tedious journey of life, I believe and decree that GOD is with me and He will meet all my needs. Thank you Lord for carrying me through all my trials and tribulations over the years. Thank you for those abundant blessings on the way. Continue to help me to be a blessing to your people. Let Your Holy Spirit forever lead and guide me. I pray in the miraculous Name of Jesus, Amen."

THE MIDDLE GAME

The firefights with the Veterans Administration Regional Office (VARO) were as fierce as heated combat battles in Vietnam. The letter below was submitted to the VARO director regarding my benefits:

David M. Williams
PO Box 27551
Detroit, MI 48227

August 30, 2013
Department of Veterans Affairs Regional Office
477 Michigan Ave.
Detroit, MI 48226-2591
Attn: Mr. David Leonard, Director
Reference: VA File No. 26446226

Dear Mr. Leonard:

Enclosed is copy of my letter to President Obama minus exhibits. (Exhibit 1) I am very frustrated and concerned about the delay in your response to demands by BVA!! Please associate the enclosed medical evidence regarding my lumbar spine disability (Exhibit 2) with my claims folders remanded to your office by Judge Bethany L. Buck on May 30, 2013.

Judge Buck stated in remand that, "This claim must be afforded expeditious treatment. The law requires that all claims that are remanded by the Board of Veterans' Appeals for Veterans claims for additional development or other appropriate actions must be handled in an expeditious manner." I believe your office is not obeying this law and are not acting in good faith. I remain prayerful that this correspondence will implore you to follow the law. Thank you in advance for your expeditious re-adjudication of my claims.

Sincerely,
David M. Williams
Vietnam Veteran, 25th Infantry Division
Enclosures

David M. Williams
PO Box 27551
Detroit, MI 48227
August 28, 2013
Honorable Barack Obama
1600 Pennsylvania Avenue NW
Washington, DC 20500

Dear President Obama:

I agree with you wholeheartedly that our aim for the 50th Anniversary events should be, "Just to celebrate the accomplishments of all of those folks whose shoulders we stand on and then remind people that the work is still out there for us to do." You also said that a way to honor Dr. King is to do "the day-to-day work to make sure this is a more equal and more just society."

As a follow –up to your sentiments, I decided to again ask your assistance. I have pursued this matter for about the last 5 years and I am certain many other veterans are likewise being victimized. I am 66 years old and continue to suffer excruciating daily pains, emotional and financial distress/hardships. I am a native of Montgomery, Alabama and met Dr. Martin Luther King Jr. at the age of eight in his living room. He told a group of church boys called, The Crusaders, three things that I vividly remember and I have used as a compass for my life. Dr. King said, "Always keep GOD first, try to get a good education and always give something back to your community." I continue to fight daily in Detroit for equality and justice for all.

The only times I have received an expedited response from the VARO has been when your office has intervened on my behalf. It's 3:00A.M. and I have tossed and turned all night due to aches and pains throughout my body. My claims have been in appeal process for a long time. Although having meager financial resources, I am paying private physicians to help VARO facilitate remands ordered by BVA. (Exhibit 1) Also, I have enclosed copy of report from MRI lumbar spine exam and consultation note of Dr. Grias, a physiatrist.(Exhibit 2) Physiatrists, or rehabilitation physicians, are nerve, muscle, and bone experts who treat injuries or illnesses that affect how you move. I did not ask to go to war in Vietnam!!! I was drafted in Montgomery and subjected to great discrimination because of my strong opposition to the war. I believe, my civil rights and other similarly situated veterans are severely and unjustly being violated. Please read my recent letter to General Allison Hickey. (Exhibit 3) I am prayerful you will urgently assist me. With your intervention on my behalf, I believe VARO will comply with BVA remand actions and expeditiously re-adjudicate my disability claims.

I fervently believe that prayer is the key that unlocks all the treasures of the Kingdom of GOD. It is the key that He has placed in our hands and invited us to use to combat adversity. Let's pray: The Lord is our Shepherd and we shall not want! Oh Merciful and Almighty GOD, please bless and keep secure President Obama, his family and his staff. Cover him with Your blood and give him Your wisdom needed to lead this country. Touch Congress and help them to get on one accord with Your appointed leader. Lord, I want to thank you for what you have already done. I am not going to wait until I see results or receive rewards, I am thanking you right now. I am not going to wait until I feel better or things look better, I am thanking you right now. I am not going to wait until people say they are sorry or until they stop talking about me, I am thanking you right now. I am not going to wait until the pain in my body disappears, I am thanking you right now. I am not going to wait until my financial situation improves, I am going to thank you right now. Continue to keep us in the palm of Your

Hand and bless me in this situation immediately. We pray in the Awesome Name of Jesus, Amen.

President Obama, thank you for all you have done and for your consideration. I know GOD appointed you to lead America during this turbulent time. You will be successful!!!

Sincerely,
David M. Williams, Vietnam Veteran
25th Infantry Division
Enclosures – Exhibits 1-3

The letter below was sent to President Obama regarding my book:

PO Box 27551
Detroit, MI 48227
February 15, 2013
Honorable Barack Obama
1600 Pennsylvania Avenue NW
Washington, DC 20500

Dear President Obama:

I am a disabled Vietnam Veteran and I humbly request you will read the article below. With your assistance, I plan to get my book in urban schools throughout the nation, starting here in Detroit. I believe my book will help curtail violence by our youths in these urban cities!! A copy was sent to you last year. When schools are visited, each student will be asked to share their book with their parents or even read with their parents. This book will not only serve as a learning tool for students but will provide encouragement, bonding and great educational history for parents. President Obama, if you may have noted in my book, your message and ideas are prominently featured throughout my book.

Humbly Submitted,
Dave Williams

* Without Faith, Nothing Is Possible

For the Presidents' Day Holiday February, 2013 and as a "Highlight to Black History Month," these sentiments were shared. One writer said, "Whenever we open the Bible, listen to a sermon, or pause to pray, it's a wonderful practice to say, Lord Jesus speak to me, I'm ready to listen and eager to obey." In Isaiah 55:8-9 are found these words, "For My thoughts are not your thoughts, Nor are your ways My ways," says the Lord. For as the heavens are higher than the earth, So are My ways higher than your ways, And My thoughts than your thoughts.'" (NKJ)

Dr. Creigs Beverly, Professor Emeritus, Wayne State University said, "Both David (Dave) Williams and I grew up in Montgomery, Alabama. We each personally knew the Reverend Dr. Martin Luther King, Jr. and we experienced the Civil Rights Movement firsthand via the Montgomery Bus Boycott. Though grounded geographically in the red clay of Alabama, our developmental paths were quite different. You will read his story in the pages to follow and I am convinced after having done so, you will more fully appreciate your own life and your search not only for self, but also for community."

What readers are saying about, How To Pull Yourself Up from Rock Bottom To Success!! "One reader said, "You owe it to yourself, our ancestors, and our children to get a copy of this book and share a copy with one or more of your contacts." Another reader called this book, "An amalgamation of African American History within Biblical underpinnings." Finally, one reader said, "This book gave me a more vivid portrait of both White and Black national leaders dependence on GOD's wisdom in performing their roles. I now have a better appreciation for the Bible and GOD's words. I have rededicated my life to Christ and started attending church."

Here are some insights and thoughts from this book:

Dave Williams said, "At the age of eight in Montgomery, I met Dr. Martin Luther King, Jr. in his living room with a group of church boys called the Crusaders. This was prior to the Montgomery Bus Boycott. He told us three things which left an indelible print on my heart and guided my life to this day. He said, 'Always keep GOD first, try to get a good education and always give something back to your community.' I have helped fight for justice and equality in Alabama/US since that date."

"The slave preacher, Nat Turner, believed that GOD had called him to lead his people out of slavery. Turner believed that if you believed in something badly enough, you can make it come true. Turner said, ' I was ordained for some great purpose in the hands of the Almighty. The Spirit instantly appeared to me and said the serpent was loosed and Christ had lain down the yoke he had borne for the sins of men and I should take it on and fight against the Serpent.'"

Dr. Benjamin Elijah Mays was an outspoken critic of segregation and major mentor to Dr. Martin Luther King, Jr.. He was president of Morehouse College from 1940 until 1967. Dr. Mays was a minister who focused on the dignity of all human beings and the disparity between American ideals and social practices. These were the key messages of Dr. King and the Civil Rights Movement. One of my favorite quotes of Dr. Mays is, "It must be born in the mind that the tragedy in life doesn't lie in not reaching your goal. The tragedy lies in having no goal to reach. It isn't a calamity to die with dreams unfulfilled, but it is a calamity not to dream. It is not a disaster to be unable to capture your ideal, but it is a disaster to have no ideal to capture. It is not a disgrace not to reach the stars, but it is a disgrace to have no stars to reach for. Not failure, but low aim is a sin."

In Chapter 16, President Reagan said, "My fellow Americans: A few hours from now in the East Room of the White House, I'll be hosting a reception honoring the memory of a man who played a truly historic role in expanding the freedom we enjoy in America. Dr. Martin Luther King, Jr., was born into a world where bigotry and racism still held sway. Before he died, he had touched the conscience of a nation and had contributed immeasurably to the human rights of black Americans. He was a man of character and a man of courage."

President Clinton said in Chapter 11, "Knowing the thoughts and ideas of my fellow Americans is very important to me as we face the challenges ahead. I believe that our nation has made a great deal of progress since I took office. I am proud of what we have done to reduce the deficit, expand our economy, improve educational opportunities, and empower hardworking Americans to make the most of their own lives. As we work to protect our shared values, meet our common challenges, and ensure peace and security at home and abroad, I hope you will remain involved."

In the prologue, President Obama said,

"Dear Mr. Williams:

The victory we achieved on November 4 means so much to so many — but to all of us, it is a stirring affirmation of our country's most fundamental promise: America is a place where anything — we choose to dream together, anything for which we choose to work together — is possible. Ours was never the likeliest campaign for the presidency. We didn't start with much money or many endorsements. Our campaign was not hatched in the halls of Washington — it was built by working men and women, students and retirees who dug into what little savings they had to give five dollars and ten dollars and twenty dollars to this cause. It grew from the millions of Americans who volunteered, and organized, and proved that more than two centuries later, a government of the people, by the people and for the people has not perished from the Earth."

Dr. Mary Jane McLeod Bethune was an American educator and civil rights leader born in 1875. She started a school for Black students now known as Bethune-Cookman University. It is located in Daytona Beach, Florida. Chapter 7 includes portions of what is referred to as her, "Last Will and Testament." I conclude with the following from Dr. Bethune:

I LEAVE YOU FAITH.

Faith is the first factor in a life devoted to service. Without faith, nothing is possible. With it, nothing is impossible. Faith in GOD is the greatest power, but great, too, is faith in oneself. In 50 years the faith of the American Negro in himself has grown immensely and is still increasing. The measure of our progress as a race is in precise relation to the depth of the faith in our people held by our leaders. Frederick Douglass, genius though he was, was spurred by a deep conviction that his people would heed his counsel and follow him to freedom. Our greatest Negro figures have been imbued with faith. Our forefathers struggled for liberty in conditions far more onerous than those we now face, but they never lost the faith. Their perseverance paid rich dividends. We must never forget their sufferings and their sacrifices, for they were the foundations of the progress of our people."

CHAPTER 25
Thank You, Lord, for Carrying Me

After receiving the following two letters from the Department of Veterans Affairs, Detroit Regional Office, I felt strongly the power of GOD working behind the scenes on my behalf. I got that spiritual revelation I had been seeking and the Holy Spirit told me that GOD was turning things around. I knew my breakthrough and victory were imminent! I believed I was not only getting help from above but also from the White House. I fervently believed that just as we were leaving Vietnam with a convoy, I had a convoy leading me across the finish line in this battle with the VA. All I had to do was keep praying, move myself out of the way and stand still and let GOD be GOD. Ephesians 6:13 proclaims, "Therefore put on the full armor of GOD, so that when the day of evil comes, you may be able to stand your ground, and after you have done everything, to stand." I felt I had done everything I could do and it now was in GOD's hand and the Board of Veterans' Appeals!!! The letter below was received on 9-20-12:

Department Of Veterans Affairs
VA Regional Office
477 Michigan Ave.
Detroit, MI 48226-2591
September 17, 2012

Dear Mr. Williams:

Your appeal is being placed on the docket of the Board of Veterans' Appeals for disposition. This means that your records are being transferred to the Board in Washington, D.C., so that the Board can reach a decision on your appeal. Appeals are considered by the Board as promptly as possible, in docket order. Once the appeal has reached the Board of Veterans' Appeals, it takes months to review it. The time it takes to complete this appellate review process will vary depending upon the current backlog at the Board.

If you have requested to appear personally at a hearing before the Board of Veterans' Appeals, you will receive further information by separate letter. If you want to appear personally and give testimony concerning your appeal and you have not already requested the hearing, you must submit your request within 90 days of the date of this letter, or by the date that the Board issues a decision in your case, whichever comes first. Any new request for a hearing or to appoint or change representatives or any additional evidence should not be submitted to this office, but should be mailed directly to Board of Veterans' Appeals (014), 810 Vermont Avenue, NW, Washington, DC 20420. Please see 38 C.F.R. 201304 for further details concerning the time limits described above.

Sincerely,
Keith Sekuterski
Veterans Service Center Manager

The next letter was received on 9 -29- 12 and read:

Department Of Veterans Affairs
VA Regional Office
477 Michigan Ave.
Detroit, MI 48226-2591
October 1, 2012

Dear Mr. Williams:

Your inquiry to President Barack H. Obama concerning your appeals was referred to the Department of Veterans Affairs (VA) Regional Office in

Detroit on September 26, 2012, because your records are located in this office. You submitted a Notice of Disagreement (NOD) on August 25, 2008, requesting service connection for hypertension and malaria. We denied your request on June 2, 2009, and you continued your appeal on July 14, 2009. You submitted a NOD on June 16, 2010, requesting service connection for 13 conditions. You also submitted a NOD on July 20, 2011, requesting service connection for ischemic heart disease. We denied both requests on October 20, 2011, and you continued both appeals on November 17, 2011. We have certified that your file is ready to be sent to the Board of Veterans' Appeals (BVA) in Washington, D.C. Once they receive it, the next step will be for them to review all three of your appeals, and make a decision.

If you have any additional questions or concerns, please feel free to visit our office, which is located on the twelfth floor of the Patrick V. McNamara Federal Building, at 477 Michigan Avenue in Detroit. You may also telephone toll-free 1-800-827-1000, where a veterans service representative will be happy to assist you.

Sincerely,
David Leonard
Director
By Direction of the Under Secretary for Benefits

*I Declare I Will Enjoy GOD's Favor And Abundant Blessings

2 Corinthians 9:8 reads, "And GOD is able to bless you abundantly, so that in all things at all times, having all that you need, you will abound in every good work." (NIV) This verse indicates and I believe that GOD wants us blessed and favored and He will provide all we need. When GOD wants to bless us, He does it in His timing. All we have to do is (1) keep reading and studying His Words: (2) keep believing , worshipping and praying daily to Him. GOD said it and I believe it that, "Our best days are ahead and imminent (really close)!!" Someone said, "If you keep on doing what you have always done, then

you will keep on being what you always been." Nothing changes positively unless you seek GOD and He helps you make a change. GOD can be trusted to always be there for us. It comes as no surprise, but it's not the same case with people – people let us down. For this reason, we should turn to GOD first and foremost in our trials, because He is the one that can ultimately turn our trials into blessings. Regardless of the situation you may be facing, GOD can provide you the right solution. He wants you to turn to Him so He can solve your problem. Always remember that GOD cares about you and He loves you and has a great plan and purpose for your life.

Psalm 30:5 states, "For his anger lasts only a moment, but his favor lasts a lifetime: weeping may remain for a night, but rejoicing comes in the morning." 2 Corinthians 6:2 reads, For he says, "In the time of my favor I heard you, and in the day of salvation I helped you. I tell you, now is the time of GOD's favor, now is the day of salvation." (NIV) In the New Living Translation, the Bible exclaims in Hebrews 3:15, "Remember what it says: Today when you hear his voice, don't harden your hearts as Israel did when they rebelled." Today is the day of salvation for each of us because tomorrow is not promised. "Go ahead and declare right now that I am GOD's vessel, I will obey His Words, do His will and achieve my divine assignment. I will have a great finish on this earthly journey for GOD is so good! I will forsake those things behind me and endure this race to receive that great prize that GOD has waiting for me. GOD will always provide all my needs and His justice will restore/redeem me. I will forever trust Him and will make Heaven my home."

All GOD's children are preordained for victory!! As a child of GOD, we have His power working in and through us. We have the power to overcome all the negative, self-defeating forces of the world. When we activate our faith, we tap directly into GOD's unlimited strength and have opened the door for GOD to move supernaturally on our behalf. When things come against us, instead of complaining and giving up, faith causes us to rise up and say, "No weapon formed against me shall prosper. I am able to do all things through Christ who gives me strength. I declare I will enjoy GOD's favor and abundant blessings for the rest of my life!!!"

OUR PRAYER

I will always trust GOD for He has never failed me. Jesus, thank you for Your blessings You allow Your children to receive. Help us to remain in Your Words and be obedient servants. Father, thank you for filling me with Your conquering power. I choose to live in faith and declare Your promises over my life. I choose to follow Your Words. I choose Your ways knowing that You have good plans for me In Jesus' Name I receive Your gifts, Amen.

 * GOD is always working behind the scenes to make our dreams and goals a reality. All we have to do is trust Him and obey His Words! GOD told the Israelites that He led them through the wilderness to test whether they would obey His Commandments. GOD sometimes allows us to face trials to test our hearts to see if we will obey His Words. If we always trust GOD, He will meet all our needs and some of our desires He wants us to have. This is spelled out in the following passage: Deuteronomy 8: 1-19 read, "Be careful to follow every command I am giving you today, so that you may live and increase and may enter and possess the land the Lord promised on oath to your ancestors. Remember how the Lord your GOD led you all the way in the wilderness these forty years, to humble and test you in order to know what was in your heart, whether or not you would keep his commands. He humbled you, causing you to hunger and then feeding you with manna, which neither you nor your ancestors had known, to teach you that man does not live on bread alone but on every word that comes from the mouth of the Lord. Your clothes did not wear out and your feet did not swell during these forty years. Know then in your heart that as a man disciplines his son, so the Lord your GOD disciplines you. Observe the commands of the Lord your GOD, walking in obedience to him and revering him. For the Lord your GOD is bringing you into a good land—a land with brooks, streams, and deep springs gushing out into the valleys and hills: a land with wheat and barley, vines and fig trees, pomegranates, olive oil and honey: a land where bread will not be scarce and you will lack nothing: a land where the rocks are iron and you can dig copper out of the hills. When you have eaten and are satisfied, praise the Lord your GOD for the good land he has given you. Be careful that you do not forget the Lord your GOD, failing to observe his commands, his laws and his decrees that I am giving you this day. Otherwise, when you eat and are satisfied, when you

build fine houses and settle down, and when your herds and flocks grow large and your silver and gold increase and all you have is multiplied, then your heart will become proud and you will forget the Lord your GOD, who brought you out of Egypt, out of the land of slavery. He led you through the vast and dreadful wilderness, that thirsty and waterless land, with its venomous snakes and scorpions. He brought you water out of hard rock. He gave you manna to eat in the wilderness, something your ancestors had never known, to humble and test you so that in the end it might go well with you. You may say to yourself, 'My power and the strength of my hands have produced this wealth for me.' But remember the Lord your GOD, for it is he who gives you the ability to produce wealth, and so confirms his covenant, which he swore to your ancestors, as it is today. If you ever forget the Lord your GOD and follow other GODs and worship and bow down to them, I testify against you today that you will surely be destroyed."

"Thank you Lord" for carrying me through my storms. I will forever give You the Honor and Praise! Although trials and tribulations may have you disgusted at this time, GOD has promised He will never leave you nor forsake you. He will continue to manifest His goodness and He will take care of all your needs. Right now stop worrying and complaining about what you don't have and how miserable life is. GOD is ready to give you your miracle. Right this moment, go ahead and thank Him. Remain prayerful and continue to trust Him to answer your prayers in His timing. Our weakness makes it imperative that we depend on GOD. He knows what is best for us and always come to our rescue in the time of need. He is an on time GOD and there is no need to worry or fear. With GOD's help, we will succeed at any endeavor we may be involved.

The Bible says that we are more than conquerors through Christ. Romans 8:37 – 39 state, "No, in all these things we are more than conquerors through him who loved us. For I am convinced that neither death nor life, neither angels nor demons, neither the present nor the future, nor any powers, neither height nor depth, nor anything else in all creation, will be able to separate us from the love of GOD that is in Christ Jesus our Lord." So rise up and see yourself as an overwhelming champion in Jesus! You can be and you will be victorious through Him. The problems that so often intimidate and defeat many people can't have a firm hold on you if you're sold out completely to Christ. Someone who belongs completely to Christ knows the strength and victory that comes through Him. Here's something to remember today: if Christ is on your side, it doesn't really matter who is against you! The opponents you face don't really matter, and don't amount to much, when Christ is standing next to you. Romans 8:31 states, "If GOD is for us, who is against us?"

*Someone once said, "Tell me whom you walk with and I'll tell you who you are." This simply means that, "A man is known by the company he keeps or birds of a feather flock together." You can't hang out with Al Capone and think you will be an angel in your other activities. At some point in our lives, many of us find ourselves overcome with the desire to become a better person. While we are all uniquely capable of navigating this world, we may nonetheless feel driven to grow, expand, and change. This innate need for personal expansion can lead us down many paths as we develop within the context of our individual lives. Yet the initial steps that can put us on the road to evolution are not always clear. We understand that we want to be better but have no clear definition of "better." To ease this often frustrating uncertainty, we can take small steps, keeping our own concept of growth in mind rather than allowing others to direct the course of our journey. And we should accept that change won't happen overnight—we may not recognize the transformations taking place within us at first.

Becoming a better person in your own eyes is a whole-life project, and thus you should focus your step-by-step efforts on multiple areas of your existence. Since you likely know innately which qualities you consider good, growing as an individual is simply a matter of making an effort to do good whenever possible. Respect should be a key element of your efforts. When you acknowledge that all people are deserving of compassion, consideration, and dignity, you will treat them in the manner you want to be treated.

When you approach your daily duties with an upbeat attitude and positive expectations, you make the world a brighter, more cheerful place. Sometimes when people face challenges, they try to seek comfort in things that are familiar to them. It may be work, an activity or relationships: and of course, we all know about "comfort food." But, those things only bring temporary comfort. True comfort is only found in a relationship with Jesus. Webster's dictionary states that comfort means to give strength and hope: to ease grief or trouble. No matter what difficulty you may be facing today, GOD wants to bring you comfort. Like a mother cares for her child, GOD wants to give you strength, hope and confidence. So today, turn to GOD and receive His love. Let go of things that would hold you back. Let Him heal your heart and give you strength for the future. Let Him empower you to rise up and overcome every obstacle in Jesus' name! Isaiah 66:13 reads, "As a mother comforts her child, so will I comfort you." (NIV)

GOD can bless you in a way that no one else can do. The Holy Spirit activates those gifts GOD has placed inside of you. I learned that no matter how you try, you can't do anything on your own and need divine guidance. Sometimes you have to change your way of living and your environment in order to maximize your GOD given talents. Yes, that old sage was correct who said, "The darkest hour of the day is just before dawn." I fervently believe you can't control what may happen in your life but you can determine that you will face all your challenges boldly and lean totally on GOD to provide all your needs and some of your desires. As you maintain a strong faith and pious attitude, GOD will give you those blessings He wants you to have. GOD will help you to overcome any adversity that comes your way.

Always remember, when you travel with GOD, you won't get lost!!! He always knows the way and is always on time. John 14:6 reads, "Jesus saith unto him, I am the way, the truth, and the life: no man cometh unto the Father, but by me." The prophet Isaiah said in chapter 30 and verse 21, "Your own ears will hear him. Right behind you a voice will say, 'This is the way you should go,' whether to the right or to the left." (NLT)

My life's history is based on never backing away from challenges and despite the prolonged drama with the VA, I was inspired to go full steam ahead to help GOD'S children! I am on my last mile of this earthly journey and I want to complete GOD's will. I want to utilize my talents to the fullest and cross the finishing line exhausted and empty because I left it all on the field of my earthly life. I will be prepared to enter eternity and enjoy everlasting life with my Heavenly Father!!!

Another one of my favorite Scriptures is Psalm 37:23-24 which says that, "The steps of a good man are ordered by the Lord and He delighteth in His way. Though he may fall, he shall not be utterly cast down for the Lord holds him in his hand." Success in life does not just come to those who have a dream but it is achieved by those who thirst for it and passionately pursue their goals.

In essence, with GOD's help, they perform the actions needed to actualize their dream. Sometimes in life, GOD leads us to change our ideas or directions. At this point in our lives, many of us may find ourselves overcome with the desire to become a better person and move reverently to the next level. While we are all uniquely capable of navigating this world, we may nonetheless feel driven to grow, expand, and change. Always hear GOD's voice and obey His instructions.

John 13:5-17, 34-35 read, "After that, He poured water into a basin and began to wash the disciples' feet, and to wipe them with the towel with which He was girded. Then He came to Simon Peter. And Peter said to Him, 'Lord, are You washing my feet?' Jesus answered and said to him, 'What I am doing you do not understand now, but you will know after this.' Peter said to Him, 'You shall never wash my feet!' Jesus answered him, 'If I do not wash you, you have no part with Me.' Simon Peter said to Him, 'Lord, not my feet only, but also my hands and my head!' Jesus said to him, 'He who is bathed needs only to wash his feet, but is completely clean: and you are clean, but not all of you.' For He knew who would betray Him: therefore He said, 'You are not all clean.' So when He had washed their feet, taken His garments, and sat down again, He said to them, 'Do you know what I have done to you? You call Me Teacher and Lord, and you say well, for so I am. If I then, your Lord and Teacher, have washed your feet, you also ought to wash one another's feet. For I have given you an example, that you should do as I have done to you. Most assuredly, I say to you, a servant is not greater than his master: nor is he who is sent greater than he who sent him. If you know these things, blessed are you if you do them. A new commandment I give to you, that you love one another: as I have loved you, that you also love one another. By this all will know that you are My disciples, if you have love for one another.'"

One of the most asked questions when one who is retiring or stepping off the stage of a movie or sports career or practically any professional vocation is: What would you have done differently in your career? These final sentiments are written to take you personally on my convoy home and prepare you for a self-evaluation of your walk with GOD. One of the most difficult assignments one may have to do in a college class or sometimes in an employment situation is to give or complete a critical self-evaluation. The main thing is to not appear to be bragging but to give a humble and truthful assessment.

Never put yourself down but you should always show your strengths and weaknesses. Then tell what you enjoyed most and what you now think you should have done in a different manner. I continue to fervently believe that with faith in GOD, one can rise above life's circumstances and feel GOD working out adverse situations for us favorably.

When 2014 began, I had great expectations and was looking forward to what GOD would do in this new season in my life. There were new territories I wanted to explore and I had several plans I wanted to fulfill. We are nearing the end of the year and I'm still battling with issues that I have been dealing with for years. Nothing has changed so far! This year is almost over, I've done all I know to do and nothing has happened. Today, the Holy Spirit told me I'm the problem. I have relied too much on myself trying to make things happen. He told me it's time for me to back off! He said, "Step aside and let GOD do what He's been trying to do for you all along. Let Him complete the work He started (Philippians 1:6)." In Ephesians 6:14 New Living Translation, Apostle Paul encourages us to "Stand your ground. You know GOD has promised to bless you, so stand firm in your faith that He will do exactly that!" The prophet in Habakkuk, 2:3, NLT: "This vision is for a future time. It describes the end, and it will be fulfilled. If it seems slow in coming, wait patiently, for it will surely take place." GOD's purpose for us always will be fulfilled. I fervently believe and declare our blessings are on the way!!!

In an e-mail I received on September 14, 2014 from Pastor Joel Osteen, he said, "Your imagination is a wonderful gift that GOD's given you! With it, you can envision opportunities and new beginnings long before they become a reality in your life. When you apply your faith this way, your imagination isn't about "day dreams" — it's a tool that helps you deepen your relationship with GOD. And when you pursue GOD and worship Him through your imagination, you plant seeds of hope for the dreams you carry in your heart. Each time you throw aside doubts, or fears about getting your hopes up, you set into motion an awesome, supernatural process. I know how difficult this can be. It's risky to imagine GOD doing the incredible or the impossible. If we never dream, we don't have to worry about being disappointed. But consider this: as powerful as our imaginations can be, GOD is able to do so much more than you can ever imagine. Victoria and I want to encourage you today to take a step of faith and to imagine... imagine all the wonderful, supernatural and great things GOD could do in your life. How bold are you willing to be? How big are you willing to dream? There's no greater joy than encouraging people to put their trust in Jesus and to expect Him to do great things in their lives. Every day, as a ministry, that's what we're doing all over the world — and it's not because of me and Victoria. It's because of friends like you who "see" the power of hope. Thank you for your support! Remember, don't be afraid to believe GOD for BIG things in your life and in the lives of your loved ones. Victoria and I want you to know that we are believing with you. Together, let's put our faith into motion...and be amazed at what GOD will do!"

Let's pray: Lord, thank you for a good night sleep and waking me early this morning in my right mind and eager to give praises and Thanksgiving to You. You have always been by my side and provided me protection and met all my needs. Lord thank you for healing my infirmities and soothing all my aches and pain. Help me to continue to trust You. Help me to continue to study Your Words and be an obedient servant. Forgive me of my sins, clean me up and use me for Kingdom building for the rest of this journey to help save the lost. Thank you Almighty GOD and I will go on in the Name of Jesus, Amen.

* An e-mail to one of my contacts reads:

Hello VB,

Everyone has a story that they can share with others. Many people share their story with others by writing a book. When you tell your story in writing, it is not totally about your writing ability but your creativity in telling your story is quite essential. Writing your story can help you quench that thirst to validate your life. Freely allow your writing to guide you in telling your story and try to make an accurate account of events. Self-talk therapy in a journal can help us to bring serenity in our lives and may fulfill a need to have your voice heard by others. Writing of your personal experiences weekly or monthly in a journal will help you tremendously in completing your book.

I have always admired your analytical and thoughtful insights. I am certain that you will enjoy this book project and will share it with your grandchildren, other relatives, friends and acquaintances. First of all, this book is authored by divine wisdom and tells succinctly how GOD has no respect of persons. What He has done for others He'll do for each of His children. Success in this discourse is learning your divine assignment and trusting GOD to help you complete it. My precursor to social work began at the age of eight in Montgomery, when I met Dr. Martin Luther King Jr. in his living room with a group of church boys called the Crusaders. This was prior to the Montgomery Bus Boycott. He told us three things which left an indelible imprint on my heart and guided my life to this day. He said, "Always keep GOD first, try to get a good education and always give something back to your community."

Even after getting married the first time and having to leave Howard University, "The Mecca of Black intellects," I did not lose focus of my divine assignment. Even after seeing many deaths in Vietnam, getting divorced from my first wife, terminated from my job and kicked out of Wayne County Circuit Court, I remained resolved to complete my divine assignment. I believe when we do what the Holy Spirit tells us to do and are in GOD's will, we should not be concerned about opposition or consequences. My divine assignment is to advocate for the least of these and try to help create Dr. King's "Beloved Community." One of the most important ingredients for "Success" is the internal belief that you will succeed. Success begins with your beliefs and thoughts. You can't change your life nor help others until you change your mind to a positive mode. As Dr. Benjamin Mays said, "It must be borne in the mind that the tragedy in life doesn't lie in not reaching your goal. The tragedy lies in having no goal to reach. It isn't a calamity to die with dreams unfulfilled, but it is a calamity not to dream. It is not a disaster to be unable to capture your ideal, but it is a disaster to have no idea to capture. It is not a disgrace not to reach the stars, but it is a disgrace to have no stars to reach for. Not failure, but low aim is a sin."

We all have things that we've learned: skills, talents, life experiences, wisdom. You have a wealth of knowledge that GOD has entrusted you with. You are not supposed to keep that to yourself. You should be passing that on to somebody else. We have a responsibility to transfer what we know to the next generation. Please take liberty to share your thoughts and comments after you have read my book.

There is no book ever written that has endured as well or transformed as many people lives as the Bible!!! By daily reading GOD's Words and obeying them, you will learn His will for your life. GOD will also bestow His favor upon you and direct you to your preordained destiny. With GOD's help, anyone can pull themselves up or overcome any adversity they may encounter on this earthly journey. Someone once said and I deeply agree with their sentiment that, "If you conceive it, believe it, then you can achieve it." This section tells of my perseverance and belief in GOD to give me victory. By GOD's Anointment, nature, disposition and desire, I am a divine servant trying to give of myself to help other children of GOD. We all want the best life we can have. We really are our brothers and sisters keepers. An old adage goes, "Teach Me and I'll learn: show me and I can do." A Chinese proverb states, "Give a man a fish and you feed him for a day. Teach a man to fish and you feed him for a lifetime." Hold on and keep trusting GOD, your change is going to come.

Faith in GOD is one of the key components to "Success." Faith enables us to enjoy GOD's blessings in our lives as well as help us to overcome trials and adversities when they come our way. The Holy Spirit is heavy on me today on this Valentine Day, 2014. I feel GOD mightily working out my situations. I believe this year, 2014, will be a year of "Increase and Restoration." GOD wants me and all His children to move to the next level. My GOD is a GOD of increase. I believe He wants to increase our capacity for distribution so we can help the less fortunate. I hear GOD saying, "Obey My Words and your 'Success' is imminent! I have heard your prayers and the prayers of many others crying out for help. I have heard you asking, seeking, and knocking and I am now coming in response to your cry. Your access is granted, walk in My abundance and help My people!!! Many people will see my handiwork and be transformed. This will be a year of Increase and Restoration!" Luke 3:10-11 read, "And the people asked him, saying, What shall we do then? He answereth and saith unto them, He that hath two coats, let him impart to him that hath none: and he that hath meat, let him do likewise."

Let's pray: Almighty GOD, I pray for peace, love and joy for all Your children today. Help them at this moment to have all their needs met. Help them to turn everything over to You, seek Your face and receive Your Favor! Lord, I have heard Your voice and request You will give me more boldness to do Your will. Please continue to bless me so that I will be a blessing to others. Keep me uplifted so that I may have words of encouragement for Your children. I pray that everyone who reads these words be blessed and transformed to help save lost souls, in Jesus Name, we submit this request, Amen.

During President Barack Obama's last campaign for "The White House," many persons in communities throughout America were skeptical about his being re-elected. I felt very confident that he was going to win. The following is an excerpt from e-mail sent to my contacts on July 1, 2012:

* "On November 6, 2012, I am fervently confident that President Barack Obama will be re-elected as the 45th President of 'These United States!!!' First Lady Michelle Obama recently offered a rare public reflection on her religious faith, telling a conference of the African Methodist Episcopal Church in Nashville, Tennessee that the life of Jesus Christ is a model for democratic organizing. 'It's kind of like church,' Obama said. 'Our faith journey isn't just about showing up on Sunday for a good sermon and good music and a good meal. It's about what we do Monday through Saturday as well, especially in those quiet moments, when the spotlight's not on us, and we're making those daily choices about how to live our lives.

We see that in the life of Jesus Christ. Jesus didn't limit his ministry to the four walls of the church. He was out there fighting injustice and speaking truth to power every single day. He was out there spreading a message of grace and redemption to the least, the last, and the lost. And our charge is to find Him everywhere, every day by how we live our lives. Citizenship like the practice of faith is not a once-a-week kind of deal. Democracy is also an everyday activity and being an engaged citizen should once again be a daily part of our lives. Time and again, history has shown us that there is nothing – nothing – more powerful than ordinary citizens coming together for a just cause.'

The major reason I believe President Obama will be re-elected is not because of anything he has accomplished or what he may produce in a second term, but I fervently believe in 'Divine intervention.' Yes, GOD works in mysterious ways, His wonders to perform!! President Obama has done some great things which I'm sure he will highlight regularly before November 6th. No matter what tactics Fox News, Karl Rove and their band of Mitt Romney fanatics use, their hate and embellished untruths will not work. No amount of money can be used to defeat the 'Favor of GOD' President Obama has on his re-election campaign. 'For with GOD nothing shall be impossible.' (Luke 1:37)"

The following e-mail was received from President Obama and his sentiment touched me deeply and provided me some much needed inspiration on this day:

From: The White House< no-reply@correspondence.whitehouse.gov>
To: davewms43@yahoo.com
Sent: Wednesday, January 30, 2013 2:32 PM

Dear Dave:

I want to thank you for your message and for holding me in your prayers. My family and I are honored that so many Americans have supported us in this special way. Our country faces enormous challenges, but each day I am uplifted by the enduring spirit of the American people. I know we will meet these challenges if our optimism and hope are met with the necessary will and hard work. We understand that 'The strength to go on produces character. Character produces hope. And hope will never let us down,' (Romans 5: 4-5). In these times of trial and opportunity, I deeply appreciate your prayers for our country, my family, and me. May GOD bless you.

Barack Obama

I often wrote President Obama when VA was slowly addressing my appeal and any response I received from his office was heartwarming. On November 20, 2013, the following was received via e-mail from The White House:

The White House
1600 Pennsylvania Ave NW • Washington, DC 20500 • 202-456-1111

"Yesterday was the 150th anniversary of the Gettysburg Address. And to mark Lincoln's historic, moving speech, President Obama sat down and penned a very personal, handwritten tribute for display at the Lincoln Presidential Library."

President Obama's handwritten tribute stated, "In the evening, when Michelle and the girls have gone to bed, I sometimes walk down the hall to a room Abraham Lincoln used as his office. It contains an original copy of the Gettysburg address, written in Lincoln's own hand. I linger on these few words that have helped define our American experiment: 'a new nation, conceived in liberty, and dedicated to the proposition that all men are created equal.' Through the lines of weariness etched in his face, we know that Lincoln grasped, perhaps more than anyone, the burdens required to give these words meaning. He knew that even a self-evident truth was not self-executing: that blood drawn by the lash was an affront to our ideals: that blood drawn by the sword was in painful service to those same ideals. He understood as well that our humble efforts, our individual ambitions, are ultimately not what matter: rather, it is through the accumulated toil and sacrifice of ordinary men and women — those like the soldiers who consecrated that battlefield — that this country is built, and freedom preserved. This quintessentially self-made man, fierce in his belief in honest work and the striving spirit at the heart of America, believed that it falls to each generation, collectively, to share in that toil and sacrifice.

Through cold war and world war, through industrial revolutions and technological transformations, through movements for civil rights and women's rights and workers' rights and gay rights, we have. At times, social and economic changes have strained our union. But Lincoln's words give us confidence that whatever trials avoid us, this nation and the freedom we cherish can, and shall, prevail," Barack Obama

One of the most triumphant moments or rather, a time of jubilation in my life occurred on March 26, 2014. The following letter was received:

Department of Veterans Affairs
Chairman, Board of Veterans' Appeal
Washington, DC 20420
March 20, 2014

Mr. David M. Williams
Post Office Box 27551
Detroit, MI 48227

LOVE KEEPS ON GIVING!!!

Dear Mr. Williams:

Thank you for correspondence of August 28, 2013, which was addressed to President Barack H. Obama, and was received at the Board of Veterans' Appeals (Board) on March 5, 2014, concerning your appeal.

On May 30, 2013, the Board granted in part, denied in part, and remanded in part your case. The remand action was necessary to assist you with the development of the appeal and to ensure the record is complete. The claims file was returned to the Regional Office in Detroit, Michigan, where development will be completed, and the appeal will be reviewed. I have forwarded your correspondence to that office for review and direct reply to you.

When the development is finished, the Regional Office will re-adjudicate the appeal. If any part of the decision remains unfavorable, the case will be returned to the Board for a comprehensive review of the entire record, according to its place on the docket.

The statements and evidence in support of your appeal that were enclosed with your correspondence have also been forwarded to the Detroit Regional Office to be considered and associated with your file.

I hope the information I have provided is helpful. Please let me know if I can be of any further assistance.

Sincerely,
Laura H. Eskenazi
Executive in Charge

This letter brought confirmation that GOD was still working behind the scenes for my good. GOD smiled on me and assured me again that He is close to His children in their time of need. Again, I exclaim, GOD may delay our request but He will never disappoint our trust!!!

According to historical documentation, Black History Month, now also known as African American History Month, was created in 1926 in the United States, when historian Carter G. Woodson and the Association for the Study of Negro Life and History announced the second week of February to be "Negro History Week." This week was chosen because it marked the birthday of both Abraham Lincoln and Frederick Douglass. "Woodson created the holiday with the hope that it eventually be eliminated when Black History became fundamental to American History. Negro History Week was met with enthusiastic response: it prompted the creation of Black History clubs, an increase in interest among teachers, and interest from progressive whites. Negro History Week grew in popularity throughout the following decades, with mayors across the United States endorsing it as a holiday." In 1976, the federal government acknowledged the expansion of Black History Week to Black History Month by the leaders of the Black United Students at Kent State University in February of 1969. The first celebration of Black History Month occurred at Kent State in February of 1970. Six years later in 1976, the expansion of Negro History Week to Black History Month was recognized by the U.S. government. Former President Gerald Ford urged Americans to "seize the opportunity to honor the too-often neglected accomplishments of Black Americans in every area of endeavor throughout our history."

It would be remorseful if I ended this "Reflection" without mentioning a couple of my friends, two solid citizens and less known historical Black figures of Montgomery, Alabama. They contributed greatly to the Civil Rights Movement and influenced my life immensely. The first person we will introduce to my readers is Sam Cook and we will culminate with Dr. E. D. Nixon.

SAM COOK

One of the shrewdest businessmen I have ever met, a very spiritual person and a gentleman and scholar is Samuel George Cook. He was born on June 11, 1935 in Montgomery, Alabama. Several pictures of Sam appear in my original text photo gallery. He is not only pictured with me but also with Dr. Martin Luther King Jr. and his wife, Mrs. Coretta King. Sam graduated from Alabama State University where he earned his Bachelor and Master's degrees.

Sam was always a sharp dresser and could astutely discuss local and national issues with any college professor. Sam was one of my mentors who taught me and others he came in contact with many valuable life lessons. He was a close acquaintance of Dr. A. G. Gaston, one of Alabama's first million-aires. Sam told me that he earned money for college by working at one of Mr. Gaston's funeral facilities. He called Mr. Gaston, grandpa and often carried him to football games in Birmingham, Alabama when Alabama State was play-ing. In addition to working for Montgomery Community Action Agency, Sam owned a restaurant and also operated a taxi service during his illustrious career. Sam always believed his every action would lead to victory and "Success."

Sam often told me, "In order to be successful all you needed was Jesus and a dollar." It took me a short while to understand what Sam meant but sub-sequently I did. I learned that Sam was saying that when you trust Jesus, He could multiply that dollar into thousands or even millions. This utterance by Sam reminded me of one of the great Biblical miracles!!! One of the places it is found is Matthew 15:29-38: it reads, "Jesus left there and went along the Sea of Galilee. Then he went up on a mountainside and sat down. Great crowds came to him, bringing the lame, the blind, the crippled, the mute and many others, and laid them at his feet: and he healed them. The people were amazed when they saw the mute speaking, the crippled made well, the lame walking and the blind seeing. And they praised the GOD of Israel. Jesus called his disciples to him and said, 'I have compassion for these people: they have already been with me three days and have nothing to eat. I do not want to send them away hungry, or they may collapse on the way.' His disciples answered, 'Where could we get enough bread in this remote place to feed such a crowd?' 'How many loaves do you have?' Jesus asked. 'Seven,' they replied, 'and a few small fish.' He told the crowd to sit down on the ground. Then he took the seven loaves and the fish, and when he had given thanks, he broke them and gave them to the disciples, and they in turn to the people. They all ate and were satisfied. Afterward the disciples picked up seven basketfuls of broken pieces that were left over. The number of those who ate was four thousand men, besides women and children." If Jesus performed that kind of miracle then, He could still do it for us today. Hebrews 13:8 states, "Jesus Christ the same yesterday, and today, and forever."

As I write today on February 24, 2014, the last week of African Ameri-can/Black History Month, I am upset with the VA and my attorney. I thought about Sam always telling me to not get angry but fight harder for change when injustice is done! This letter was just taken to VA office:

Department Of Veterans Affairs
VA Regional Office
477 Michigan Ave.
Detroit, MI 48226-2591
Attn: Mr. Keith M. Sekuterski, Veterans Service Center Manager

Dear Mr. Sekuterski:

The letter below was hand-delivered to your office on 2-1-14! This letter is being submitted today by hand-delivery to advise your office that my attorney has withdrawn as my attorney effective upon receipt of this notice!!! His attached letter regarding list of evidence that is being submitted to BVA should be ignored. I want my case immediately sent to BVA. Your SSOC notice response was signed on 1-31-14 advising that 30 days was not needed to turn in additional evidence!! During this final week of Black History Month, the struggle for African Americans and similar situated veterans continues and I am extremely frustrated and very disappointed in the Veterans Administration. I still know how to fight! Veterans Deserve Better!!! Thank you kindly for your expeditious consideration!!!

Sincerely,
David M. Williams

After I returned home, I finished reading an article Sam sent me from a VA facility in Tuskegee, Alabama — where he now lives. Sam still motivates me although he's a thousand miles away. The article appeared in The Tuskegee News on February 13, 2014 and is entitled, "Cook remembers driving Dr. King to the Selma March." A portion of the article reads as follow: "When asked if Black History Month is still significant, civil rights activist and military veteran Sam Cook believes it is the best month for our youth today. 'We have to tell the youth about the past, if we do not, they will not know and will not remember.' While working at his grandfather's funeral home, Cook became active in the Civil Rights Movement and helped drive the citizens to and from the different locations for rallies. 'I can remember just like it was yesterday the first time I met Dr. King,' Cook recalled. 'He was such a humble man. When the plans were started to march from Selma to Montgomery, his main concern was the safety of the people.' Cook was the one that drove Dr. King and the main leaders to Selma before the march. Cook, along with James Orange, James Leon Hall and Bernard Lee, all worked together for the movement.

Cook feels that Black History must be kept in the forefront for today's youth. He believes that if they knew the history, they would not make some of the mistakes they make. 'At the time we were making plans for the march, I did not know that we were going to make history, I was just a part of the historical march.' Cook has gone back every year for the march, except when he was in the United States Army. He has been blessed to have met so many every year in Selma. 'If we get our youth involved in issues today, imagine what historical events they could be a part of tomorrow,' he commented." Sam Cook expired on January 10, 2016.

One writer said that, "Failure is only a detour on the road to Success." History is full of examples of people who have done great things but failed several times before they succeeded. From Thomas Edison who had a few failures, after all he did hold 1093 patents for different inventions, to NBA great Michael Jordan who was cut from his high school team! The list is numerous. If we would study some of the lives of successful people, we would learn that their real strength was their tenacity to keep getting up after a failure. Although they may have had innate talent, their refusal to quit led them to be a "Success."

DR. EDGAR DANIEL NIXON

I got a chance to meet with Dr. E.D. Nixon in his home when I sought the Alabama House of Representatives in 1985. He gave me an autographed picture with him and First Lady Eleanor Roosevelt taken in 1941 which I will always cherish. Anna Eleanor Roosevelt was the longest-serving First Lady of the United States, holding the post from 1933 to 1945 during her husband President Franklin D. Roosevelt's four terms in office. I later used this photograph in one of campaign literature which was widely distributed in Montgomery. I called Dr. E. D. Nixon, "The Forgotten Hero."

According to historical documentation, Dr. E. D. Nixon was born on July 12, 1899, in Lowndes County, Alabama to Wesley M. Nixon and Sue Ann Chappell Nixon. His adolescent years were spent in Montgomery, Alabama. Nixon's mother died when he was a boy, and he and his seven siblings lived with several family members as youths. He received little formal education but numerous honorary degrees. He stood about six feet, four inches tall, and possessed a charismatic spirit and a deep baritone voice. He had a natural ability to organize and to rally people around a cause. In 1926, Nixon and his first wife, Alease (who died in 1934), had a son, E. D. Nixon Jr. (1928-2011), an actor who went by the stage name Nick La Tour. His second wife, Arlette Nixon, became a fixture at his side in the Montgomery Civil Rights Movement.

During the 1920s, Nixon began working as a Pullman sleeping car porter. Porters assisted passengers boarding trains and also carried their luggage. Sleeping car porters assisted those passengers who took residence in the sleeping compartments of the trains. Widely considered desirable jobs among African Americans for the high wages and travel opportunities they offered. The Brotherhood of Sleeping Car Porters (BSCP) union helped these Pullman porters to enter the small middle class of Black America. During his travels on the trains, Nixon was exposed to the less restrictive communities and social practices outside the Deep South, with its entrenched Jim Crow racial policies. It also introduced him to the BSCP, a union that advocated better wages and working conditions for black railway workers, and acquainted him with its influential leader, A. Phillip Randolph. It was through these connections and experiences that Nixon was inspired to become an activist. Nixon quickly became a disciple of Randolph, and his philosophies greatly influenced Nixon's later Civil Rights work in Alabama. Randolph believed that the Civil Rights Movement was "wholly inadequate" to rectify the racial problems in America and more governmental action was needed.

It was during the 1940s, Nixon's community activism began in honest in Montgomery, where he and a group from the Madison Park community in North Montgomery organized the Alabama Voters League and worked to increase voter registration among the city's African American population. Through the Alabama Voters League, the outspoken Nixon organized and launched a march of about 750 people on the Montgomery County Municipal

Court House in 1944 to raise awareness of impediments to Black voting. In 1945, he was elected as the president of the Montgomery chapter of the National Association for the Advancement of Colored People (NAACP) and just two years later became the state president of the organization.

Nixon was politically astute and negotiated successfully with white city leaders to gain marginal advances in employment for Blacks in city governmental agencies. It is said that during the 1950s, Nixon was instrumental in convincing the Montgomery Police Department to hire Blacks by agreeing to support a white candidate who was sympathetic to the fight for Black Civil Rights. It was about this time that Nixon began to openly question the segregated seating restrictions on city buses and the refusal of bus companies to employ Black drivers. He and other members of the Montgomery branch of the NAACP began to look for a test case to challenge the legality of Montgomery's segregation laws.

On December 1, 1955, Rosa Parks, a seamstress and secretary for the NAACP in Montgomery, was arrested for refusing to surrender her seat to a white man. Nixon was notified of the arrest and when he telephoned to inquire about Parks' arrest, his inquiry was met with racial epithets and the police refused to speak with him. Undeterred, Nixon sought help from civil-rights attorney Clifford Durr and his wife Virginia to gain information about the arrest and accompany him to post bail for Parks. Nixon put his house up as bond collateral for her release.

A few days later, Nixon consulted with the Durrs, attorney Fred Gray, and other local Black leaders, and they decided that Parks' arrest would serve as the case to challenge the state's segregation policy in Montgomery. A short time later, Nixon and a group of Montgomery-area clergy and civic leaders, including Civil Rights leader Ralph Abernathy, founded the Montgomery Improvement Association (MIA). Minister and Civil Rights leader Dr. Martin Luther King Jr. was elected president of the organization. MIA provided a focal point for activism in Montgomery's Black community and its leaders organized the Montgomery Bus Boycott, in which the city's Black citizens refused to ride public transportation for an astounding 381 days. During the boycott, Dr. Martin Luther King Jr.'s home was bombed on January 30, 1956, and Nixon's home was bombed just two days later, although this event did not receive nearly as much attention as the King bombing.

After the success of the boycott, which lasted more than a year, MIA continued to serve the community by conducting voter-registration drives and hosting workshops on nonviolent protest methods. Nixon had been elected as the treasurer of MIA at the group's founding, but later quit the organization after a dispute with some of MIA's leaders. His departure likely related to the class-based schism in leadership within the Black community. Most of the leadership positions in the movement were held by well-educated middle-class Black men, whereas less-educated and lower-class Black men and most women were relegated to support positions. Nixon opposed this division and on June 3, 1957, disassociated himself from the organization in protest.

Economically, Nixon was middle class, but was considered of lower-class status because of his lack of formal education. Despite Nixon's departure from MIA, he continued to be an activist for the Black community, although never to the degree of his involvement with the Montgomery Bus Boycott. By the late 1960s, Nixon had lost much of his political clout and faded into the background without any recognition or fanfare for his major contributions to the Civil Rights Movement. He worked as the recreation director of a public housing project after the 1960s in relative obscurity, although he did receive a few awards for his Civil Rights work in his later years.

Nixon died on February 25, 1987 at Baptist Hospital in Montgomery. People from all walks of life came to the funeral of this Civil Rights icon at Bethel Baptist Church in Montgomery. Nixon generally has been overlooked by historians, and his importance in the bus boycott has been downplayed by some participants associated with it. Long-overdue recognition was finally bestowed on this early Civil Rights hero when the Montgomery County Public School System named an elementary school in his honor in 2001.

Words are quite powerful! They can cause one to experience a number of emotions, both positive and negative. But always remember that when you face any circumstance firmly and stand on GOD's Words, victory is imminent if it is GOD'S will. Our GOD is a faithful GOD. He will not allow anything to happen to us that He does not have a purpose for it. He always has your back! He will carry you through your storms and any adversity that may come your way. So my brothers and sisters, no matter what, keep moving forward boldly each day with GOD and you will cross "The Finishing Line!!"

I always try to stay positive and I still believe that there is a way to live in this world in peace. I am certain that by reading the Bible daily you will receive relief from difficult thoughts and circumstances in your life. Joshua 1:8-9 state, "This book of the law shall not depart out of thy mouth: but thou shalt meditate therein day and night, that thou mayest observe to do according to all that is written therein: for then thou shalt make thy way prosperous, and then thou shalt have good success. Have not I commanded thee? Be strong and of a good courage: be not afraid, neither be thou dismayed: for the Lord thy GOD is with thee whithersoever thou goest."

Always try to share love and be a good influence on people you come in contact with on your journey of life. It is a fact that our thoughts and actions are like stones dropped into still waters, causing ripples to spread and expand as they move outward. The impact you have on the world is greater than you could ever imagine. A smile at a stranger passing by, a compliment given to a contact, an attitude of laughter, or a thoughtful act of kindness will send ripples that spread among your loved ones and associates, out into your community, and finally throughout the world.

1 Corinthians 4:15 -18 read, "For all things are for your sakes, that the abundant grace might through the thanksgiving of many redound to the glory of GOD. For which cause we faint not: but though our outward man perish, yet the inward man is renewed day by day. For our light affliction, which is but for a moment, worketh for us a far more exceeding and eternal weight of glory: While we look not at the things which are seen, but at the things which are not seen: for the things which are seen are temporal: but the things which are not seen are eternal."

Pat Croce, the former minority owner and president of the Philadelphia 76er's once said, "I believe that customer service is a lost art in our society. People appreciate and compliment great service because we don't get it on a continuous basis. It's so easy. All you have to do is adhere to the golden rule— treat everyone as you want to be treated. Put yourself in the other person's shoes. His ten commandments include: (1) Say hello and goodbye, common courtesy. (2) Say a person's name. (3) Opportunity sometimes knock softly, so you truly have to listen. (4) You have to communicate. (5) Everyone like a good, clean environment. (6) Be prompt, don't disrespect other's time. (7) Think success. (8) Feel good about yourself. (9) Make your work fun. (10) Never put off for tomorrow, what you can do today."

Galatians 5:22-23 reads, "But the fruit of the Spirit is love, joy, peace, longsuffering, gentleness, goodness, faith, meekness, temperance: against such there is no law." It has been said that, "Joy is love singing, peace is love resting, patience is love enduring, kindness is love sharing, goodness is love's character, faithfulness is love's habit, gentleness is love's touch, and self-control is love in charge." Forgiveness is one of the key principles that Jesus taught his disciples in what we call the Lord's Prayer. It states, "Our Father, Who art in heaven, hallowed be Thy name. Thy Kingdom come, Thy will be done on earth as it is in heaven. Give us this day our daily bread and forgive us our debts as we forgive our debtors. And lead us not into temptation, but deliver us from evil. For Thine is the kingdom and the power, and the glory forever, Amen." Jesus meant that part about GOD forgiving us as (in the same way as) we forgive others! In fact, right after He taught His disciples that prayer, He said this in Matthew 6:14-15: "For if you forgive men when they sin against you, your heavenly Father will also forgive you. But if you do not forgive men their sins, your Father will not forgive your sins." Jesus' kingdom is all about forgiveness. When you became a Christian that's what it was all about – GOD forgiving your sin. When you believed that Jesus was the Christ, the Son of the Living GOD: when you accepted the idea that you were a sinner and needed to change your life (repent): when you confessed Jesus as your Lord and Master: and when you allowed yourself to be baptized of Christian baptism and risen up to a new life – your sins were all removed. GOD removed them from you as far as the East is from the West. He buried them in the very depths of the sea and promised He would not remember them ever again. Jesus shed his blood so that our sins would be forgiven. His blood covered ALL our sins, and GOD remembered them no more. Now, as servants of the most High GOD, He calls on us to do the same to those who have sinned against us. Ephesians 4:32 tells us to "Be kind and compassionate to one another, forgiving each other, just as in Christ GOD forgave you." (NIV)

After being incarcerated for 27 years, Nelson Mandela was released in 1990. He served as President of South Africa from 1994 to 1999. One of the most memorable quotes that Mandela often said was, "Our deepest fear is not that we are inadequate. Our deepest fear is that we are powerful beyond measure. It is our light, not our darkness that frightens us most. We ask ourselves, 'Who am I to be brilliant, gorgeous, talented, and famous?' Actually, who are you not to be? You are a child of GOD. Your playing small does not serve the world. There is nothing enlightened about shrinking so that people won't feel insecure around you. We were born to make manifest the glory of GOD that is within us. It's not just in some of us: it's in all of us. And when we let our own light shine, we unconsciously give other people permission to do the same. As we are liberated from our own fear, our presence automatically liberates others." My advice to every person I come in contact with personally or through e-mails is, "Never give up on those dreams and don't be complacent about pursuing what GOD has placed in your heart. No matter how long it's been, no matter how impossible things looks, if you'll stay in faith, believe in GOD and wait on Him, your appointed time for your abundant blessings will arrive. GOD is never a second late but His time may differ from your time! GOD placed that dream and vision into your heart and if it's His will, He will bring it to pass. So hold on to that vision today and declare that my time is coming. I know that GOD is working on my behalf and I will fulfill my divine destiny!"

Let's pray: Lord, direct my steps each day and continue to lead me home to dwell with You eternally. Help me to walk in Your perfect will in order to have what You want me to have and do what You want me to do. Forgive me of my sins and give me Your favor as I get closer to my Heavenly Home. Almighty GOD, Our Lord and Savior, thank you for Your truths today. I receive Your promises in Your Word and I believe my best days are ahead. I feel You working out my situations and I know victory is mine. I will continue to wait on You and I ask that You clean my heart with Your Holy Spirit so that I can pursue Your perfect plan for my life. Help me to continue to let my light shine so others can see Your good works. Lord, continue to bless my loved ones and contacts. Forgive us of our sins and save the lost. I will forever give You the glory, honor and praise, Amen.

The following letter I received from one of my spiritual contacts brought me encouragement and I hope it does the same for you:

Dear Dave:

It may seem like others around you have no problems. As you look at their lives, you may wonder why things are always so good for them. They seem to move from one great experience to the next, while you're struggling to get by and keep your head above water. From a distance you start thinking things like, it's not fair. Why can't I get a break? When is it going to be my turn? If you've ever had these thoughts, I want to let you in on a little secret. We all face challenges and problems! We all face obstacles that tempt us to be discouraged, to settle for less or to give up hope. But the important thing is what we do when those challenges come our way. With every problem, we have a choice: Will I still believe GOD is a good GOD and that He has great things in store for me, or will I settle for less than GOD's best?

When you face challenges, especially really significant ones, it's easy to slide into survival mode, but we're not supposed to stay there! Even in your most difficult season, there is still opportunity. GOD has given you everything you need to succeed. He wants you to do more than survive: He wants you to THRIVE! I want to encourage you to choose to fill your mind with GOD's promises and His expectations for your life. This is really the key to thriving! Don't let your problems shape your expectations. You can live with confidence knowing that great things are coming your way! This is your moment to BREAKTHROUGH...this is your moment to thrive!

I believe that you can start new and fresh today. Remember, if you've slid into a survival mentality, don't stay there. Go deeper and get planted. It all comes back to a simple choice: believe GOD is who He says He is! We love you and want you to know we're praying for you. Thank you so much for your support of this ministry. Always remember that when you are feeling burdened and overwhelmed by circumstances, continue to trust GOD and know that with GOD, all things are possible. There is no one that can keep you from your destiny: no bad break, no disappointment, no mountain, no illness can stop you from your goal. So keep on hoping, keep on praying and keep moving forward because with the help of GOD, you can handle whatever comes your way!!!

GOD Bless

CHAPTER TWENTY-SIX
The Endgame: New Levels Of Joy

In the last days, the Bible tells us that there will be much turmoil: wars and rumors of wars: humanity showing disrespect and lack of love for each other. My intense Vietnam style firefights with the VA remained the peak of my mental stimulation. It appears that we are in the last days and we are heading fast to self-destruction. 2 Timothy 3:1-17 read, "This know also, that in the last days perilous times shall come. For men shall be lovers of their own selves, covetous, boasters, proud, blasphemers, disobedient to parents, unthankful, unholy, Without natural affection, trucebreakers, false accusers, incontinent, fierce, despisers of those that are good, Traitors, heady, high-minded, lovers of pleasures more than lovers of GOD: Having a form of Godliness, but denying the power thereof: from such turn away. For of this sort are they which creep into houses, and lead captive silly women laden with sins, led away with divers lusts, Ever learning, and never able to come to the knowledge of the truth. Now as Jannes and Jambres withstood Moses, so do these also resist the truth: men of corrupt minds, reprobate concerning the faith. But they shall proceed no further: for their folly shall be manifest unto all men, as theirs also was. But thou hast fully known my doctrine, manner of life, purpose, faith, longsuffering, charity, patience, Persecutions, afflictions, which came unto me at Antioch, at Iconium, at Lystra: what persecutions I endured: but out of them all the Lord delivered me. Yea, and all that will live Godly in Christ Jesus shall suffer persecution. But evil men and seducers shall wax worse and worse, deceiving, and being deceived. But continue thou in the things which thou hast learned and hast been assured of, knowing of whom thou hast learned them:

And that from a child thou hast known the holy scriptures, which are able to make thee wise unto salvation through faith which is in Christ Jesus. All scripture is given by inspiration of GOD, and is profitable for doctrine, for reproof, for correction, for instruction in righteousness: That the man of GOD may be perfect, thoroughly furnished unto all good works."

The Bible provides us with many examples of how GOD will use our suffering for our good and to His glory. Paul went through many hard times in the Bible. In 2 Corinthians 11:24- 27 Paul says, "Of the Jews five times received I forty stripes save one. Thrice was I beaten with rods, once was I stoned, thrice I suffered shipwreck, a night and a day I have been in the deep: In journeys often, in perils of waters, in perils of robbers, in perils by my own countrymen, in perils by the heathen, in perils in the city, in perils in the wilderness, in perils in the sea, in perils among false brothers: In weariness and painfulness, in watchings often, in hunger and thirst, in fastings often, in cold and nakedness."

1 Peter 4:12-16 read, "Beloved, do not be surprised at the fiery trial when it comes upon you to test you, as though something strange were happening to you. But rejoice insofar as you share Christ's sufferings, that you may also rejoice and be glad when his glory is revealed. If you are insulted for the name of Christ, you are blessed, because the Spirit of glory and of GOD rests upon you. But let none of you suffer as a murderer or a thief or an evildoer or as a meddler. Yet if anyone suffers as a Christian, let him not be ashamed, but let him glorify GOD in that name."

Through GOD, we have the power to overcome everything that may cause us to be depressed or feel hurtful. GOD often uses our weaknesses and sufferings as His opportunity to show His strength and also to perform great and mighty things through us. The sickness of Lazarus provided an opportunity for GOD to make His glory known in deeper ways. John 11:4 reads, "When Jesus heard that, he said, This sickness is not unto death, but for the glory of GOD, that the Son of GOD might be glorified thereby." So when going through times of adversities and tribulations, keep persevering, give your best efforts and trust GOD to lead you to victory. GOD can lift you up and give you "Success" whenever He chooses. No matter what, always give GOD the glory for His grace and mercy!!!

Regardless of what has happened in your past, you can come to the conclusion today that the past is behind you. With GOD's grace, a new season of blessings is in your future. Sometimes, what may look like a misfortune is simply GOD positioning you for a better opportunity. GOD is always in control of our lives. Just because your prayer has not been answered today, tomorrow may be your day! Always remember that in order to have a healthy body, mind and soul, we must feed on GOD's Words every day!

The last Christmas card I received from my brother, Dr. Booker T. Williams Jr., before he expired on April 10, 2009, included this poem by an unknown author: He entitled it,

"A CHRISTMAS PRAYER FOR YOU ALL."

I said a Christmas Prayer for you
Because the season's near.
I didn't ask for riches
But for gifts so much more dear.
I asked for joyful gatherings
With your family all around,
And for carols to inspire you
With their old familiar sound.
I asked for quiet moments
In your heart on Christmas morn,
For a special time to celebrate
The Savior who was born.
I asked for friends and family to send their best
That you might know they care and share:
I asked for peace and love and hope,
And I know GOD heard my prayer.

My brother concluded his Christmas greetings by writing, "Always give love, forgiveness and peace. I feel you today and I value your thoughts." His words always brought me a ray of hope! In summation, it has been said that the darkest hour of the day is just before dawn. Continue to lean and depend on GOD, He will smile on you and provide spiritual guidance during your tribulations. A portion of one of the great inspirational hymns by Rev. James Cleveland follows:

GOD HAS SMILED ON ME

"GOD has smiled on me, He has set me free. GOD has smiled on me, He's been good to me. He is the source of all my joy, He fills me with His love. Everything that I need, He sends it down from above."

God loves blessing His children and all He wants us to do is always give Him the glory! It is my desire that throughout this book God will use my words to serve as an appetizer to the readers. I hope God will use my words as a preservative to give a lasting beneficial value to mentally stimulate readers on this earthly journey. Finally, I pray that God will purify my words to assure that they will be rightly received and touched the hearts of unsaved readers. Let's pray: Thank you Lord for always being near to provide my needs. May these shared "Reflections" of my life lead lost souls to GOD and the goodness of reading and obeying His Words. Help us to get in Your will and by reading this book, may some wayward children find the path to Your divine destiny for their lives, Amen.

Excerpts from a letter I received on April 7, 2014, from the Department of Veterans Affairs read:

Board of Veterans' Appeals
Washington, DC 20420
Date: 04/03/14
David M. Williams
PO Box 27551
Detroit, MI 48227

Dear Appellant:

The Board of Veterans Appeals (Board) has received your Department of Veterans Affairs (VA) claims file, and your appeal has been returned to the Boards docket. Since your appeal was previously remanded for additional development by the originating agency, we will expedite action on your case. Although we will make every effort to decide your appeal as quickly as possible, the time needed to render a decision can vary depending on a number of factors, including the complexity of the appeal, whether a hearing was requested, whether there is a question regarding the status of representation, and whether further evidentiary development is required. Please be assured that your case will be acted upon as expeditiously as practicable.

The Board has employees available to answer questions about the status of your appeal. Please feel free to contact us at (800) 923-8387. The Board's hours of operation are 8:00 a.m. to 4:30 P.M., Eastern time, Monday through Friday. Any questions about factual or legal matters involved in your appeal should be directed to your representative, if you have one.

Sincerely yours,
Bruce P. Gipe
Director, Office of Management, Planning and Analysis

This was surreal!!!! It was as though the VA was wishing me a Happy Birthday for April 3rd was my birthday. After reading this letter I felt resurrected and I affirmatively declare to each of you to, "Be encouraged today because GOD is working behind the scenes on your behalf to solve your problems. Delight yourself in Him — find joy in serving Him and make your heart moldable in His hands. Don't settle for mediocrity because GOD knows what's in you and His plan is to finish the work He began in you when you delight yourself in Him! GOD always wants your best and you can rest assured that GOD has His best blessing for you on the way!!"

Psalm 37:4-5 read, "Delight yourself also in the Lord, and He will give you the desires and secret petitions of your heart. Commit your way to the Lord [roll and repose each care of your load on Him]: trust (lean on, rely on, and be confident) also in Him and He will bring it to pass." (AMP)

Throughout this book, I have tried to demonstrate that GOD is awesome and He is always working behind the scenes for our good. He wants to bless all His children abundantly. So attach your hand to His hand and receive GOD's best. GOD wants us to always think positive, obey His Words and tell Him our needs through prayer. Romans 4:17 says in part, "calleth those things which be not as though they were." Job 42:10 - 16 read, "And the LORD turned the captivity of Job, when he prayed for his friends: also the LORD gave Job twice as much as he had before. Then came there unto him all his brethren, and all his sisters, and all they that had been of his acquaintance before, and did eat bread with him in his house: and they bemoaned him, and comforted him over all the evil that the LORD had brought upon him: every man also gave him a piece of money, and everyone an earring of gold. So the LORD blessed the latter end of Job more than his beginning: for he had fourteen thousand sheep, and six thousand camels, and a thousand yoke of oxen, and a thousand she asses. He had also seven sons and three daughters. And he called the name of the first, Jemima: and the name of the second, Kezia: and the name of the third, Kerenhappuch. And in all the land were no women found so fair as the daughters of Job: and their father gave them inheritance among their brethren. After this lived Job an hundred and forty years, and saw his sons, and his sons' sons, even four generations."

I'm humble and grateful that GOD allowed me to be the vessel to write this book and "All The Glory Goes To GOD." Below is a portion of a letter that was sent to VA director, General Eric Shinseki and his resignation letter below was my only response. His resignation letter was received by e-mail on 5-31-14 from one of my contacts!!!

"Top Aide Says Obama is 'Madder than Hell' about VA Scandal" — 5-18-14

AP- White House Chief of Staff Denis McDonough says President Obama is very upset about reported cover-ups at veterans' hospitals and long waits for treatment at VA facilities that have drawn widespread scrutiny. "The president is madder than hell. I've got the scars to prove it," McDonough said in an interview with CBS News' "Face The Nation" that was broadcast Sunday. In testimony on Capitol Hill last week, Veterans Affairs Secretary Eric K. Shinseki said he was "mad as hell" about reported problems with the VA, including allegations that clinics in Phoenix and Fort Collins, Colo., schemed to conceal the records of patients who endured long waits for treatment. "We have seen obviously the reports out of places like Phoenix and Fort Collins and North Carolina, and we're going to get to the bottom of those things, fix them and ensure that they don't happen again," McDonough said. He also defended Shinseki." General Shinseki continues to work this every single day," McDonough said, "and he will continue to work these issues until they're fixed."

David M. Williams
PO Box 27551
Detroit, MI 48227
January 13, 2014
Office of Secretary of Veterans Affairs

General Eric Shinseki, Director
810 Vermont Ave. NW
Washington, DC 20420

Dear Director Shinseki:

Please peruse the letter to President Obama and the letter I sent to NCC PAC regarding their illegal deduction from my disability check. I believe VARO and NCC are harassing and discriminating against me illegally. I have called VA billing center several times to no avail. I have left several messages for Mr. Donnelly at 313-471-3913, the VARO employee handling my appeal but he has not returned calls to advise me when my claims will be re-adjudicated. I pray you will intervene on my behalf ASAP.

Sincerely,
David M. Williams
Vietnam Veteran, 25th Infantry Division
Enclosure
David M. Williams
PO Box 27551
Detroit, MI 48227

January 4, 2014

Honorable Barack Obama
1600 Pennsylvania Avenue
Washington, DC 20500

Dear President Obama:

One of our mentors was Senator Ted Kennedy. I got a chance to take a cherished photo with him when he campaigned here in Detroit when Secretary of State, John Kerry, was running for President. He once said, "All of my life, the teachings of my faith have provided solace and hope, as have the wonders of nature, especially the sea: where religion and spirituality meet the physical. This faith has been as meaningful to me as breathing or loving my family. It's all intertwined. My faith and the love of following its rituals, has always been my foundation and my inspiration. These foundations have been shaken at times by tragedy and misfortune, but faith remains fixed in my heart, as it has been since my childhood days. It is the most positive force in my life and the cause of my eternal optimism. I have fallen short in my life, but my faith has always brought me home. Life can be violent and grim, but I think of the Resurrection and I feel a sense of hope. I believe if you have a warm and embracing heart, faith can have a powerful impact on your outlook." Although I have been fighting with the Detroit VARO for over five years, I still have faith and my hope is strong!!!

My case was remanded by BVA on May 30, 2013 for certain actions to be performed. After these actions were completed, BVA ordered that my case be given preferential and expeditious re-adjudication of my claims. This letter is written to request your assistance to end this stalling scheme by VARO. I know you are tired of my letters and if I had any other idea how to get VARO to show justice, I would. Please review the enclosed sampling of over five years of evidence and previous data submitted to you. I humbly pray that you will immediately order Detroit VARO to re-adjudicate my claims. Thank you kindly and may 2014 be a great year for you, your family and administration.

Sincerely,
David M. Williams, Combat Vietnam Veteran

This e-mail was received on Saturday, May 31, 2014: US Department of Veterans Affairs <veteranshealth@public.govdelivery.com> wrote:
This morning, I resigned as Secretary of Veterans Affairs. My personal and professional commitment and my loyalty to Veterans, their families, and our survivors was the driving force behind that decision. That loyalty has never wavered, and it will never wane.

Over the course of the last five-and-a-half years, you have made significant and lasting progress in expanding access for Veterans, in significantly decreasing the backlog in Veterans' claims while building the system that will end the backlog in 2015, and in bringing an end to Veterans' homelessness. We have come a long way together in bringing this Department into the 21st Century in ways that will serve Veterans well into the future. Yet, there is more work to be done, and I have no doubt that you will achieve all that you set about doing in the interest of Veterans.

I have been privileged to have served as your Secretary and am deeply grateful to the employees and leaders who have placed the interests of Veterans above and beyond their own self-interests: who are serving with dignity, compassion, and dedication: and who live by VA's core values of Integrity, Commitment, Advocacy, Respect, and Excellence. I know that you will provide your support and loyalty to Acting Secretary Sloan Gibson, who is now your leader. In fact, I expect it. Thank you. May GOD richly bless all of you, Veterans, and this great country of ours.

Eric K. Shinseki

When you are angry, frustrated, and confused, always turn to GOD. Let Him handle all your situations! Romans 5:1-11 read, "Therefore being justified by faith, we have peace with GOD through our Lord Jesus Christ: By whom also we have access by faith into this grace wherein we stand, and rejoice in hope of the glory of GOD. And not only so, but we glory in tribulations also: knowing that tribulation worketh patience: And patience, experience: and experience, hope: And hope maketh not ashamed: because the love of GOD is shed abroad in our hearts by the Holy Ghost which is given unto us. For when we were yet without strength, in due time Christ died for the ungodly For scarcely for a righteous man will one die: yet peradventure for a good man some would even dare to die. But GOD commandeth his love toward us, in that, while we were yet sinners, Christ died for us. Much more then, being now justified by his blood, we shall be saved from wrath through him. For if, when we were enemies, we were reconciled to GOD by the death of his Son, much more, being reconciled, we shall be saved by his life. And not only so, but we also joy in GOD through our Lord Jesus Christ, by whom we have now received the atonement."

The Holy Spirit provides us with the power for restoration and forgiveness of sins. It is our comforter and guides us to righteous living. It is so very true that the more we obey GOD, the more He will give us His abundant blessings. GOD's mercies are from everlasting to everlasting. Psalm 103:17-18 state, "But the mercy of the Lord is from everlasting to everlasting upon them that fear him, and his righteousness unto children's children: To such as keep his covenant, and to those that remember his commandments to do them." You cannot control what may happen in your life but you can determine that you will face all your challenges boldly and lean totally on GOD. As you maintain a strong faith and GODly attitude, GOD will provide your needs to overcome any adversity that comes your way.

Following is an excerpt from a letter sent to VARO:

September 14, 2014
Detroit VARO
477 Michigan Ave. – 12th Floor
Detroit, MI 48226
Attn: Director David Leonard

Dear Mr. Leonard:

I have studied hard and trained constantly to be in both good physical and mental condition throughout my life. A former mentor once told me and I believed him immensely then and even more today, "If your body is weak and out of shape, your mind will also be the same!" I have fought injustices my entire career since meeting Dr. Martin Luther King Jr. at the age of eight (8). I have always wanted to be successful and pursued a career in social work after Dr. King spoke to a group of church boys in his living room. We, all being 8 to11 years old, formed a church group called "The Crusaders!" I vividly remember, this was the summer of 1955 before the historic Montgomery Bus Boycott. Dr. King said," Always Keep GOD first, try to get a good education and always give something back to your community." When I received my Masters' in Social Work from Wayne State University as an "Honor Graduate," I couldn't help from thinking about Dr. King's advice many years ago on getting a good education!!! I also recall that Dr. King spoke out on the war in Vietnam in 1967. He received many threats and upset many politicians and other leaders in America because of his refusal to remain silent regarding the Vietnam War. He said that, "a time comes when silence is betrayal."

It really hurts my heart to get this type of result from VARO! This is not fair and there is no reason VARO continues to act illegally and disgracefully regarding my claims. "I am one vet who still knows how to fight!!!" VA Secretary, Robert A. McDonald said, "There's no higher calling in life than serving Veterans. I see leadership of VA as an opportunity to improve the lives of men and women I care deeply about." I still believe he will help veterans like me and similarly situated veterans get fairness and justice. We put our lives on the line and over 58,000 soldiers even lost their lives in the Vietnam War. Combat Infantry Soldier, Dave Williams was only spared by the grace of GOD!!!"

Let's pray: Almighty GOD, thank you for bringing me to another level on this journey. I plead Your mercy to help me to continue to trust and obey You as I travel to the end of this earthly domain. As I persevere and try to encourage my brothers and sisters, let Your will be done in and through me. Lord, thank you for my ups and downs on this journey of life. You have led me all the way and I'm much obliged and offer You many thanks. Right now, I ask You to have Your way in my life. Please forgive me of my sins and those who have trespassed against me. Lord, I surrender my all to You today and I know You have made great plans for the rest of my life. Thank you Most Kind Master for blessing me from my early existence to this moment. You have been so good to me and I will forever give You the glory and praise. I submit everything to You and I stand firmly on Your Words in 1 Peter 5:6-7, "Humble yourselves therefore under the mighty hand of GOD, that he may exalt you in due time: Casting all your care upon him: for he careth for you." O Merciful Father, thank you for leading me into a place of rest and peace today. I surrender my brokenness to You and open my heart to receive Your healing and favor. Lord, have mercy on the sick and those who are grieving the loss of a loved one today. Soothe their heartaches and pain and let them know You are with them. Jesus, I ask at this moment that You will touch our hearts and minds and help us to get in Your will and let You handle every situation. Help us to read and obey Your Words and receive Your power to navigate the rest of this earthly journey. We ask these and other blessings in Jesus' Name, Amen.

* It is often said that "Confidence comes not from always being right but from not fearing to be wrong." God Always Has Ideas And Dreams For His Children To Achieve.

The following is a poem called "If," written in 1895 by British Nobel laureate Rudyard Kipling:

If you can keep your head when all about you are losing theirs and blaming it on you: If you can trust yourself when all men doubt you, but make allowance for their doubting too: If you can wait and not be tired by waiting, or, being lied about, don't deal in lies, or being hated don't give way to hating, and yet don't look too good, nor talk too wise:

If you can dream—-and not make dreams your master: if you can think—-and not make thoughts your aim, if you can meet with Triumph and Disaster and treat those two impostors just the same: if you can bear to hear the truth you've spoken, twisted by knaves (dishonest persons) to make a trap for fools, or watch the things you gave your life to, broken, and stoop and build'em up with worn-out tools:

If you can make one heap of all your winnings and risk it on one turn of pitch-and-toss, and lose, and start again at your beginnings, and never breathe a word about your loss: if you can force your heart and nerve and sinew to serve your turn long after they are gone, and so hold on when there is nothing in you except the will which says to them: "Hold on!"

If you can talk with crowds and keep your virtue, or walk with Kings—-nor lose the common touch, if neither foes nor loving friends can hurt you, if all men count with you, but none too much: if you can fill the unforgiving minute with sixty seconds' worth of distance run, yours is the Earth and everything that's in it, and—-which is more—-you'll be a Man, my son!"

Our destiny and reason for living are wrapped up tightly in our dreams, ideas and desires. God designed every member of the human race to have dreams. Yes, God is the source of all our dreams. Every person must come to Jesus for his or her dream to make sense. In fact, without Jesus, you might follow a dream for your life that God never put in your heart. Jesus said in John15:15, "I am the vine: you are the branches. If you remain in me and I in you, you will bear much fruit: apart from me you can do nothing." (NIV) God always has ideas and dreams for His children to achieve. If we pray and listen to Him with a heart that is thankful, God's revelation of these dreams will be manifested to us. Always follow the Bible's advice as recorded in John 2:5, "His mother saith unto the servants, Whatsoever he saith unto you, do it." (KJV) The power, energy and creativity needed to fulfill our dreams must flow from Jesus.

One of the crucial question an individual may want answered is, "How do I know which dreams in my heart are from God?" Here is the answer. You will know it's God's dream if:

1. It is bigger than you.
2. You can't let it go.
3. You would be willing to give everything for it.
4. It will last forever.
5. It meets a need nobody else has met.
6. It brings glory to God.

When we give GOD our best, He will always return the favor! There is nothing in this world like GOD's wisdom. Today, without hesitation, if you haven't, turn everything over to GOD. Let GOD restore your spirit, body and soul. Pastor Jamal Harrison Bryant, a Morehouse man, great orator and the Shepherd at New Birth Missionary Baptist Church in Metro Atlanta, said on a visit to Detroit in 2014: "Although Detroit is in Bankruptcy Court, GOD is going to abundantly bless this city." He also gave an unforgettable spiritual formula for GOD's children which is: "Imagination + Articulation = Manifestation." This means that when GOD gives us an idea, if we believe in our heart that we have a worthy dream/idea, we can articulate to GOD to confirm and we may share with an unselfish, spiritual believer, if it is in GOD's will, He empowers you to make this idea a manifestation. Another way of saying this formula is, "Through the power of imagination, I envision my dreams unfolding. I cultivate my dreams in my consciousness and activate my plans for divine manifestation."

Finally, we must always try to share love with everyone we have contact with on life's journey. We are all GOD's children and deserve respect. We are mandated to love GOD and love our sisters and brothers. Matthew 26:22-40 exclaim, "Master, which is the great commandment in the law? Jesus said unto him, Thou shalt love the Lord thy GOD with all thy heart, and with all thy soul, and with all thy mind. This is the first and great commandment. And the second is like unto it, Thou shalt love thy neighbour as thyself. On these two commandments hang all the law and the prophets." A few words of encouragement may save a lost soul from their evil ways. Without a shadow of doubt, I fervently believe that when you have trials or reach "Rock Bottom," if you hold on to GOD's hand, He will allow you to have His Favor and rebound to have "Success!!!"

In order to overcome the adversities and trials that may come your way on this earthly journey of life, you have to trust GOD and persevere. No one is promised a bed of roses as you navigate your journey of life. I learned this thoroughly from my first arrest at age 15 during the Civil Rights Movement with Dr. Martin Luther King Jr.: Great cultural lessons were learned from the Detroit Riots of 1967: Another cumbersome memory was the expulsion from college for allegedly being part of a group trying to incite a riot in 1968 after Dr. King's assassination: This expulsion caused me to be drafted into the Army in 1969 and sent to Vietnam: A 30-day stay in the hospital for malaria in Vietnam had a blessed message and helped me to get an early exit from Vietnam: A surprising and hurtful divorce in 1980 taught me costly lessons: Termination from my first job after graduate school was quite unfair but gave me many creative dreams afterwards. Throughout the many difficulties I faced on this journey, I have never given up on GOD and He always has been near to rescue me before I drowned!

The Bible states in Psalm 118:8 that, "It is better to trust in the LORD than to put confidence in man." When you put your trust in people, they oftentimes will fail you. However, when you put your trust in GOD, the One who created you, who knows you and who cares about, you can totally depend on Him. GOD will never let you down. The Bible also tells us in Proverbs 18:24 that there is a friend that sticks closer to you than a brother. That friend is Jesus. He is the very lover of your soul. He loved us so much that He willingly came down from His glorious throne in heaven to live and then die so that we might live again with Him. He now is in heaven interceding before GOD the Father on our behalf. Now, that's someone that you can really trust. If you have a need, Jesus says that all you must do is "Ask, and it will be given to you." (Matthew 7:7) But, there is a stipulation on the matter. When you ask, you must trust GOD to do what you ask. This is noted in Matthew 21:22. "And whatever things you ask in prayer, believing, you will receive." Sometimes it is not easy to trust GOD. When things seem to be going wrong, when people let you down, when you're hurting, when your finances are not good, when you or someone you love is sick, or when various trials and problems come your way, it can be difficult to trust GOD to take care of things. But in order to get through this life here on earth, we must trust GOD. We must have faith in the One who knows all and who wants to take care of our every need. So, what can we do to increase our faith so that we can trust Him? Romans 10:17 tells us that faith comes by hearing the Word of GOD. If you are having problems trusting GOD pray often and every day you need to read GOD's Words and learn more about Him.

The following letter was sent to President Obama prayerfully again requesting his intervention to get Detroit's VARO to act expeditiously:

Personal and Confidential
David M. Williams - Claim #26446226
PO Box 27551
Detroit, MI 48227
October 13, 2014

Honorable Barack Obama
1600 Pennsylvania Avenue

Washington, DC 20500
Dear President Obama:

Please read the enclosed letter that was sent to VA Secretary Robert A. McDonald on September 7, 2014. Detroit's VARO Director David Leonard received a second remand order from the Board of Veterans' Appeals (BVA) in July, 2014 and had appointment scheduled for me with Dr. Suganthini Krishnan-Natesan on August 27, 2014. Dr. Natesan is an internal medicine and infectious disease physician. I kept this appointment and Dr. Natesan submitted Director Leonard her response before September 4, 2014. As of today, my claims have not been approved and I have not received a SSOC notice. In his remand order, BVA Judge ordered my claims to be adjudicated expeditiously or sent back to BVA for a decision. Seven years of fighting for deserved benefits is long enough!!! I am being grossly mistreated and humbly request your immediate intervention to end this nightmare! Thank you kindly for your prompt and positive consideration.

Sincerely,
David M. Williams, Vietnam Veteran - 25th Infantry Division
Enclosure – Copy of Letter to VA Secretary Robert A. McDonald"

On Friday, January 2, 2015, I received the following from the Office of Senator Stabenow:

United States Senator Debbie Stabenow - Michigan

Dear David,

I am writing to update you on the status of your inquiry about resolution of your remanded appeal. Recently, I received an interim response from Department of Veterans Affairs stating they have received my inquiry and are in the process of reviewing your case. As soon as I receive a final determination, I will let you know.

I hope this information is helpful. If you have questions or concerns, please contact JoAnn Papenfuss in my Northern Michigan Office at 231-929-1031.

Sincerely,
https://outreach.senate.gov/iqextranet/Customers/quorum_stabenow-iq/dssign-debbie.gif
Debbie Stabenow
United States Senator

It's 4:56 A.M. on May 2, 2015 and I heard GOD's voice saying, "Get Up and Listen!" The following is part of the message I received. Yes, it appears that the world is in uproar. Wars and rumors of wars: Over 6,000 deaths so far known from earthquake on April 25, 2015 in Nepal, a city in the Himalayan foothills: Rioting started April 27, 2015 in Baltimore, Maryland because of the murder of a Black young man, Freddie Gray, where 6 police officers were charged: On April 28, 2015 the Supreme Court heard oral arguments on gay marriage: global warming debate continues and on and on... GOD is still in charge and wants us to seek Him while we still have a chance. When you are blessed, it is your duty to become a blessing to my children. The following appeared in an e-mail sent to some of my contacts on April 25, 2015.

* ALWAYS FILL YOUR MIND WITH THE WORD OF GOD.

"Let's pray: Lord, thank you for touching my heart today. Father, thank you for opening doors for me that no one can close and telling me my victory is on the way!!! I know that You are faithful and You are a rewarder of those who diligently seek You. Fill us with Your peace, joy and favor as we seek You daily. Help us to always lean and depend totally on You. I hear Your voice saying fear not, obey Me, and give You the glory and You will meet all our needs. Help us to listen to You more deeply, obey You more readily, and glorify You more fully. Let us no longer be afraid to reach out and touch another life with Your love and grace. Lord, encourage us, like You did Your Disciples, to follow Your will and be a blessing to Your children. Thank you Lord for restoring

hope in our lives and peace to our minds. You are our Savior and Our awesome
GOD. We offer this prayer in the Name of Jesus, Amen.

Baltazar Gracian was a Spanish Jesuit and baroque prose writer and phi-
losopher. Gracian was the son of a doctor but in his childhood lived with his
uncle, who was a priest. He assumed the vows of the Jesuits in 1633 and dedicated himself to teaching in various Jesuit schools. He acquired fame as a
preacher and one of his noted quotes stated, "True friendship multiplies the
good in life and divides its evils. Strive to have friends, for life without friends
is like life on a desert island... to find one real friend in a lifetime is good fortune: to keep him is a blessing."

Colossians 3:2 reads, "Set your minds on things above, not on earthly things."
(NIV) On our earthly journey, GOD warns that we will have trials and tribulations. The good news is that He also promises to deliver us from them all! Now,
He doesn't say that He will deliver us instantly, or the way we expect, or on our
schedule. It is easy to get discouraged when things don't happen when we want
them to happen or the way we had hoped they would. But when you feel like
trouble is surrounding you, that's when you have to dig your heels in and say,
Lord I'm depending on You!!! GOD is a good GOD and He is always on time!
GOD wants You to be abundantly blessed. He wants you strong in order for you
to help His children. It doesn't matter what's happening in the world around you,
GOD's Word is always true. He wants you to always fill your mind with the Word
of GOD. Let His truth empower you because His ways are always higher than
our ways. You may be discouraged at this moment but GOD is working behind
the scenes on your behalf to make your dream become a reality!!!

GOD loves us so much that He will meet all our needs and some of our
desires if they are in His will. 1 Chronicles 16:34 exclaims, "Oh, give thanks
to the Lord, for He is good! For His mercy endures forever." Sometimes we
make mistakes or sin on our daily walk but GOD kindly forgives and offers
His grace and mercy. Whatever our preordained assignment is or whatever
we may attempt to do on this earthly journey, it will not be a "Success" without
GOD's help and His intervention."

My VA appeal was again sent to the Board of Appeals in Washington, DC
on April 16, 2015. Doing this period of hand-to-hand combat with the VA, I
often have to remind myself that, "The darkest hour of the day is just before
dawn. Just continue to lean and depend on GOD, He will deliver your break-

through on time. GOD is never a second late!!!" About 12:00 noon, GOD brought me spiritual encouragement when I received the following e-mail from The White House:

May 1, 2015

Dear Mr. Williams:

Thank you for writing to President Obama. The President appreciates your taking the time to share your views and concerns. We received your correspondence and forwarded your information to the appropriate agency for further review. You may also find assistance by visiting www.USA.gov or calling 1-800-FED-INFO.

Sincerely,
The Office of Presidential Correspondence

I was denied my benefits by BVA and representing myself, I filed my appeal to the United States Court Of Appeals For Veterans Claims (CAVC) which was docketed on November 20, 2015. According to instructions for self-represented appellants notice received on December 11, 2015, I was told that my appeal may be better presented if I was represented by an attorney. CAVC instructions said, "When we docketed your appeal, we put your name and address on our Internet web site, so lawyers may write you offering to represent you." I received about 20 letters from attorneys and the following solicitation letter convinced me to hire an attorney ASAP!

12-11-15

Dear Mr. Williams:

The U.S. Court of Appeals for Veterans Claims' docket sheet indicates that you have filed an appeal and that you are proceeding with your appeal at this time pro se, that is, without legal representation. I wish to introduce myself to you in this regard.

I am a former VA attorney, having been both Associate Counsel at the Board of Veterans' Appeals in Washington, DC (writing appellate decisions for signature by a Veterans Law Judge, the same type of decisions on appeal to the Court) and a Rating Veterans Service Representative, a Rating Board Member, writing and signing my own rating decisions at the Wichita, Kansas VA regional office. Given this extensive experience, I know veterans benefits law, and I truly seek to "put veterans first." I am also an Army brat. My father is retired career military, a Command Sergeant Major.

VA's Office of General Counsel represents Secretary McDonald with respect to your appeal. Since VA has an attorney fighting against you, you should have an attorney fighting for you, particularly one who comes from inside VA, understands how VA and the Court 'think,' and is committed to providing personal, hands-on attention to your appeal. Given this commitment to excellence, I take only a limited number of cases out of thousands of appeals filed each year, which means that I give you and your appeal the focused attention required in this situation. You will always get me, not some assistant or associate, and that's something a big law firm just cannot provide. You're not just another case to me.

If you would like to discuss your appeal and the possibility of my representing you in this matter before the Court, and maybe even back before VA, please call me at the phone number listed above. I take appeals from all across America. Rest assured that there is no charge to you, no legal fee, just to chat about your appeal. I look forward to hearing from you. I hope we speak soon."

Again, I thanked God and said, "Father, You said the path of the righteous gets brighter and brighter. You said no good thing will You withhold because I walk uprightly before You. I still believe that because I delight myself in You, You will give me the secret petitions of my heart. Thank you Lord for being in control of my life, Amen." Although this process was continuing to be tedious, I kept my faith in God strong and I remain prayerful that my victory was coming.

Luke 14:33 reads, "In the same way, those of you who do not give up everything you have cannot be my disciples." (NIV) In my opinion, one of the greatest hymns of invitation to surrendering your life to GOD or church membership is called, I Surrender All written by Judson DeVenter in 1896. The song in its entirety follows:

> All to Jesus I surrender: All to Him I freely give: I will ever love and trust Him,
>
> In His presence daily live.
>
> Refrain: I surrender all, I surrender all: All to Thee, my blessed Savior, I surrender all.
>
> All to Jesus I surrender: Humbly at His feet I bow, Worldly pleasures all forsaken:
>
> Take me, Jesus, take me now.
>
> All to Jesus I surrender: Make me, Savior, wholly Thine: Let me feel the Holy Spirit,
>
> Truly know that Thou art mine.
>
> All to Jesus I surrender: Lord, I give myself to Thee: Fill me with Thy love and power:
>
> Let Thy blessing fall on me.
>
> All to Jesus I surrender: Now I feel the sacred flame. Oh, the joy of full salvation!
>
> Glory, glory, to His Name!

I believe, at this moment in time is a good time for us to invest in eternity. Without question, divine connection is of more value than any amount of money. Money can't provide total happiness or freedom from illness. With GOD's grace and guidance, "Success" is imminent. It is my prayer that you will agree to abide in Jesus and help make a difference in the spiritual lives of others. When GOD is first in your life, He works behind the scenes on your behalf. He orders our steps and prepares the right breaks on our journey of life. Psalm 18:30 states, "As for GOD, His way is perfect: The word of the Lord is proven: He is a shield to all who trust in Him." So try to think on positive things daily. Things that will build you up and encourage you. Things that will give you more hope and faith in GOD. Then, you will find dreams of a better tomorrow and your best days will soon arrive in GOD's timing. I admonish you today to stay in faith and keep trusting in GOD.

CHAPTER TWENTY-SEVEN
My Final Thoughts

As I reflect today in this New Year of 2016, I thank GOD again for my mother who is deceased, and mothers around the world. Mothers are "GOD's Most Precious Gifts!" Dr. Creigs Beverly, my former professor at Wayne State University School of Social Work stated in the Foreword to this book, "When David asked me to write the Foreword to his book, I was at first reluctant to do so. My reluctance to do so was based on the passage of so many years when our lives never crossed. I therefore felt that I couldn't do justice to his book. Decades had passed since I had seen him. At that moment the realization hit me that time and distance from a person are not nearly as important as the foundation established when first you met." Let's never forget, "The lessons learned in your past and the people who helped you. They are always a part of your future!"

Regardless of our race/ethnicity, gender, socioeconomic status or our situational issue, GOD is always ready to meet our needs. When we spend daily time in GOD's Words and obey Him, we get closer to GOD. His Holy Spirit transforms our lives. We view our lives differently. We think and act with more peace and love with our contacts. The closer we get to GOD, the easier the road to "Success" becomes! Jesus said in John 15:5, "Apart from me you can do nothing." One of the underlying messages of this book is to have GOD's faith filled Words bring you encouragement to help you achieve your preordained destiny and become a "Success." I fervently believe that our greatest source of wealth evolves from our relationship with GOD. The wonderful truth is, GOD blesses those who walk in faith and believe in Him for victory. GOD always shows favor to those who strive to help the least of our society. I love to read the history of people who give their all to make this a better world.

To me, being a blessing to others is one of the most important spiritual principles on this journey of life. The ultimate challenge and value of a man's life is what he leaves for posterity. It bears repeating that any communication that I received from President Obama brought me not only mental stimulation but spiritual enlightenment and personal encouragement. On June 8, 2015, the following e-mail was received from President Obama with Senator Edward Kennedy's letter attached:

The White House
Washington

On a day in early September of 2009, I received the following letter from Senator Edward Kennedy. He'd written in May of that year, shortly after he learned that his illness was terminal. He asked that it be delivered to me upon his death. It is a letter about the cause of his career—what he called "that great unfinished business of our society"—health care reform. "What we face," he writes, "is above all a moral issue: that at stake are not just the details of policy, but fundamental principles of social justice and the character of our country."

Senator Kennedy never stopped asking what he could do for his country. Today, tens of millions of Americans are better for it. And while Teddy didn't live to see his life's work signed into law, more than five years after its passage, the spirit of his words ring true. This is, fundamentally, about the character of our country. Doing right by one another. It's who we are.

Tomorrow, I will deliver remarks about health care in America. Get a history of where we've been, and let me know you'll be watching.

Thank you,
President Barack Obama

Edward Kennedy
Massachusetts
United States Senate
Washington, DC 20510-2101
May 12, 2009

Dear Mr. President,

I wanted to write a few final words to you to express my gratitude for your repeated personal kindness to me – and one last time, to salute your leadership in giving our country back its future and its truth. On a personal level, you and Michelle reached out to Vicki, to our family and me in so many different ways. You helped to make these difficult months a happy time in my life. You also made it a time of hope for me and for our country.

When I thought of all the years, all the battles, and all the memories of my long public life, I felt confident in these closing days that while I will not be there when it happens, you will be the President who at long last signs into law the health care reform that is the great unfinished business of our society. For me, this cause stretched across decades: it has been disappointed, but never finally defeated. It was the cause of my life. And in the past year, the prospect of victory sustained me—and the work of achieving it summoned my energy and determination.

There will be struggles—there always have been—and they are already underway again. But as we move forward in these months, I learned that you will not yield to calls to retreat—that you will stay with the cause until it is won. I saw your conviction that the time is now and witnessed your unwavering commitment and understanding that health care is a decisive issue for our future prosperity. But you also reminded all of us that it concerns more than material things: that what we face is above all a moral issue: that at stake are not just the details of policy, but fundamental principles of social justice and the character of our country.

And so because of your vision and resolve, I came to believe that soon, very soon, affordable health coverage will be available to all, in an America where the state of a family's health will never again depend on the amount of a family's wealth. And while I will not see the victory, I was able to look forward and know that we will—fulfill the promise of health care in America as a right and not a privilege.

In closing, let me say again how proud I was to be part of your campaign – and proud as well to play a part in the early months of a new era of high purpose and achievement. I entered public life with a young President who inspired a generation and the world. It gives me great hope that as I leave another young President inspires another generation and once more on America's behalf inspires the entire world. At the Denver Convention where you were nominated, I said the dream lives on. And I finished this letter with unshakable faith that the dream will be fulfilled for this generation, and preserved and enlarged for generations to come.

With deep respect and abiding affection."

*WORDS OF ENCOURAGEMENT FOR 2016

Over the last six months, my weight has gone from 255 pounds to 225 pounds. I am so proud and thankful that I set a goal and God helped me to achieve it. Now I must admit, it was not difficult after the first couple of weeks. I walked a 20-minute mile 4 times a week. I began to eat more vegetables, fruits and mostly baked foods in small portions. I tried to drink at least 32 ounces of water daily and ate nothing after 7:30 pm unless it was a banana. The hard part is now, keeping the lost weight off! I truly believe that if we trust God in everything, He will make the desires of our heart a reality. Today, I'm requesting that you join with me and submit that problem, that situation or that challenge over to God that you want solved for Him to handle. He has been waiting on you to bring your desires to Him for His intervention. He can and will meet all your needs.

Psalm 57:1-3 read, "Be merciful unto me, O GOD, be merciful unto me: for my soul trusteth in thee: yea, in the shadow of thy wings will I make my refuge, until these calamities be overpast. I will cry unto GOD most high: unto GOD that performeth all things for me. He shall send from heaven, and save me from the reproach of him that would swallow me up. Selah. GOD shall send forth his mercy and his truth."

Pastor Joel Osteen said, "Going through tough times, you don't know what God may be preparing you for. God challenges you to help you grow. Know that God would not have allowed a challenge to happen if He did not plan for something good to come from it. It may be ten years before you realize the benefit that God provided.

Your attitude has a great impact on whether you move forward on God's path or stay put. Don't go around complaining, 'God, why am I always getting these bad breaks?' instead, stay in faith. Just say, 'God, I know You're in complete control of my life. And no matter how tempted I am to be disappointed, I will not be a victim.' I will not be negative, blaming other people. I know You've got me in the palm of Your hand. And I believe one day I will look out and see how this all turned out for my benefit."

OUR PRAYER

Oh Merciful Father, we come into Your presence with worship, adoration and surrender. You are an Awesome God and make sense of all our concerns. You have the answer to all our circumstances and You want to bless the lives of all Your children. Almighty God, give us Your wisdom to make the correct decisions throughout 2016. Right now Lord, we ask You to have mercy on us. Give us more love, joy and peace throughout our world. Help us to keep You first in our lives and study Your Words daily. Right now, we vow that no matter what may happen from day to day, we will obey and trust You Lord. We know the battle belongs to You. We believe You will give us total victory over every situation we may face this year and the rest of this earthly journey. Give us Your favor and keep us in the palm of Your hand. In Jesus' Name we offer this prayer, Amen.

As I conclude these "Reflections," I fervently testify that there is power in the illuminating Words of GOD. As it is often said, the past cannot be erased and we should not allow our past to poison our current situation nor our future. GOD is still in control and if you keep your faith in Him, GOD will take that negative situation, turn it around, and use it for your advantage. It pays great dividends to always trust and obey GOD. John 15:5 -7 state, "I am the vine, ye are the branches: He that abideth in me, and I in him, the same bringeth forth much fruit: for without me ye can do nothing. If a man abide not in me, he is cast forth as a branch, and is withered: and men gather them, and cast them into the fire, and they are burned. If ye abide in me, and my words abide in you, ye shall ask what ye will, and it shall be done unto you."

Without question, I feel certain when you finish reading these "Divine Words" given to me by GOD to share with His children, you will go forth having more faith in GOD and sharing copies of *How To Pull Yourself Up From Rock Bottom To Success* with your relatives and contacts!" In my humble opinion, this book will be a great gift for any occasion!!! It paints an accurate picture of GOD's love for each of us. GOD's unconditional love always lead us to victory. GOD is an awesome GOD and He can do amazing things beyond our highest expectations. As I complete this book, I praise GOD and exclaim, "Hallelujah, Hallelujah, Thank you Lord For Your Blessings!" I testify today, as always, GOD hears His children's prayers and brings abundant blessings (Success) in His timing!!! Yes, GOD uses a single moment to transform lives for the better!! GOD is always working, even when we have no idea what He's doing. He loves to bless us with His amazing, awe-inspiring goodness, even when we least expect it, or when things don't seem to be going the right way. I proclaim and decree "Success" is on the way for you: Amen, Amen, and Thank you Lord!!!

THE FINAL WORD!

Always remember to never think that Satan, negative people who you come in contact with on life's journey or any adversity can stop you from achieving "Success!" GOD is always good and He will help us to triumph. As is recorded in 2 Corinthians 2:14, "Now thanks be unto GOD, which always causeth us to triumph in Christ, and maketh manifest the savour of his knowledge by us in every place." So, my brothers and sisters, hold on to your dreams, keep praying daily and stay in the will of GOD. He will give you those things you believingly ask for in your prayers. You may ask, "Dave, how do you know this is true?" I am glad you asked: "If He did it for me, He'll do it for you. Yes, it's a fact, GOD Brought Me Up From Rock Bottom To Success!"

In my opinion, good documentation and creativity are the first ingredients to writing a high quality book. After you have gotten your thoughts and ideas organized, you then formulate your plan and then it's go time to beginning chapter 1!!! Give your best efforts and always trust GOD to do what you can't! On this Memorial Day, May 25, 2015, I have thoughts of my bout with Malaria in Vietnam and I prayerfully remember deceased loved ones and contacts. I thank GOD for covering me in Nam and for the shoulders of contacts I now stand who guided me in truth over the years. GOD's Word is truth and learning to face truth in every situation is the road to victory. It was their love, wisdom and encouragement that helped me to stretch my faith and become the vessel GOD preordained. I will always cherish their memories and my comrades who made the ultimate sacrifice in uniform. My VA benefits continued to be denied by BVA. After VA scandal was disclosed that immensely troubled President Obama, a new VA Secretary Robert McDonald was appointed. The battle changed course when on November 19 2015, I appealed my case to the U.S. Court of Appeals for Veterans Claims. About 25 veterans' attorneys from across the U.S. contacted me to represent me in the Veterans' Appeal Court. I hired law firm which I was led by the Holy Spirit to trust. I felt relieved and my faith was increased. I declared again that I am a living witness that GOD always win every battle and sometimes gives us "Double For Our Trouble!!"

On May 2, 2016 the following was received from my attorney regarding my appeal to the U.S. Court of Appeals for Veterans Claims:

Mr. Williams,

Per your request, attached find the assessment memo I have prepared for the settlement conference to take place on May 16, 2016. The memo succinctly covers the most important arguments I believe VA made in developing your case. I will be in touch to discuss the status of your case and can go through these arguments in detail after that conference. Again, please keep this memo confidential and do not share with anyone at this time.

On May 6, 2016, I sent the following letter (minus exhibits) to my attorney by US Mail:

Dear Attorney:

The memory of Detroit VARO lying acts, deliberate deception and protracted stalling tactics weigh heavy on my heart and mind today! I was unable to sleep at all last night. I was led by God to write these final words to you about 3:00am. I vividly remember a 2nd Lieutenant telling my platoon before we departed for Vietnam, "Never leave a stone unturned and always stay focused on your objective. Be a critical thinking soldier, then victory and your return home alive are inevitable!!!" To have read the enclosed documents regarding my clinical records denied by VA numerous times, still caused me to be depressive and hurtful. I believe this and other acts by VA/BVA may be criminal and acts of malfeasance which is defined as "The performance by a public official of an act that is legally unjustified, harmful, or contrary to law." (Exhibit 1)

The enclosed portion from remand order dated May 20, 2013 indicated that VA stated, "The examiner ultimately determined that there was no evidence of malaria. Service treatment records do not currently include records from the hospitalization referenced in the August 1970 record." I still wish my near death experience with malaria was a dream! Exhibit 3 is my statement in support of claims dated 12-16-13 which summarize errors of VA/BVA in developing my case and dictate immediate approval of my benefits. Thank you kindly for your comprehensive consideration and may God bless you and your team abundantly in my case and in your future career.

Recently, my PTSD benefits were increased: I pause to offer praise and thanksgiving to my Awesome God. Again, I must repeat that when we have faith and trust in God, we eventually will declare victory and will have "Success" in His timing!!! I fervently believe that God will abundantly blessed me double for my trouble with the VA dishonesty. I want to at this moment thank Dr. Mark Faber at Henry Ford Medical Center in Detroit, Michigan for his medical care. He is a renowned physician but my appreciation is extended also for his allowing me to ventilate my concerns about mistreatment by the VA. This helped me tremendously during a trying time of my life. It is my prayers that God blesses Dr. Faber with a long life to continue to serve His children.

"Success" is intentional, it does not happen by chance. Make sure you ask GOD, "Is this idea or plan I have in Your will?" We begin planning for a successful life during our early childhood growth and development. We learn to make positive steps to reach our preordained destiny from our parents, teachers and childhood mentors. GOD has a good plan for each of His children lives. When we have faith in GOD, study and obey His Words, GOD will guide us to victory and His plan for our lives. GOD loves us and hears our prayers. He is the Master of time and our situations. He wants us to have His best blessings on our earthly journey. The late Aretha Franklin and others made the following song popular, "The Lord Will Make A Way." A couple of lines state: "I know the Lord will make a way, Yes He will. I know the Lord Will make a way, Yes, He will. He'll make a way for you, He will lead you safely through, I know the Lord will make a way, Yes He will." Although I have not been the best father in the world or a renown social worker, I have trusted God and tried to always give my best efforts. Even, when I was homeless and without employment, I never lost hope. God always came to my rescue and provided my needs. I have never fled from challenges and my God has always intervened on my behalf.

After our stay on earth is completed, GOD wants us to have an eternal home with Him! John 3:16 exclaims, "For GOD so loved the world that he gave his one and only Son, that whoever believes in him shall not perish but have eternal life." (NIV)

The following was taken from remarks I gave at the "Homegoing Services" for my mother-in-law, Ms. Patsy Williams in 2005. The Holy Spirit guided me heavily during the writing of these thoughts.

LIFE REFLECTIONS GROM A SON-IN-LAW

Two persons I most admired and had the privilege of meeting in their living room in Montgomery, Alabama were Dr. Martin Luther King Jr. and Ms. Patsy Williams. When I was growing up in Montgomery during the Civil Rights Movement, Black people had to really struggle to make ends meet. I met Ms. Patsy in 1963. From that time until my last visit with her during the 2004 Thanksgiving holidays, I learned a lot from Ms. Patsy. She believed in keeping paramount in her life her faith, her family, and her community. She loved her children, grandchildren, nieces, nephews, sisters, brothers and all her relatives, friends and associates and would help anyone who asked if she could.

What I admired most about her was that she was a hard worker and although a single parent, she provided for her family. They may not have always had the best things in life but Ms. Patsy always kept food in the cabinets and a roof over their heads. She always tried to encourage each of them to pray and trust GOD to meet their every need. Ms. Patsy knew and lived Luke 1:37 - For with GOD nothing shall be impossible. She was prepared for the end because she loved GOD and treated everyone with love and respect. Yes, Ms. Patsy knew Jesus as her personal Savior and I feel certain, the angels in heaven are rejoicing with her right now. Ms. Patsy had great concern about her community and country. She often expressed her opinion to me about how she felt things could be improved. As I continue to fight for justice and equality for African Americans, I will never forget her great humor and the lessons I learned from her.

Many Christians believe and I concur that when we live a devout life, death is our ticket to live with GOD eternally. The New Testament teaches that the resurrection of Jesus is a foundation of the Christian faith. The resurrection established Jesus as the powerful Son of GOD and is cited as proof that GOD will judge the world in righteousness. GOD has given Christians "a new birth into a living hope through the resurrection of Jesus Christ from the dead." Christians, through faith in the working of GOD are spiritually resurrected with Jesus so that they may walk in a new way of life. One minister put it this way, "Each day we have on this earth is a gift from GOD but ultimately everyone has to be prepared to face death and judgment. Through the triumph of the cross and resurrection, Jesus has already dealt with both of those. Unfortunately, multitudes of people who do not know Jesus as their Lord and Savior are putting their hopes in the wrong places. In the secular West, we put our confidence in government and science. We define security in terms of money in the bank. Globally, billions of people blindly follow religions that will never lead them to eternal life."

Dr. Martin Luther King Jr. said, "Every now and then I guess we all think realistically about that day when we will be victimized with what is life's final common denominator — that something we call death. We all think about it.

And every now and then I think about my own death, and I think about my own funeral. And I don't think of it in a morbid sense. Every now and then I ask myself, "What is it that I would want said?" And I leave the word to you this morning. If any of you are around when I have to meet my day, I don't want a long funeral. And if you get somebody to deliver the eulogy, tell them not to talk too long. Every now and then I wonder what I want them to say. Tell them not to mention that I have a Nobel Peace Prize, that isn't important. Tell them not to mention that I have three or four hundred other awards, that's not important. Tell him not to mention where I went to school. I'd like somebody to mention that day, that Martin Luther King, Jr., tried to give his life serving others. I'd like for somebody to say that day, that Martin Luther King, Jr., tried to love somebody. I want you to say that day, that I tried to be right on the war question. I want you to be able to say that day that I did try to feed the hungry. I want you to be able to say that day that I did try in my life to clothe those who were naked. I want you to say, on that day, that I did try, in my life, to visit those who were in prison. I want you to say that I tried to love and serve humanity."

In 1973, Dr. Mary McLeod Bethune was inducted into the National Women's Hall of Fame. In 1974, a sculpture was erected in her honor in Lincoln Park, Washington, D.C. by sculptor Robert Berks. Engraved in the side is a passage from her "Last Will and Testament." It states, "I leave you love. I leave you hope. I leave you the challenge of developing confidence in one another. I leave you a thirst for education. I leave you a respect for the use of power. I leave you faith. I leave you racial dignity. I leave you a desire to live harmoniously with your fellow men. I leave you, finally, a responsibility to our young people." (Please refer to chapter 7 for more information on Dr. Bethune's last will.)

I state again that, "Sooner or later, everyone must exit this life! Lord, we are calling on You right now to help us get prepared for our exit. You have promised that You would never turn away anyone who calls on You. For Your Words say, 'Whoever shall call on the name of the Lord will be saved!' We believe and we are sorry for our unbelief! Save us Lord and forgive us of our sins from this world and prepare us for Your eternal kingdom. In the book of Psalms, David often asked GOD to intensify his awareness of life's fragility. He said in Psalm 39:4- 6: 'Lord, make me to know my end, and to appreciate the measure of my days. Let me know and realize how frail I am – how transient is my stay here. Surely every man walks to and from: each one heaps up riches, not knowing who will gather them.' (AMP) David's increased awareness of his own fragility increased his desire to know GOD, the only Life that is lasting! This confirmed for David the utter uselessness of allowing himself to be in turmoil due to seeking earthly riches. You can be encouraged that life's uncertainty makes us more aware that we will be home with the Lord soon. We must try to understand the positive changes GOD may want us to make in order to have a more fulfilled life. Some things aren't done for you to understand. GOD does not make mistakes. He is always good and His decisions are preordained. Don't fear death! GOD wants you to know that He is standing right by your side. His strength is by you to carry you through your earthly journey. He wants you to know that not only did Jesus die to abolish the power of death, but the power that any fear of death may hold over you as well. His Words explain that Jesus became like us so that, by going through death, He might, 'Make of no effect him who had the power of death, that is, the devil: And also that He might deliver and completely set free all those who through the fear of death were held in bondage throughout the whole course of their lives.' Hebrews 2:14-15

With GOD, death is not a termination, it is a transition, from this earthly life to life with Him which is eternal and will never cease. Death is for the Christian a setting free from the bondages of our physical bodies and the sin of this world. Death gives us the freedom to be with GOD. Rejoice – you may be leaving one home, but in GOD's grace you are going to a better one."

Let's pray: "Heavenly Father, thank you for Your revelation. Let Your power of victory over death and over the fear of death, now deliver me from all bondage. No longer will apprehension over the passage from this life into Your Life in heaven, make me sick or afraid. For to be absent in the body is to be at home with You. I praise You for the renewal of my mind and the new freedom I now feel to go on in Your name. Lord, I will trust You and honor You forever, in Jesus' Name, Amen."

According to God's Words found in Joshua 1:8, "This Book of the Law shall not depart from your mouth, but you shall meditate in it day and night, that you may observe to do according to all that is written in it. For then you will make your way prosperous, and then you will have good success." (NKJV)

Never forget that Satan always fight the hardest when he knows GOD has great plans for you. Finally, I salute my three children, Shanera Smith, Marnard and Orantes Williams. Although, I may have not been the father you desired, I daily thank GOD for each of you. It is my fervent prayer that GOD's Favor chase each of you down and help you to know GOD and trust Him to help you and your loved ones achieve your divine destiny. The great emancipator, Harriet Tubman said, "Love thy neighbor is a precept which could transform the world if it was universally practiced." This ends my dialogue to "Success" and I hope it will help you tremendously, Amen. Please take liberty to share a copy or two with your contacts!!!

A copy of the following letter was received from VA Board of Veterans' Appeals on December 26, 2017.

Department of Veterans Affairs
Board of Veterans' Appeals
Washington, DC

December 20, 2017
Casey Walker, Esq.
VA Disability Group, PLLC
251 North Rose Street, Suite 200
Kalamazoo, MI 49007

Dear Mr. Walker:

Thank you for your correspondence of October 3, 2017, which was received at the Board of Veterans' Appeals (Board) on the same date, concerning Mr. David M. Williams. Your correspondence has been associated with Mr. Williams' file.

On March 16, 2017, the Board remanded Mr. Williams' case. For your information, I am enclosing a copy of the Board's decision. The remand action was necessary to assist Mr. Williams with the development of the appeal and to ensure the record is complete. The claims file was returned to the Regional Office in Detroit, Michigan, where development will be completed and the appeal will be reviewed. I also note that you have requested a copy of the contents of Mr. Williams claims' folder. I have forwarded your request to the Detroit Regional office.

When the development is finished, the Regional Office will re-adjudicate the appeal. If any part of the decision remains unfavorable, the case will be returned to Board for a comprehensive review of the entire record, according to its place on the docket.

I note your submission of VA Form 21-22a. Our database has been updated to reflect that you are Mr. Williams' representative.

Your request for the Board to allow 90 days to submit evidence and argument prior to deciding the claim is of record.

I hope the information I have provided is helpful. Please let me know if I can be of any further assistance.

Sincerely,
David C. Spickler
Principal Deputy Vice Chairman
Board of Veterans' Appeals

On September 18, 2018 the following e-mail was sent to my attorney:

Attorney Walker,

Someone from CAVC called, I forgot name, stated that my case is being re-docketing as petition for extraordinary relief. Assigned to Chief Judge Davis, I remain prayerful this fight is about to end!

The Lord said in Matthew 11:28-30, "Come unto me, all ye that labour and are heavy laden, and I will give you rest. Take my yoke upon you, and learn of me: for I am meek and lowly in heart: and ye shall find rest unto your souls. For my yoke is easy, and my burden is light." Without question, I believe that when you focus on GOD and consider what behavior pleases Him, you are acting wisely. By studying His Words and following His Biblical viewpoint, you are setting yourself on the pathway to a lifetime of "Success."

On October 10, 2018 the following e-mail was sent to a few close friends, "FYI and prayers: I'm rounding third base and headed for home. Hope you guys are doing great and I'm sharing the enclosed letter:

October 9, 2018
United States Court of Appeals For Veterans Claims
625 Indiana Ave. – Suite 900
Washington, DC 20004-2590
Case No. 18-3331

Dear Clerk of the Court:

Please associate this evidence with my case file. To me, the epitome of the VA dishonesty and prolonged injustice occurred in March, 2014. Their action was quite hurtful and very deceitful. VA memorandum dated November 1, 2013 stated, "1. We have determined that information to corroborate veteran's clinical records from Convalescent Center in Cam Ranh bay, Vietnam unavailable for review.' (Exhibit 1, RBA pages 2269 – 2270)

When I read this memorandum and subsequently found my medical records that VA said were burned, I felt very humiliated, became depressive and realized that VA had blatantly breached the confidentiality law. If not for fate, these documents which were sent to my former attorney who had withdrawn, would have never been obtained. My former attorney, John Walus withdrew from representing me on February 24, 2014. I received copy of his certified letter to VA on February 25, 2014. Without question, VA had these documents in their system since 1972 when I first applied for benefits for Malaria. VA illegally sent boxes of my records to attorney Walus on March 4, 2014. Exhibit 2 includes related medical records from RBA pages 1276 – 1290. My attorneys and I had sought this information since 2007. As I reflect on this near-death experience with Malaria, my faith is renewed. I can still hear one of my former drill sergeants yelling to a bunch of recruits, "Don't ever leave a stone unturned nor allow anything within your power to rely on chance."

Humbly Submitted,
David M. Williams, Vietnam Veteran
Enclosures – Exhibits 1 and 2

The following completes this edition to my story. In a recent letter, (2-21-19) to my brother on his birthday, I wrote: Happy Birthday, Bill. You are getting a prophetic excerpt from my last chapter manuscripts. It will be submitted to publishers as soon as VA re-adjudicate my claims. On November 6, 2018, I had two reasons to be joyful. First, I learned that the Democratic nominee for Michigan's Governor, Gretchen Whitmer had won her election. Then, I read online that Chief Judge Robert N. Davis of the United States Court Of Appeals For Veterans Claims, stated in his order that, "After further review, the Court re-docketed this as a petition for extraordinary relief. The Court apologizes to Mr. Williams for the delay in the adjudication of his case." Judge Davis went on to say, "Ordered that Mr. Williams, within 30 days from the date of this order, identify which of the claims listed in the July, 2014 Board decision are still pending. It is further ordered the secretary, within 30 days from the date Mr. Williams files his response, file an answer to the petition that addresses its specific allegations and provides any documentation necessary to aid in the Court's resolution of this matter."

During my vigorous canvassing, literature distribution and volunteer work for the Democrats, I had sent in several letters to the Detroit newspapers. A portion of one letter reads, "As a combat veteran of the Vietnam War, I know the importance of having good people in command. With less than a month to our General Election, Tuesday, November 6th, it's time for all hands to get on deck to ensure a fighter for Michigan is elected to lead our state. No campaign is perfect, but I'm proud of the fact that Governor's candidate, Gretchen Whitmer and Garlin Gilchrist, her running mate, are taking the time to make their rounds throughout Michigan to hear the concerns of citizens statewide. I'm doing my part to help them!!!

Voting rights and anti-gerrymandering efforts are already under renewed attack, along with millions of Americans' health care and protections from pre-existing conditions. Brett Kavanaugh might never have to face the voters, but we can defeat hundreds of his top allies in the states and prevent his rulings from destroying the values we hold dear – if we act fast. Finally, we're looking for your help in winning this election."

In the Detroit Free Press endorsement of Gretchen Whitmer for Governor on October 28, 2018, they wrote, "Politics shouldn't be this hard. Sure, we have serious disagreements about important things. But it shouldn't take a massive terror attack or a natural disaster to remind us that those differences are neither as numerous nor as important as the priorities we share. We all aspire lives as good or better than our parents', and hope that our children's good fortune will exceed our own. We all want safe roads, safe schools and safe drinking water. We all want to live in a society that rewards hard work, penalizes cheating and treats innocent victims with compassion. Gretchen Whitmer is the sensible choice to be Michigan's next governor."

Governor Gretchen Whitmer was sworn in on January 2, 2019 as the 49th governor of Michigan. She said in her inauguration speech, "Of course, what truly makes Michigan special are the people who call it home. Our diverse cultures, backgrounds, and experiences that strengthen the fabric of our communities. Grit. Humility. Dreaming up something new. Building it with our own two hands. That's how we became a hotbed of innovation and created music that moved the world. It's why Michigan will be forever associated with names like Reuther, Ford, and Aretha.

And it's why, a century after we led a global manufacturing revolution, we still have the best workforce on the planet – from our farmers and factory workers, to our incredible state employees, who work tirelessly every day to keep Michigan going strong. There's no place in the world like Michigan. No people like Michiganders. And no question that Michigan has as much God-given potential as any place on Earth. But while potential is universal, opportunity is not. And right now, in Michigan, too few have the opportunity they deserve. That's not easy to admit, but we have to be clear-eyed about the challenges we face. Now is the time to confront our problems head-on and say – in one voice – let's get it done.

We have always defied the odds. And we are going to do it again, together. We are going to prove that our shared future is more powerful than the issues that divide us. If we put our differences aside and get to work, we will come back stronger than ever. At a time when too many people want to separate us by building walls, we here in Michigan are going to get back to building bridges together. We can do great things when we work together. I know I didn't get here on my own. I'm here because, over the past year, the people of Michigan showed up. At town halls, at rallies, and in record numbers on Election Day. I am so grateful that you did. But our work is just beginning. That's why, today, I'm asking you to keep showing up. Keep showing your passion for our state – and demanding action from our leaders. And let's join forces, as Michiganders, to build bridges together... Over waters. Between parties. And to a brighter future for all. Let's get to work Michigan!"

It is my prayers that Governor Whitmer will allow GOD to use her talents to be a blessing to the least of His children. In Genesis 12:2 are found these words, "I will make you into a great nation, and I will bless you: I will make your name great, and you will be a blessing."

The following information was taken from a blog site for veterans. "VA takes forever to act on some veteran claims. The Court of Appeals for Veterans Claims (CAVC) does a better job than anyone of holding at least the BVA accountable. A Veteran filed the First Petition for Writ of Mandamus in 1792 with CAVC. The Court **denied this Revolutionary War Veteran's Writ** challenging the Government's slow handling of Veteran Pensions. The Writ of Mandamus is an Order from a Court directing an Executive Branch Official to take a certain required action. CAVC has the authority to issue a Writ of Mandamus pursuant to a statute called the All Writs Act. To seek that relief, you have to file what is called the 'Petition For a Writ of Mandamus.' The Court has issued the Writ less than a handful of times in its young history. However, here are the legal elements of a Writ of Mandamus. A Word of Caution: telling you the 'Elements' to a legal claim is like telling you the list of ingredients for a good lemon meringue pie – I am telling you what goes into the pie, but not how to put the ingredients together to make the pie. I'd love to tell you the 'how' of this type of filing, but because **the Court has only issued the Writ a handful of times in its history**, I don't know that anyone can tell you how to succeed with a Petition for a Writ of Mandamus.

(1) The petitioner must lack adequate alternative means to attain the desired relief, thus ensuring that the writ is not used as a substitute for the appeals process,

(2) The petitioner must demonstrate a clear and indisputable right to the writ, and

(3) The Court must be convinced, given the circumstances, that the issuance of the writ is warranted. If you are alleging "delay" is the basis for your Petition for a Writ of Mandamus, then you have an "extra" element:

(4) The petitioner must demonstrate that the alleged delay is so extraordinary, given the demands on and the resources of the Secretary of the VA, that it is equivalent to an arbitrary refusal to act."

The following information was taken from the CAVC website on November 21, 2018.

"General Docket United States Court of Appeals for Veterans Claims"
Case Number:18-3331
Docketed: 06/19/2018
David M. Williams v. Robert L. Wilkie
Appeal From: Department of Veteran Affairs
Fee Status: fee paid

Case Type Information:

07/23/2018 — Clerk's stamp order granting appellee's motion that the proceedings on this appeal are stayed pending ruling on appellee's motion to dismiss (RW) 08/15/2018 Appellant's response to Appellee's motion for stay of proceedings (with exhibits) (RW) 08/23/2018 ORDERED that the appellant, within 20 days after the date of this order, file a response discussing whether the circumstances in this instant case warrant the equitable tolling of the 120- day judicial-appeal period. If the appellant fails to do so, the Court may dismiss this appeal without further notice. Proceedings on this appeal are stayed until further order of the Court. (CMB) (RW) 08/25/2018 Appellant's response to the Court's August 23, 2018, order (RW) 09/18/2018 Notice of Re-docketing as petition for extraordinary relief (APS) 09/18/2018 Assigned case to Chief Judge Davis (APS) 10/06/2018 RECEIVED: Correspondence from Petitioner (RW) 10/09/2018 RECEIVED: Correspondence from Petitioner (RW) 11/06/2018 ORDERED that the July 23, 2018, stay imposed in this case is lifted. It is further ORDERED that the Secretary's July 23, 2018, motion to dismiss is DISMISSED as moot. It is further ORDERED that Mr. Williams, within 30 days from the date of this order, identify which of the claims listed in the July 2014 Board decision are still pending. It is further

ORDERED that the Secretary, within 30 days from the date Mr. Williams files his response, file an answer to the petition that addresses its specific allegations." My writ of mandamus was denied by Judge Davis in CAVC and VA ordered to re-adjudicate my benefits.

Pastor Joel Osteen said, "It's not how much you have: it's what you're doing with what you have. Don't believe the lies that your gift is too small, you are too old, or you're not qualified. It's not a competition. When you're looking left or right, you're not able to look up to God. Now is your moment to take what God has given you and begin to develop and release it. And as you release your gifts, God will multiply your influence, your resources, and your talents."

God is in control and He has seen your afflictions and wants to shift things in your favor. All of us struggle, at different levels, with the problem of unbelief. Perhaps, like Abraham and Sarah, you've prayed for something for years, but God has not answered. Life is passing you by while you wait. You struggle with doubt as you often wonder whether He is hearing your prayers. You may have suffered some tragedy, such as the loss of a close loved one, and you wonder, "Where was God when this happened?" Maybe it's a family problem that has dragged on for years. As in my case, an ongoing fight with the VA for earned benefits. I have often wondered, "Why doesn't God do something? Why doesn't He answer?" Sometimes I've struggled with doubt when I've needed some small thing that would be easy for God to provide, something which I knew would further His work, and yet in spite of my prayers, God did not answer.

The Lord's word to Sarah speaks to all who struggle with unbelief and that's all of us. Genesis 18:11-14 reads, "Abraham and Sarah were already very old, and Sarah was past the age of childbearing. So Sarah laughed to herself as she thought, 'After I am worn out and my lord is old, will I now have this pleasure?' Then the Lord said to Abraham, 'Why did Sarah laugh and say, 'Will I really have a child, now that I am old?' Is anything too hard for the Lord? I will return to you at the appointed time next year, and Sarah will have a son."

How could anything be difficult for the Lord, who spoke the universe into existence? And if nothing is difficult for Him, then how can we persist in our unbelief? This story of Abraham and Sarah waiting all these years for the promised son teaches us an important spiritual lesson: God brings us to the end of our strength so that we will trust in His ability to do the impossible.

Our faith should be so strong that it is proactive and will empower our thoughts and bring them into manifestation in our daily lives. James 1:6 reads, "But when you ask, you must believe and not doubt, because the one who doubts is like a wave of the sea, blown and tossed by the wind."

Sometimes the wheels of justice move slowly. Hold on to your faith, keep trusting God and expecting victory: God will always deliver and answer your prayer!!! After over 12 years of playing chess with the VA for my benefits, they offered me a settlement on December 9, 2019. God words in Isaiah 61:7 exclaims, " For your shame ye shall have double: and for confusion they shall rejoice in their portion: therefore in their land they shall possess the double: everlasting joy shall be unto them."

There is nothing that gives a parent more satisfaction than the love and achievements of their children. All parents want to have good bonding with their child/children. They try to provide the love, warmth, and comfort that the child wants and needs in every phase of their development. It makes them quite proud to see their children finish high school and college. When our children start working, and living independent of us, we feel sometimes lonely in our empty nest. There is no better feeling than to hear from them and know they are doing good and making a success of their lives. On a recent birthday, the following was expressed to my brother Bill, by his daughter Ashley: "No matter how you slice the pie I am amazed by you. Thank you for all that you do and have done. This man has made sacrifices beyond belief to show me unconditional everlasting love from the day of my existence. Words cannot touch how important my Daddy is to me. I am so blessed to have you in my life and I thank God every day for you. May He continue to bless you with a healthy, happy life. Love you always. 😊"

When I read Ashley's words, I thought about the story of the "Prodigal Son." The story begins with a man who has two sons. The younger son asks his father for his portion of his inheritance. Once received, the son promptly sets off on a long journey to a distant land and begins to waste his inheritance on wild living. When his money ran out, a severe famine hits the country and the son finds himself in dire circumstances. He takes a job feeding pigs. Eventually, he grows so destitute that he even longs to eat the food assigned to the pigs. The young man finally comes to his senses and decides to return to his father and ask for forgiveness and mercy. The father who has been watching and waiting, receives his son back with open arms of compassion. He is over-joyed by the return of his lost son. In Luke 15: 20 – 24, we find these words, "And he arose, and came to his father. But when he was yet a great way off, his father saw him, and had compassion, and ran, and fell on his neck, and kissed him. And the son said unto him, Father, I have sinned against heaven, and in thy sight, and am no more worthy to be called thy son. But the father said to his ser-vants, Bring forth the best robe, and put it on him: and put a ring on his hand, and shoes on his feet: And bring hither the fatted calf, and kill it: and let us eat, and be merry: For this my son was dead, and is alive again: he was lost, and is found. And they began to be merry." So don't wait to hit "Rock Bottom" come to your senses, and decide to run to God's open arms for compassion and mercy today!!! Your "Success" is imminent.

Thank you Lord, thank you Lord, I just want to thank you Lord!!! The following prayer was shared with family, friends and contacts. It was written as self-therapy the next day after my father had passed. I wrote, "As we gather today, Oh Merciful Father, we want to first say 'Thank you!' You have brought us from a mighty long way and You have blessed us over the years abundantly. Jesus, we ask humbly that You will guide and strengthen each family member and contacts here today as we complete our earthly journey. Let us all re-member the love, smiles and work ethic of our deceased father and loved one. May we use his memory to allow our candles to shine and make this a better world. Thank you Master for teaching us that it is only through You that we can receive eternal life.

As we depart, let each of us realize that in order to enter Your Kingdom, we must be Christ-Like. Help us to use our head and our heart in our daily relations. With Your Holy Spirit overshadowing us, we will be blessed and we will liberally share our blessings with others. Thank you Lord for Booker T. Williams Sr. and the lessons he taught us. There is no question, he had God's favor, Amen.

The chorus of an old gospel hymn goes, "He touched me, Oh He touched me, And oh the joy that floods my soul! Something happened and now I know,

He touched me and made me whole." From the beginning of this book to the end, it was my desire to show readers we must obey God's Words. Hebrews 12:2 reads, "Looking unto Jesus the author and finisher of our faith." Yes, God is the author and finisher of these words. Dave Williams was just His anointed vessel to write this project. I couldn't close this discourse without writing my epitaph. Hopefully, it will read: He Lived! He Loved! He Received Eternal Life!

The eulogy I shared with my family after learning of my uncle George Williams' demise on April 8, 2019 follows: " Matthew 25:23 reads, 'His lord said unto him, Well done, good and faithful servant: thou hast been faithful over a few things, I will make thee ruler over many things: enter thou into the joy of thy lord.' Aunt Gussie, Cousin Linda and other relatives and friends, I can hear Uncle George singing to us today," Have thine own way, Lord! Have thine own way! Thou art the potter, I am the clay. Mold me and make me after thy will, while I am waiting, yielded and still.' Today is not a sad day but a day for rejoicing for Grandma Ada and Grandpa Clark Williams' baby boy, George has joined them in Heaven. My dad was the oldest child and Uncle George was the baby. They were always close and Uncle George was like my second daddy. I wished I could be there physically but due to health and other challenges, I am there spiritually and penned these Holy Spirit given words of love. Uncle George loved God, loved his family and all God's children and was an anointed son of God. I have patterned my life after Uncle George from a teen until this day. I became an ordained deacon and served in Vietnam. Uncle George was a soldier in the US Army for 30 years. I will always remember the life lessons he taught especially about waiting on the Lord. My most rewarding experience was the summer I spent with Uncle George while I attended a class at Lackland Air Force Base in San Antonio, Texas. I got to know the man and enjoyed learning from him about having a personal relationship with God. I can hear him reading to St. Stephens church family, Deuteronomy 31:6 – 'Be strong and of good courage, do not fear nor be afraid of them: for the Lord your God, He *is* the One who goes with you. He will not leave you nor forsake you." I can hear him saying, get right church and let's go home. I can hear him telling me and you: Psalm 27:14, "Wait on the Lord: Be of good courage, And He shall strengthen your heart: Wait, I say, on the Lord!" Uncle George labored in God's vineyard with his mind, body and soul and was ready for Heaven's rewards. I close with one of my favorite poems by Edgar A. Guest.

"People Liked Him"

People liked him, not because
He was rich or known to fame:
He had never won applause
As a star in any game.
His was not a brilliant style,
His was not a forceful way,
But he had a gentle smile.

And a kindly word to say.
Never arrogant or proud,
On he went with manner mild:
Never quarrelsome or loud,
Just as simple as a child:
Honest, patient, brave and true:
Thus he lived from day to day,
Doing what he found to do.

In a cheerful sort of way.
Wasn't one to boast of gold
Or belittle it with sneers,
Didn't change from hot to cold,
Kept his friends throughout the years,
Sort of man you like to meet
Any time or any place.
There was always something sweet.

And refreshing in his face.
Sort of man you'd like to be:
Balanced well and truly square:
Patient in adversity,
Generous when his skies were fair.
Never lied to friend or foe,
Never rash in word or deed,
Quick to come and slow to go
In a neighbor's time of need.

Never rose to wealth or fame,
Simply lived, and simply died,
But the passing of his name
Left a sorrow, far and wide.
Not for glory he'd attained,

Nor for what he had of pelf,
Were the friends that he had gained,
But for what he was himself.

I salute you Uncle George, I love you and also plan to make Heaven my home." A photo of Uncle George and his siblings appears at the end of this book.

Psalms 116:1-5 exclaim, "I love the LORD, because he hath heard my voice and my supplications. Because he hath inclined his ear unto me, therefore will I call upon him as long as I live. The sorrows of death compassed me, and the pains of hell gat hold upon me: I found trouble and sorrow. Then called I upon the name of the LORD: O LORD, I beseech thee, deliver my soul. Gracious is the LORD, and righteous: yea, our God is merciful."

OUR CLOSING PRAYER

Our Father, Almighty God, Our Lord and Merciful Savior, we come today to say we love You. Thank you for the many blessings You have given us from our birth until this moment. Thank you for those abundant blessings on the way. We desire to praise You and now place our earthly concerns in Your hands. Forgive us of our sins, we repent and turn away from all iniquities. Fill us with Your Holy Spirit and help us to serve You the rest of our days on this earthly journey. We give You the glory, honor and praise. May we live with You eternally we pray, in Jesus' name, Amen.

Psalms 136:1-6 states, "O give thanks unto the LORD: for he is good: for his mercy endureth forever. O give thanks unto the GOD of GODs: for his mercy endureth forever. O give thanks to the Lord of lords: for his mercy endureth forever. To him who alone doeth great wonders: for his mercy endureth forever. To him that by wisdom made the heavens: for his mercy endureth forever. who spread out the earth upon the waters, for his mercy endureth forever." Hallelujah! GOD'S mercy endureth forever and He has allowed us to be a "Success."

IF I DID IT, YOU CAN DO IT TOO.

ƆƐƆ 2/8/11
Ɖᴅᴡ

The Obama's

Thank you for your support
and friendship.

We made history together in
2010, and I look forward to
continuing that work in the
weeks and months ahead.

Happy New Year, from my
family to yours.

2020

Vice President
Kamala Harris

President Joe Biden

LOVE KEEPS ON GIVING!!!

School of Social Work

Development and Alumni Affairs
5447 Woodward Avenue, Detroit, Michigan 48202
313-577-8887

WAYNE STATE
UNIVERSITY

October 29, 2020

Mr. David M. Williams
PO Box 35521
Detroit, MI 48235

Dear Mr. Williams:

Thank you for your gift to the School of Social Work. Through your generous support, you are strengthening our mission to advance social work knowledge and prepare a diverse student body for practice that promotes social justice.

The School of Social Work empowers social change in Detroit through teaching, research and continuing education programs that benefit the community, with emphasis on social, economic and environmental justice. The urban context provides compelling experiences that develop professional competence and prepare our students to uphold the core values of the social work profession. With more than 600 local agencies in partnership with the school, this year we have students placed in 314 field agencies. They are assisting children, youth, adults and families while gaining practical knowledge and skills to serve in careers that help to shape the quality of life in their communities.

Your support means so much as overall employment of social workers is projected to grow more than 10 percent in this decade, reflecting an increased need for professionals who focus on children and families, aging, health and behavioral health, interpersonal violence and community, and policy and program development. Your important investment is providing enriching opportunities and experiences that enhance our students' learning, training and service as they work directly with the community.

If you have any questions about the impact of your gift, please contact me at 313 577 4429 or kwilloughby@wayne.edu. Thank you again for your generous support.

Sincerely,

Katy Willoughby

Katy Willoughby
Individual Giving Officer
School of Social Work

P.S. Your receipt for tax purposes will be mailed separately, if applicable. Please call 313-577-2263 if you have any questions about the receipt.

WAYNE STATE UNIVERSITY

Skylar Herbert Endowed Scholarship
in the
School of Social Work

Skylar Herbert

During the coronavirus pandemic in April of 2020, donor David Williams, MSW '97 was so moved by the story of Skylar Herbert that he created this scholarship in Skylar's honor. This is Skylar's story.

Skylar was Michigan's youngest victim to succumb to the coronavirus, according to the state's Department of Health and Human Services (as of July, 2020). Skylar was the only child of two veteran first responders LaVondria, who has been a police officer for 25 years, and her dad Ebbie, who has been a firefighter for 18. Skylar's grandmother, Leona Pennell-Herbert, said that Skylar was an energetic and joyful kindergartener. She said Skylar was very bright and called her a "smart little cookie."

This scholarship has been created by the generosity of David to ensure that Skylar's legacy lives on. As an alumni of the school, it is David's intent that this scholarship aid in relieving the financial obligations that many students face while working to complete their degrees at the School of Social Work.

Thank you for All That
You have done
For me.
love, Ashton Johnson 8-16-18

Thanks Ashton, you write well. MAY
GOD HELP YOU TO DO GOOD IN SCHOOL AND
HAVE A GREAT FUTURE. LOVE AND MY PRAYERS,
GRANDPA DAVE 8-19-18

HAPPY ANNIVERSARY PAT – GOD'S MOST PRECIOUS GIFT TO ME.

Forever and Always!!!

Thank you card from Governor Gretchen Whitmer

WHITMER GILCHRIST FOR MICHIGAN

Presorted Standard
U.S. Postage
PAID
Permit #1002
Detroit, MI

Dear Friend,

I wanted to reach out and thank you for your support. Thanks to your contribution, we're in a strong position as we approach November. We will continue to improve our infrastructure, keep our economic recovery strong, and fight for working families across the state.

I'm working as hard as I can to keep Michiganders and our state moving forward. We will continue to do that in 2022 and beyond-- but I need you to keep fighting alongside me.

Thank you!

April, 2022

1**2**59****************ALL FOR AADC 481
David Williams
PO Box 35521
Detroit, MI 48235-0521

Dave and Governor Jennifer Granholm October, 2001

Uncle George — US Army

Part of Williams paternal roots; Left to right – Uncle George, Aunt Ada, Uncle Buddy. Dad – Booker T. Williams

Judge Damon Keith

Senator Ted Kennedy

Cobo Hall - Detroit Economic Club
9-22-03

John Kerry

Dave - 48 Year old Slam Dunk King!

My Favorite Sports Moment -
Babe Ruth 2nd Place Tournament Winner

1983   Uncle Bill   ALABAMA
         CP   STATE
                      CUBS

Detroit Special Night To Salute Rosa Parks – 11-28-99

Rosa Louise McCauley Parks was born on February 4, 1913 and expired on October 24, 2005. The United States Congress honored her as "the first lady of civil rights" and "the mother of the freedom movement." Shown in picture above are guests top right, Martin Luther King III and bottom left, Evander Holyfield, former boxing heavyweight champion.

CPSIA information can be obtained
at www.ICGtesting.com
Printed in the USA
BVHW052036100723
667029BV00002B/3